Collie Concept

Ch. Wickmere Rapunzel, by artist Betty Clewis. Rapunzel is one of the
few Collie bitches to have gone Best in Show (under Alva Rosenberg). The collage
shows her at four months, eighteen months, and at almost twelve years. She was a joy
to own and show—a once in a lifetime dog for any breeder.

Dedication

To those who protect the honor of the Collie as a companion, working dog and a show ring competitor, I respectfully dedicate this book.

The Breeder

An Artist, modeling in plastic clay, or conjuring with marble, brings forth a conception that the World acclaims a triumph. He deals, however, with his materials direct, and they respond to his lightest touch, as he toils toward a preconceived Ideal.

There is no resistance to his manipulations. What, then, should be our estimate of one who has first to conceive the figure in his brain?...whose only tools are the laws of Heredity, Selection, In-breeding, Outcrossing and alimentation?...whose only materials are the flesh and blood, approachable only by indirection?...who battles against the stubborn forces of Atavism, or reversion to ancestral form?...who seeks, and succeeds in producing a creature pulsative with life, exquisitely fashioned down to the most minute detail, not only a thing of beauty in itself (which Artists try, sometimes with ill success to reproduce on canvas or in bronze), but a creation that serves as well, the highest utilitarian purpose? The breeder of Animals directs the Spark of Life itself. *The possibilities of his art are almost infinite.*

This treatise appeared in the December, 1925, National Geographic magazine and is a valid sign of honor to those individuals who proudly wear the badge of a BREEDER.

A DOG AND A KID

No one will invent and no one ever did
A happier pair than a dog and a kid.

For doubt can't bedim nor can worry befog
The gay zestful way of a kid and a dog.

Athrob with adventure, their hearts beat as one,
Their pulses resurge with the rhythm of fun.

They swing into action as impulse may bid,
"Today is the day" for a dog and a kid.

Oh God, clear the pathway along which they jog
And smooth out the bumps for a kid and his dog.

And make of the world tnat they wander amid
A place truly fit for a dog and a kid.

Berton Fraley

Collie Concept

by Mrs. George H. "Bobbee" Roos

with illustrations by Dahlis Roy

1988
Alpine Publications, Inc.
Loveland, Colorado, USA

Table of Contents

Foreword

All the truly great Collies I vividly recall had one attribute in common—class!

Maybe it is that undefinable element so often repeated (seven times) in the Collie standard—expression! Class, expression, elegance and balance distinguish the really great ones that transcend beyond equal technical perfection of type and soundness as defined by any standard, written or pictured. The best Collie judges, whether all-breed judges as the late Alva Rosenberg, or our better specialty judges of the past century, have not only adhered to the standard but have had the ability to recognize *class* and *beauty*. As a result, perhaps the most beautiful breed of dogs has evolved in the modern Collie.

But there is another and perhaps more important aspect of this beautiful and gentle breed of dogs. Collies instinctively love children and children love them. As a child, how I was fascinated by the stories of Albert Payson Terhune! I thought our own "farm type" Collie was wonderful, but with bits to eat and petting, I also lured the neighbor's purebred Collie to visit me. I don't know which one I liked most, but they both liked me. Have you ever seen a Collie that did not like children and would not tolerate their foolishness as well as protect them, if necessary, even from a spanking?

While to the child almost all Collies are loving and good natured, to the prowler or thief the Collie is a large, instinctively suspicious dog that will bark. This alone may deter the thief.

To almost everyone, the Collie is a beautiful dog, whether a show specimen or not. These qualities have endeared the Collie to the public in the past and have made it a popular breed in spite of new breeds and a shift from rural to urban life.

Stephen J. Field
Parader Kennels

x

Albert Payson Terhune with three of his Collies: Sunnybank Grey Dawn (left); Ch. Sunnybank Explorer (center); and Ch. Sunnybank Sigurdson (right).

Museum copy loaned by Claire Leishman.

A Tribute to Albert Payson Terhune and Sunnybank

Who was this man who cast such a spell over his readers, both youngsters and adults, that caused them to yearn so for a Collie of their own?

Among the numerous admirers and a historian of this prolific author is Karen Phelps of Yorktown Heights, New York. Terhune's books inspired her involvement in Collies. Miss Phelps presented the following history and little known facts about Terhune as a program for her Collie Club.

Albert Payson Terhune

Albert Payson Terhune was an author and journalist for many years before he wrote his first dog story, "His Mate," for *Redbook* magazine. This story was later included in his collection of Collie tales entitled, *Lad: A Dog,* reluctantly published by E. P. Dutton and Company. *Lad* was an instant success and more than a dozen dog books were to follow. In them, Terhune extolled the virtues of Collies—their near human intelligence, their tawnygold beauty, their everlasting loyalty—and elevated the breed to a level of popularity that has spanned decades.

With only a handful of dog books, Albert Payson Terhune inspired a loyal following that has withstood half a century. He received letters by the thousands from children and adults who had been touched by the dogs he wrote about with such insight. Sunnybank, his home in Pompton Lakes, New Jersey, became a tourist attraction as visitors poured through its gates hoping for a glimpse of the famous Sunnybank Collies.

What was so special about Albert Payson Terhune? Why have his books sold more than 650,000 copies? Why are they still read today?

Irving Litvag explains it best in his Terhune biography entitled *The Master of Sunnybank:*

"Perhaps the most important thing about Terhune and the dog people is that hundreds of families came to own Collies because of him. And these big, brave, sweet-tempered animals brought much joy to those who loved them. In a very real sense, Bert Terhune was responsible for this. It is possibly one of the nicest epitaphs a writer could wish for.

...you took this Collie dog and you told stories about his greatness and goodness and love and eternal loyalty, and with your story telling skill, you made us—all the thousands or hundreds of thousands or millions of us—you made us actually fall in love with a damn dog! And he became the dog we always wanted to have and never did. Maybe even more than that—maybe he became the friend we always wanted to find, or even the brother or the father. And this authentic-imaginery dog ... this Collie dog took hold of us and won't let go."

Albert Payson Terhune died in 1942 at the age of 70 and his wife, Anice, lived on at Sunnybank until her death in 1964. The nine-and-a-half remaining acres of the estate were sold by her attorney to a realtor and her personal effects were distributed or sold to antique dealers. The proceeds from the sale went to the Albert Payson Terhune Foundation created by Mrs. Terhune to perpetuate Sunnybank as a museum. The officers of the Foundation claimed there was not enough money to carry out her wishes.

The Battle to Save Sunnybank

When the realtor announced Sunnybank was to be subdivided into nine luxury homes, area residents, headed by Claire Leishman, started a publicity campaign to prevent it. They got publicity through *Collie Cues,* a national Collie magazine, and other publications and urged everyone to write to Wayne Township to save Sunnybank from desecration.

The battle raged for several years until on April 19, 1967, the township bought Sunnybank for $145,240.93. Since then, it has been reimbursed for most of this amount by the State of New Jersey Green Acres Program.

Gradually Wayne Township ran short of money to pour into Sunnybank's restoration and two groups emerged. One of these was the Citizens for Sunnybank, made up of concerned local people. Its first donation to save Sunnybank arrived in September, 1967. Eight months later the second group, The Terhune Sunnybank Memorial

Fund, was formed. Ken Martin, former owner of *Collie Cues,* was the president and Claire Leishman, a New Jersey resident, was the secretary/treasurer. The late Ada Shirley of Oklahoma was also instrumental in the Fund's formation. The Memorial Fund strove to raise the money needed to restore the house and collect Terhune's scattered possessions. Estimates were given for reconstruction costs of the house but before the money could be raised, tragedy struck in 1969.

Two boys, who were trespassing, nearly fell through the decaying roof and Wayne Township, ultimately responsible for the property, ordered its demolition. In April, 1969, Albert Payson Terhune's beloved house was torn down.

But from that disaster hope ensued. The Citizens for Sunnybank raised money for an architect to draw up a master plan for a park. The plan showed Sunnybank's ultimate restoration, including a two-room concrete museum building duplicating the living room and music room of Terhune's home.

On October 15, 1967, the long hoped for dream became a reality. Sunnybank was opened to the public. Five days later the Sunnybank Festival, which was to become an annual event, was held. They displayed Terhune memorabilia, gave a Collie obedience demonstration and sponsored other activities. At the October, 1972 Festival, the centennial of Terhune's birthday, a monument was dedicated to his memory with his likeness in bronze placed upon a granite column.

With Claire Leishman's unswerving dedication, the Sunnybank Memorial Fund continues. Terhune's pistol, the Sunnybank trophies and a drawing of Grey Dawn with his beloved elephant are among a few of the hundreds of recovered pieces.

Many pitched in to help with Sunnybank's restoration, contributing money, free time, and labor. The lily pond, gazebo, the dog gravestones and one of the puppy pens have all been restored. Ongoing projects continue to recover the "Garden From Everywhere," the plants and the shrubbery.

The Legacy of Sunnybank

Irving Litvag, as the "Visitor," describes the mystical lure of Albert Payson Terhune's Sunnybank:

"The Visitor tried to understand why. Why had he come, what had drawn him here? Why did others feel the same draw? Why was an unimportant writer, as measured by almost any literary standard, able to take the emotions of so many readers and hold them in a grasp that defied time and the grave?

The scholars ignore him and he is not to be found in histories of American literature. Yet thousands upon thousands of readers were thrilled by him, moved by him, and remember him. Most of all, remember him. Year after year passes, decade after decade. Yet his words still live. And the people who read those words so long ago still come here to walk among the oaks and remember.

What was this strange quality that had kept Sunnybank alive for him and had brought him here, after so long, on this day? The Visitor had no answer. But he wished, fervently, that someplace there might be new children who would carry on this unexplainable love for Sunnybank that he had known since his own childhood. So that there always would be someone to remember the old glories here and the stories written about them."

There are new children. Every year letters faithfully arrive from the new generation asking about Terhune and the Sunnybank Collies. Claire Leishman, now head of the Terhune Sunnybank Memorial Fund, personally answers each one.

Sunnybank is now an official historic site and is safe at last. For years to come "Lad's" admirers will be able to stroll the restored grounds. Albert Payson Terhune is remembered: each fall he is commemorated at the annual Sunnybank Festival and Collie Club of Northern New Jersey, with Mrs. Terhune's written permission, offers a memorial trophy each year in his name for the Novice Dog and Novice Bitch class at their March Specialty. The Collie Club of Northern New Jersey also holds their summer match show at Sunnybank and once again Collies can be seen romping across the lawns.

Bibliography

Collie Cues, 6200 Bay View Avenue, Richmond Heights, CA 94805.

Litvag, Irving. *The Master of Sunnybank.* Harper & Row, Publishers, Inc., New York, 1977.

Terhune Sunnybank Memorial Fund, 290 Oakwood Drive, Paramus, NJ 07652.

Introduction

Wistful recollections of a childhood enhanced by a Collie companion send many parents on a search for one "like I had as a kid" when the time approaches for the new generation to have a dog.

Nostalgic reveries are told again by Mom or Dad as a family clusters around the newly adopted puppy cradled in loving arms.

Perhaps this cycle will be repeated again in several decades, when these youngsters prepare their own families for the acquisition of a very important canine.

By virtue of an endearing temperament and disposition, the Collie has survived many fads and fancies to consistently remain one of the most popular and well-known comrades.

Albert Payson Terhune glorified the Collie intellect and prowess through his books, now collector items. This library stimulated the desire for many young readers to own a Collie.

Terhune's influence was then compounded by the advent of Lassie as a movie and television star. Week after week the public was exposed to Collie loyalty and feats of almost human reasoning and perception. This was wholesome entertainment. Plots and storylines did not tax the imagination or insult a code of propriety.

Rudd Weatherwax, the Hollywood dog trainer, made television history with a sable and white male masquerading as the female Lassie. Following the financial success of the movie, "Lassie, Come Home," six more Lassie films were made by M-G-M- studios. When movie interest waned a television writer asked Weatherwax if he'd be interested in a series revolving around Lassie.

The pilot show was introduced in 1952 and Lassie became a star. There were five generations of Lassies, each being a son of the previous dog. The movies and syndicated re-runs of the television series continue to impress the potential dog owner. Grateful for the publicity there is one drawback for breeders to tolerate. Many prospective purchasers feel that *Collie* is synonomous with *Lassie* and *sable* and are reluctant to consider any other color.

The canine courage and loyalty touted by Terhune and depicted by Lassie are tales of fancy, but the Collie has surpassed the fiction of the written word and performances of actors to become an authentic hero.

In the twenty-five year history of the Ken-L Ration Dog Hero of The Year awards program, a Collie has earned this distinction five times.

Tang, a Collie owned by Air Force Capt. and Mrs. Maurice Dyer of Dennison, Texas, was the first recipient when the Quaker Oats Company (maker of Ken-L Ration and sponsor of the annual event) initiated this recognition for canine heroism in 1954. Tang's valor had saved the lives of five children. Four times he leaped in front of automobiles to push youngsters out of their paths. The fifth tragedy was averted when Tang stationed himself in front of a truck, barking until the driver discovered a two-year-old had climbed onto the truck and would surely have fallen when the vehicle started to move.

To decide the winner of this award, a panel of leading authorities in the animal world review the courageous acts of various dogs and select what they feel is the most heroic deed. Tang set a precedent for four other Collies to be honored at the awards banquet and received the coveted gold medal, a $1,000 U.S. Savings Bond, a gold plated leash and collar, and a year's supply of dog food.

Blaze, the second Collie to be named Dog Hero of The Year, received the honor in 1957. He had saved two-year-old Dawn from an enraged sow on the family's farm.

The selection in 1961 was Duke, an Ohio Collie who tore burning clothing off of Penny, the ten-year-old daughter of Mr. and Mrs. John Gantz, thusly credited with saving her life.

Then Buddy, owned by the Crinkley family of Budd Lake, New Jersey, saved a herd of seventy pregnant dairy goats when he herded them out of a burning barn in 1964.

In 1966, a dog so aptly named Hero of Priest River, Idaho, saved two-year-old Shawn Jolley from being trampled by a horse.

Tang, first recipient of the "Dog Hero Award" with his owner Mrs. Maurice Dyer.

Two mixed breeds have also won hero awards. Lady, a Collie/German Shepherd cross was honored in 1959, and a Collie/Malamute, Patches, was the 1965 recipient.

Fact or fiction, the Collie has a niche in dogdom from his loyalty and companionship.

1

From Baronial Castles to the White House

"The farther back you can look, the farther forward you are likely to see."   Churchill

The origin of the Collie, including its name, has been the subject of much research and equal speculation.

It has been purported that when the Romans invaded Britain they brought with them sheepdogs. These working dogs, interspersed with the animals native to that area (particularly the far North) are perhaps the ancestors of our Rough and Smooth Collies of today.

"Collie" is thought to have stemmed from the black-faced "Colley" sheep for which the dogs became respected for their aptitude in handling. The dogs then became known as the "Colley Dog." This could also be why so many people, even today, refer to our current evolution of the "Colley" herding dog as the "Scotch Collie."

For those who would like a choice, there is also the theory that the original working dog was black, and so dubbed "Coallies."

Whichever version preferred, historians do agree that the Rough and Smooth variety stemmed from common ancestors which earned their keep herding cattle and sheep in the north of Scotland.

In 1860 the tide turned for the Collie. Birmingham National Dog Show Society held classes for different varieties of herding dogs in Birmingham, England, and interest in the breed grew rapidly thereafter. Although the Collie was, and still is, known as the "working man's dog," belonging primarily to the middle class worker whose funds were limited and must be carefully budgeted to cover the breeding and exhibiting of the dogs, the breed was given a real boost by several early fanciers of royal lineage who had apparently inexhaustible resources and were able to obtain the finest specimens.

One of these was Queen Victoria, who first saw the Collies when visiting at Balmoral Castle in Scotland. With her patronage the Collie had an upsurge of acceptance and popularity.

Dahlis

1

Two Collies from Her Majesty's Kennel at Balmoral, Scotland, were imported to America by a John H. Warren. Duncan, a black-and-tan two-and-one-half-year-old, was Winners Dog at the second annual Westminster Kennel Club Show in 1878; a kennel mate, Colin, also a black and tan, placed third in a class.

Bernard W. Emmons reported in *The Collie Club of America, Its History and Development, 1886-1965* concerning the importation of Duncan and Colin: "By astute advertising they were a great attraction and drew large crowds to the show, undoubtedly stimulating interest in the breed."

Whether these dogs contributed anything beyond this publicity, I don't know, but the fanfare about their origin was another lift up the ladder in popularity for the Collie.

In 1888 J. Pierpont Morgan Sr. made his debut in Collies and subsequently imported the English sable, Sefton Hero, for which he paid the record price, at the time, of $5,000. Hero was the Winners Dog at the first Collie Club of America show, held in New York in 1894.

A fantastic but true story concerning Hero was revealed by the renowned horse artist, George Morris. Morris had been commissioned by Morgan to paint Hero's portrait and the dog was delivered to the artist's seventh floor Chicago studio by one of the Armstrong brothers who managed the Morgan Kennels, located up the Hudson River in New York State.

2 Morris stepped out of the studio for a moment. When he returned no $5,000 Collie was to be seen—but he noticed the chain lead (Hero had been tied to the radiator pipe) stretching out the open window. Morris rushed over and there was Mr. Morgan's $5,000 worth of Collie dangling in mid-air, seven stories above the ground.

Hoping that the collar would hold, or not be slipped, the artist steadily and zealously pulled the struggling Collie back over the window sill. Within a few minutes Hero was none the worse for his sudden leap out of an open window seven stories up and Mr. Morris never breathed a word of the incident until many years later.

As the dog shows grew in number and importance, so did the urge to purchase, own and breed the finest Collies bring forth the keenest competition in men like J. Pierpont Morgan and Samuel Untermeyer. It was reported that in 1904

J. P. Morgan paid $10,000 for Ch. Wishaw Clinker, and Untermeyer, a corporation lawyer, was busy signing $5,000 checks for imports. The rivalry between these two men added spice to the early days of Collie exhibition.

Collie traffic across the Atlantic was dominated by the affluent feud between Morgan and Untermeyer for several years.

The American bred class entries were defeated by the British champions and so, in a concerted effort to settle down to the task of producing homebred winners, many importations of English dogs and bitches were made from 1901 through 1909 by various fanciers who wanted to utilize the best quality in their American breeding program.

W. Ormiston Roy, a Canadian, imported Parbold Provost in 1919. Roy, a life member of the Collie Club of America, served as its President in 1923-1924. His proposal, in 1916, to amend the standard to allow weights on a Collie's ears in the show ring was defeated.

Tazewell Kennels, Washington, Illinois, housed some of the finest specimens under the guidance of Dr. O. P. Bennett, including Parbold Picador, imported in 1914. Bennett served as President of the Collie Club of America in 1917. His book, "The Collie," now a collectors item, is considered the best treatise written about the breed.

The war years of 1914 through 1918 caused much concern for the welfare and continuity of the Collie in England, but the wily British enthusiasts emerged after the Armistice with survivors to carry on the heritage of quality.

In 1921, English Ch. Magnet was imported by Miss Eileen Moretta. Whelped in 1912, Magnet was not in the flower of his youth when he arrived in the United States. Although he sired two American champions after his arrival, the impact of the "Magnet line" was most dominant through his grandson, Ch. Eden Emerald, imported by Mrs. Clara Lunt. Her prefix of Alstead was added and through this line (sire chart #1) you can see the significance which Magnet had via Emerald and Laund Legislator.

Claudia Schroder, who prepared the two sire charts, reports that the name of El Capitan of Arken is generally mispelled in pedigrees. The dog was named for the John Phillip Sousa operetta and its title march. The dam of Ch. El Troubadour of Arken was Gailly Arrayed of Arken. Her name has also been the victim of spelling errors.

Mrs. C. M. Lunt announced the dispersal of the Alstead Kennels in 1926, but another New Jersey lady, Mrs. F. B. Ilch, maintained the heady pace of importing excellent English Collies of which many were from the Laund Kennel. Mrs. Ilch produced numerous champions carrying her prefix, Bellhaven.

In 1935 Ch. Lucason of Ashtead O'Bellhaven made the front page of practically all the large daily newspapers. On September 27, while his trainer, Michael J. Kennedy, was grooming the dog near the bank of the Shrewsbury river, a 10 year old boy fell into a stream from a row boat. Mr. Kennedy could not swim but he said to Lucason, "Go get him, Rover," and Lucason, who perhaps had won more show honours in 1934 and 1935 than any other Collie of that time, immediately dived into the water and brought the boy ashore.

Ch. Silver Ho Parader, whelped in 1943, (sire chart #2) was the starting point for the "Parader" line that placed Stephen J. Field of Omaha, Nebraska, in national prominence. Mr. Field bred Lodestone Bandoliera II to Ch. Silver Ho Shining Arrow, who was a son of Ch. Honeybrook Big Parade, a Ch. Future of Arken son. Among the many Collies emanating from the Parader foundation are excellent producers and winners with prefixes found in many of the current Collies: Merrie Oaks, Teecumsee, GinGeor, Cherrivale, Glen Hill, Cul Mor, Rudh' Re', Hanover, Wickmere, Vi-Lee and Twin Creek.

Coming through the progressive line of producing studs are Ch. Parader's Bold Venture, Ch. Parader's Country Squire, Ch. Two Jays Hanover Enterprise, Ch. Glen Hill Full Dress, Ch. Gin-Geor Bellbrookes Choice, Ch. Wickmere Chimney Sweep, Ch. Antrum Alltheway, Ch. Cul Mor's Conspiratour, and two current leading sires of champion offspring, Ch. Tartanside The Gladiator and Ch. Twin Creeks True Grit.

The Gaylord and Brandwyne Collie lines were strongly influenced by Ch. Sterling Starmist and Ch. Tokalon Storm Cloud. Storm Cloud sired Poplar by Storm, who was the sire of Ch. Gaylords Mr. Scalawag. Gaylords Major Merrymaker, sire of Int. Ch. Gaylords Flyer, also sired Brandwyne Tom Foolery, who sired Ch. Brand-wyne Needless to Say, a sable dog of exquisite expression who was exported to Japan before he really had an opportunity to reach his siring potential in the United States.

It has been Ch. Brandwyne Destiny's Echo's role to carry the Brandwyne banner. Mrs. Janet Leek of New York has solidified the line through Echo's son, Ch. Pat's Bayberry Mr. Ben, owned by Marjorie Toombs; Ch. Brandwyne Bayberry Mister (by Echo out of Ch. Brandwyne Bayberry Miss); and his son, Ch. Skye's Bayberry Destiny. They have been the integral breeding tools that Mrs. Leek has used as the most promising and astute Brandwyne student to carry on the line.

The Smooth variety has accelerated so rapidly in quality in the last decade that variety competition at Specialty shows is keener. Among those who have extolled the virtues of the Smooths and worked diligently to promote them and breed for the same structural qualities as their rough kin was Miss Margaret Haserot of Ohio. She was considered to be the matriarch of the Variety. It was Miss Haserot's Ch. Pebble Ledge Bambi who convinced many Rough Collie breeders that the Smooths could be of equal quality. The interest grew with fanciers such as Tom Kilcullen, Mr. and Mrs. Omar Rees, Sandra Tuttle, Eva Rappaport, Virginia Holtz and other dedicated devotees across the United States who helped catapult the variety into the current status of quality.

Into the eighties appeared a blue smooth female to bring equality to the sexes and the variety! Ch. Lisara's Morning After, bred and owned by Lawrence and Carmen Leonard, garnered an enviable show record in specialty and all breed competition. Nine best in show, all breed, twice she defeated the rough special bitch for best opposite sex at the national specialty for the Collie Club of America and she took maternity leave from the ring to produce six champions, three smooths and three roughs.

Also contributing to the increased competition between the varieties by campaigning quality smooths are Dona Haggerty, Joyce Beddow, Dian Bendit and Sondra Calhoun.

The most dominant force was Ch. Black Hawk of Kasan, a tricolor smooth of outstanding quality and temperament. "Hawk" was Best of Breed at the Collie Club of America National Specialty,

3

won Best in Show all breed, and set an enviable siring record as his champion offspring finished across the country.

Through the years intelligent breeders have continued to produce stock to perpetuate the virtues they felt important and reveled in the publicity that assisted in pet sales. Collies appeared in advertisements, movies, on television and even resided at the White House, Grace Goodhue Coolidge had Rob Roy, a white Collie, and Lyndon B. Johnson had Blanco, also a white.

There has been an interim of many years and generations since the working dogs of the North evolved into our graceful companions and show dogs of today, but they remain essentially the same—loyal dogs of serene temperament.

4

Fig. 1. Ch. Wishaw Clinker imported from England by J. Pierpont Morgan. In a letter written by Bernard Emmons to W. Van Dyck, February 19, 1962, Mr. Emmons reported that he had just completed a 28 to 32 generation pedigree of Silver Ho Parader and the English ancestry contained practically every great Collie in history. El Troubadour twice, Alstead Eden Emerald five times, Magnet twelve times, Knocklayde King Hector (or Weardale Lord) seventeen times and Anfield Model twenty-two times. Going back to the beginning, there was Trefoil five times and the first Collies such as Duncan, Scott, Tramp, Rutland, Wolf, Eclipse, just to name a few; and, of course, Cockie several times, who Mr. Emmons said was the first sable Collie from which all of our sable Collies descend.

Fig. 2. Ch. Eclipse, the best son of Ch. Charlemagne. James Watson noted, with obvious surprise, that Eclipse sired only sable and white puppies, even when bred to tricolor bitches; he was "pure for sable."

Pedigree of CH. ECLIPSE (K.C.S.B. 12949)

		Twig	Old Twig
			Help
	Ch. Trefoil, 4523 (Mar. 19, 1873)	Bess	Byrne's Rattler
			Watts' Bess
Ch. Charlemagne, 10691 (Jan. 4, 1879) Sire			Old Cockie, 2847 (1868, pedigree unknown)
	Bissell's Maude		Ch. Mec, 2877
		Meg	Clyde
		Twig	Old Twig
			Help
	Ch. Trefoil, 4523	Bess	Byrne's Rattler
			Watts' Bess
Flirt, 9459 (litter sister of Charlemagne) Dam			Old Cockie, 2847
	Bissell's Maude		Ch. Mec, 2877
		Meg	Clyde

Fig. 3. Old Cockie, 1868

Fig. 4. Ch. Rutland, grandson of Cockie

5

Fig. 5. Ch. Charlemagne, 1879

Ch. Marcus

Blue Princess Alice

6 Ch. Anfield Model

Ch. Wellesbourne Charlie

Portington Bar None

Fig. 6. A study in heads, from Marcus to Model.

Donovan II

Fig. 7. Ch. Knocklayde King Hector. This dog was imported from England as Weardale Lord. At this time the name of a dog could be changed. This photo was taken in 1914. In researching pedigrees Bernard Emmons discovered that during this period the dogs in England were closely linebred and King Hector had Parbold Piccolo six times in five generations and Wishaw Clinker three times. *Courtesy T. Hunter.*

Fig. 8. Ch. Parbold Piccolo, who appeared so friendly and content in his new home that his importer, J. I. Behling, turned him loose to run, disappeared on the day of his arrival in the U.S. and was never seen again. It was, wrote Dr. C. P. Bennet, "perhaps the greatest loss ever experienced by the fancy in America," Oct. 1904. This dog appeared six times in five generations in the pedigree of King Hector.

Fig. 9. Ch. Bellhaven Enchanter

Fig. 10. Ch. Bellhaven Bronze Scepterson.

Fig. 11. Ch. Skye's Bayberry Destiny.

Fig. 12. Ch. Pat's Bayberry Mr. Ben. *Courtesy J. Leek.*

Fig. 13. Ch. Brandwyne Bayberry Mister. *Gilbert photo.*

Fig. 14. Laund Loyalty of Bellhaven.
Courtesy C. Schroder.

Fig. 15. Ch. Anfield Model, 1902. Model was one of the most highly touted dogs between 1900 and 1910. He was the ideal that many breeders were striving for in head and expression. The mid-west in particular was dominated by the line-breeding to Model. Unfortunately his temperament was not a virtue and this shyness attributed to the loss of favour which the Collie suffered after the end of the first World War. *Courtesy C. Schroder.*

Fig. 16. Ch. Squire of Tytton, 1904. Some breeders felt Squire was an excellent specimen but lacked the expert promotion of his contemporaries. *Courtesy C. Schroder.*

Fig. 18. Ch. Seedley Stirling, 1911. *Courtesy C. Schroder.*

10

Fig. 17. Triple Ch. Bellhaven Starbat Strongheart, sire of 13 champions; best Collie, Westminster 1923-24. *Courtesy C. Schroder.*

Fig. 19. Ch. Bellhaven Black Lucason, sire of 16 champions. *Courtesy C. Schroder.*

Fig. 20. Ch. Laund Lero of Bellhaven, first Collie to win the Working Group at Westminster, 1926. *Courtesy C. Schroder.*

Fig. 21. Ch. Southport Summit, Ch. Southport Student, Ch. Beauty of Tytton, Ch. Squire of Tytton, Ch. Anfield Model.

Fig. 22. Mrs. C. M. Lunt with Ch. Alstead Seedley Satisfaction, Genevieve Torrey with Ch. Alstead Seedley Supremacy, and Mrs. W. H. McCurdy with Ch. Seedley Stirling, 1922. *Courtesy C. Schroder.*

Fig. 23. Ch. Sterling Silverflash, world's first white Collie champion, winners bitch at 1937 CCA. *Courtesy C. Schroder.*

Fig. 24. Edwin L. Pickhardt, Sterling Collies, with Ch. Sterling Starmist (left) and Ch. Sterling Syndicate.

12

Fig. 25. Four generations of Bellhaven Collies: Triple Ch. Lucason of Ashtead O'Bellhaven (three times BOB at CCA and Westminster 1930, 1931, and 1932); his son, Ch. Bellhaven Black Lucason (sire of 16 champions); his son, Ch. Bellhaven Standard Bearer; and his son, Ch. Bellhaven Gold Standard.

Fig. 27. Undefeated Ch. Braegate Model of Bellhaven, forty times best of breed, 18 working groups, twice best in show, BOB Westminster 1944, CCA 1943. *Courtesy C. Schroder.*

13

Fig. 26. Rob Roy and Grace Goodhue Coolidge. This all-white Collie from the Island White Collie Kennels in Wisconsin was the favorite pet of President Coolidge. This Howard Chandler Christy painting hangs in the White House and is a favorite with tourists. *Courtesy of the White House Historical Association.*

Fig. 28. Beulah's Silver Don Mario of Saint Adrian, imported by James Christie. A genuine war refugee, he left his home with Nadine K. George of Beulah Collies during the 1941 bombardment of Britain. The ship on which he was scheduled to sail was torpedoed. Luckily, Don Mario had been moved to another ship and arrived safely.

```
                    Ch. El Troubadour of Arken
            Ch. Future of Arken
                    Ch. Nymph of Arken
        Ch. Honeybrook Big Parade
                    Ch. Aalveen Anchor
            Honeybrook Helen
                    Gene of Arken
    Ch. Silver Ho Shining Arrow
                    Ace of Ashstead
            Ch. Master Lukeo of Noranda,CDX
                    Ch. Lady Lukeo of Cosalta
        Silhouette of Silver Ho
                    Ch. Major Lukeo
            Ch. Heidi of Noranda
                    Ch. Lady Nan of Cosalta
CH. SILVER HO PARADER
                    Ch. Cock Robin of Arken
            Para of Sunnyheath
                    Tazewell Thumming II
        Heatherton Pal
                    Sunderland Serenader
            Bellefontaine Blondebelle
                    Bellefontaine White Bordoni
    Lodestone Bandoliera II
                    Lodestone Landmark
            Star of Lodestone
                    Lodestone Lady Leda
        Landmark Lady
                    Ch. Bergamot Bandolier
            Lodestone Lively
                    Lodestone Lucky
```

Fig. 29. Pedigree of Ch. Silver Ho Parader.

Fig. 30. Ch. Parader's Bold Venture

```
CH. SILVER HO PARADER
 ├Ch. Parader's Golden Image
 │ └Ch. Parader's Bold Venture*
 │   └Ch. Parader's Country Squire
 │     ├Ch. Two Jay's Hanover Enterprise
 │     ├Ch. Parader's Reflection
 │     └Ch. Antrum's Alltheway
 ├Ch. Kinmont Sheyne
 │ └Arrowhill Ace High
 │   ├Ch. High Man of Arrowhill
 │   └Ch. Black Hawk of Kasan
 │
 ├Ch. Teecumsee Temptor
 │ └Ch. Cul Mor's Conspiratour
 │
 │Parader's Future Sensation
 │ └Bellbrooke's Master Pilot
 │   ├Ch. Gingeor Bellbrooke's Choice
 │   ├Ravette's Wayside Traveler
 │   ├Ch. Hi Vu The Intruder
 │   └Ch. Tartanside The Gladiator
 │
 └Ch. Vi-Lee's Parading Chieftain
   └Vi-Lee's Country Chipper
     └Ch. Vi-Lee's Redd Robbyn
       └Ch. Vi-Lee's Jubilant Jonathan
         └Ch. Vi-Lee's Classic Contender
           └Ch. Vi-Lee's Myster Mac
             └Ch. Lochlomun's Interlock
               └Ch. Twin Creek's True Grit
```

```
*Ch. Parader's Bold Venture
 ├Ch. Parader's Typesetter
 │ └Ch. Glen Hill Dreamer's Nobleman
 │   └Ch. Glen Hill Emperor Jones
 │     └Ch. Glen Hill Full Dress
 │
 └Ch. Merrie Oaks Star Billing
   └Ch. Merrie Oaks Star Boarder
     └Ch. Merrie Oaks Midnite Star
       └Ch. Wickmere War Dance
         └Ch. Wickmere Chimney Sweep
```

Ch. Silver Ho Parader

This chart shows the tail male relationship of the country's most recent leading sires to Ch. Silver Ho Parader.

14

Fig. 31. Ch. Tartanside The Gladiator. *Courtesy C. Hook.*

Fig.33 A.Ch. Tartanside Apparently. Best of Breed Collie Club of America, 1985. *Ashbey photo.*

Fig. 32. Bellbrooke's Master Pilot. *Courtesy J. Giuliano.*

Fig. 34. Ch. Twin Creeks True Grit. *Courtesy B. Houser.*

15

Fig. 33. Ch. Antrum Alltheway II. *Bennett photo.*

Fig. 35. Am. Can. Ch. Glen Hill Full Dress. *Shafer photo.*

Fig. 36. Ch. GinGeor's Bellbrooke's Choice, sire of 28 rough and two smooth champions.

16

Fig. 37. Ch. Black Hawk of Kasan

Fig. 38. Am. and Can. Ch. Wickmere Chimney Sweep. *Ashbey photo.*

Fig. 39. Ch. Wickmere War Dance

Fig. 40. Ch. Lochloman Interlock. *Courtesy J. Thomas.*

Fig. 41. Ch. Merrie Oaks Midnite Star

Fig. 42. Ch. Two Jay's Hanover Enterprise

```
                                              Ch. Sterling Syndicate
                                 Gaylord's Major Merrymaker
                                              Powell's Bonnie Babe
                   Brandwyne Tom Foolery
                                              Poplar By Storm
                                 Poplar By Storm's Gem
                                              Locksley Hall's Lava
        Ch. Brandwyne Needless to Say
                                              Poplar By Storm
                                 Gaylord's Mr. Scalawag
                                              Ch. Gaylord's Gay Glory
                   Gaylord's My Bonnie
                                              Cherrivale Second Mate
                                 Cyn-San O' My Mist of the Heather
                                              Honeybrook Black Velvet
   Brandwyne Royal Destiny
                                              Ch. Sterling Syndicate
                                 Gaylord's Major Merrymaker
                                              Powell's Bonnie Babe
                   Brandwyne Tom Foolery
                                              Poplar By Storm
                                 Poplar By Storm's Gem
                                              Locksley Hall's Lava
        Brandwyne Mam'Selle
                                              Ch. Orange Man of ToKalon
                                 Ch. Poplar Golden Opportunity
                                              Ch. ToKalon Shower of Gold
                   Mon Bijou Gay Spring
                                              Brown's Lucky Boy
                                 Ch. Grosz-Schone's Black Magic
                                              Brown's Black Princess
CH. BRANDWYNE'S DESTINY ECHO
                                              Ch. Sterling Starmist
                                 Ch. Sterling Syndicate
                                              Sterling Surplus
                   Gaylord's Major Merrymaker
                                              Ch. ToKalon Stormy Weather
                                 Powell's Bonnie Babe
                                              Powell's Bronze Beauty
             Brandwyne Tom Foolery
                                              Ch. ToKalon Storm Cloud
                                 Poplar By Storm
                                              ToKalon Polly of the Follies
                   Poplar By Storm's Gem
                                              ToKalon Winter Shadows
                                 Locksley Hall's Lava
                                              Linda of Locksley Hall
   Brandwyne Caprice
                                              Ch. Gaylord's Mr. Scalawag
                                 Brandwyne The Mood Indigo
                                              Blue Jade of Ronas Hill
                   Brandwyne Skylarking
                                              Gaylord's Major Merrymaker
                                 Gaylord's Dreamboat
                                              Gaylord's Ring of Frost
        Brandwyne Sweet Song
                                 Ch. Brandwyne Can You Top This

             Brandwyne Desiree
                                              Gaylord's Major Merrymaker
                                 Brandwyne Blue Stocking
                                              Blue Jade of Ronas Hill
```

18

Fig. 43. Pedigree of Ch. Brandwyne Destiny's Echo, the male that plays an important role in continuing the Brandwyne line.

Fig. 44. Ch. Brandwyne No Foolin'

Fig. 45. Gaylord's Major Merrymaker

Fig. 47. Honey Hill Harvester.

Fig. 46. Brandwyne Tom Foolery

Fig. 48. Ch. Brandwyne Destiny's Echo, sire of twenty-two rough and one smooth champion.

2

Selecting, Purchasing, and Naming Your Collie

"A name is a kind of face whereby one is known." Fuller

The classified advertising section of a newspaper is the first source prospective dog owners usually consult to find a dog, although not always the best. Veterinarians are pleased to recommend clients who have a litter available, although many practitioners readily admit that they are unfamiliar with breed standards. In metropolitan areas there may be a referral service in the local newspaper or a breed listing in the yellow pages of the telephone directory. Officers of specialty and all-breed clubs are very willing to assist puppy buyers in locating an honorable and ethical breeder. They can also tell you the schedule of shows and matches in the area which you may attend to view Collies and meet breeder/exhibitors.

Whatever route is used to locate a Collie, the buyer wants to be assured that the dog is purebred and registerable with The American Kennel Club. When advertising in the pet or livestock column, an experienced, educated breeder is competing in an open market where there may be other litters available at a lesser price because there has been very little invested through money, time or even consideration of the suitability of the parents as to compatability of temperament or physical attributes. The latter is concerned mainly in having puppies for sale, perhaps for pecuniary reasons.

Price tags vary according to investment, calibre of the parents (one or both may be champions) and geographical areas. If a bitch's owner has shipped her across the country by air to a notable stud, he hopes to recoup some of his financial outlay. On an average you should expect to pay from $150 to $300 for a good Collie puppy as a pet. You may possibly find one for a lesser price under unusual circumstances.

If you feel that you want something a step or so higher than a pet, be very candid with the breeder and announce your plans to breed the Collie or enter the show ring, and expect to pay over $300.

Dahlis

Sales contracts can prevent any misunderstandings and assure the purchaser that there is recourse in the event a puppy would fail to pass veterinary inspection or is not acceptable within the first forty-eight hours or whatever time limit is stated in the contract. The accompanying contract samples can be modified to suit individual needs, desires and situations.

MALE OR FEMALE

Either are excellent pets and usually a seller will encourage companion owners to have the males neutered and the females spayed. Surgery does not alter the temperament or physical appearance of the Collie, and the owners do not have the worry of a female coming into season or a male becoming an itinerant Romeo. This selection is individual preference. You will hear pros and cons on either sex.

The neutering or spaying clause would not be applicable when acquiring a Collie of breeding or show quality. Since a young puppy is a gamble, it is surely reassuring to know that this is considered in the contract agreement.

WHAT AGE PUPPY?

Most breeders make an initial appraisal of their litter and select several puppies they wish to "grow out" for further observation as potential breeding and showing stock. These puppies, if they fulfill the earlier promise, may be in the price range of $500 to $1,000 at five months to one year of age.

The first round of elimination will allow some puppies to be available at quite a young age—seven or eight weeks as pets.

The fact that the breeder does not want to keep these puppies does not infer that they are rejects, physically or mentally impaired or handicapped. These are the high class companion puppies, the sale of which helps to support an expensive hobby.

A seven or eight week old puppy is very appealing but requires much more attention and care. It quickly grows out of this appealing look into the gawky, adolescent stage of two-and-a-

half to five months—not so pleasing to the eye but much easier to cope with housebreaking. This puppy has better bladder control and is on a less stringent feeding schedule than the eight-week-old.

For those who do not wish to go through the young puppy stage, a young adult is an excellent choice. Even a Collie over two years of age adjusts to a new home and environment easily and rapidly. We have had excellent results in placing elderly champions and stock which is not being used in our breeding program. These Collies spend their remaining years as the only canine member of a family.

If a Collie does not develop within the bounds of the standard, the breeder may offer the dog at a year of age, or older, for a reasonable fee. The term "bargain" may be rather demeaning, but there are many satisifed Collie owners who have acquired, and prefer, an older dog instead of an infant.

O.T.Ch. Waltstone Impulse, T.D. "Jodi" was owner handled by Maeleine Loos.

22

SALES CONTRACT FOR PET PUPPIES

On _____, _____ kennels agrees to sell the following
           date   name

_____ to _____
           breed   name

of _____for the sum of $_____
                    address

Color: _____ Sire:_____ Reg. No._____

Sex: _____ Dam: _____ Reg. No. _____

Whelped: _____ Litter Reg. #_____

    Registration papers will either be given with the puppy or will be transferred to the buyer immediately upon their receipt from AKC if they are still being processed.

    It is understood that at the time of sale this dog is *not* considered to be of show or breeding quality, but is representative of its breed and is structurally and temperamentally suited as a companion and/or obedience dog. Beginning training classes are highly recommended for any family dog to insure a happy relationship with the animal. This dog is guaranteed for 48 hrs. against any health or temperament irregularities, and it is recommended the buyer have the puppy examined by a reputable veterinarian during this period. (NOTE: any puppy going to a new home may be a bit unsure of himself until he becomes completely familiar with his surroundings.) A full refund will be given for any pup found unsatisfactory during the first 48 hrs.

    No other guarantee is given except in the case of an *hereditary* defect which develops to the extent it renders the dog unsuitable as a pet. In this instance a replacement will be given when one becomes available.

    The buyer agrees not to use this animal for breeding except by the express permission of the breeders at a later date. Neutering of the animal is recommended.

Special provisions:

Signed: _____
                           buyer

Signed: _____
                           seller

Address: _____

SALES CONTRACT FOR SHOW OR BREEDING QUALITY DOGS

On _____, _____ kennels agrees to sell
           date   name

to _____ of _____
           name   address

the following _____for the sum of $_____
                    breed

Name: _____ Whelped _____

Sire: _____ Color: _____

Dam:_____ Reg. #_____ Sex: _____

Litter or Indiv. _____ Reg. # _____

    This animal is guaranteed to be free from all hereditary defects affecting its suitability for breeding, and is guaranteed to be free of disqualifying and serious faults of a structural or temperamental nature. Health is guaranteed for 48 hrs. and it is recommended that the buyer have the animal examined by a reputable veterinarian during that time.

    A replacement or credit for the amount of purchase will be given for any animal sold for $_____ or more if the dog matures at less than the represented quality at 18 mos. of age, unless it is mutually agreed to determine this at another date.

Special Provisions of sale:

Signed: _____
                           buyer

Signed: _____
                           seller

Address: _____

NAMING YOUR COLLIE

Purebred dogs are AKC registered collectively as a litter. Transfer of ownership from the breeder of the litter to you, as purchaser, is made via the "blue slip." The blue slip, which is the individual registration for a single puppy, requires submission of two names, not to exceed twenty five letters.

Acquisition of a single Collie for the pet owner, future exhibitor, or the arrival of a breeder's litter from which they intend to keep several prospects can be a traumatic occurrence.

It or *they* must be adorned with a name—one which fits the breed, gender and personality of the individual. Originality does not concern the pet owner as it would be a hazardous guess how many Lassies, Lads, Kings, Dukes or Princesses are registered. Companion owners are urged to read the pedigree to see if it can reveal or suggest a fitting name for their proud possession.

When a puppy looks very promising and could possibly become a well-known star in the realm of showing and breeding, its owners may spend more time investigating sources for its name than they did for their children's. A dictionary, the thesaurus, astrology, racing forms, bill boards, advertisements, current events, anything and everything is used to select a name that will be remembered.

Study the list of dogs in Chapter One. These dogs were contributors to Collie history. As you have perused the book you made a personal visit with Collies that I feel were excellent examples of quality and whose owners complied with requests to furnish photographs.

How appropriate that a bitch of superb virtues would be christened "Spun Gold," our own "Rapunzel," whose collage graces the preface, and the lilting "M'Liss" and "Repartee." The firm, masculine identification of "Bold Venture," "Destiny's Echo," and "Country Squire."

A call name can be anything you desire. Perhaps the puppy was tagged as an infant due to a personality trait or an idiosyncrasy of behavior, but as it matures and shows potentiality of a "super-star" you want to christen it with a memorable name.

The automotive industry has spent a fortune researching and gathering names for new cars. Folklore and mythology are studied, and at one time even a poet was hired to, hopefully, present new ideas. Car names create an "aura." Riviera, Capri, Continental are luxurious. Mustang, Cougar and Bronco emanate from the animal world.

Many aspiring actors have changed their names in the hopes it would enhance a theatrical career. Would you have rushed to the theatre to see Marion Michael Morrison as a swashbuckling hero? As "John Wayne," nicknamed "Duke," he

24

Ch. Lee Aires Amazing Grace, Best of Opposite Sex, 1980 Collie Club of America.

was a veteran Hollywood actor who symbolized virility and heroism.

The Jockey Club publishes a book of registered race horse names and it serves as an excellent sample of how horse breeders will combine the name of the stallion and mare for originality and uniqueness. Knight's Daughter produced an excellent stakes winner, Round Table, who in turn sired Tilt Top. Then there was Alibi out of Why, by Questionnaire, and this led to the offspring, Traffic Judge and Why Lie!

When reading pedigrees one can almost name the year or era in which some dogs were registered when owners were prompted to hail an historical event, popular music, dances or prominent personages.

Mrs. Browning of the ToKalon Kennels made family connections with Storm Cloud, Still Storming, and a sable bitch carrying that tremendous coat for which ToKalon was noted, Shower of Gold.

Ch. Wee Kirk's Star Billing's top son was Ch. Merrie Oaks Star Boarder. Star Boarder's progeny out of Ch. Merrie Oaks Julep produced five champions in one litter, including the Best In Show (All Breeds) bitch, Ch. Merrie Oaks Shooting Star and a handsome black brother, Ch. Merrie Oaks Midnite Star, who played an instrumental role in the development and success of our Wickmere Collies.

Color identification can be easily made by Ch. Poplar Sleet Storm, Ch. Poplar Golden Opportunity, Ch. Arrowhill Oklahoma Redman, and Ch. Alteza The Silver Lining with her offspring Silver Treasure, Silver Mark, and Splashed With Silver.

Those who are reluctant to give up on the old standby's add a classy international flavor and Fido becomes Phydeaux.

If you have bred or purchased a puppy that exudes potential, take the time and effort to select a fitting name, for your dog may become enshrined in Collie history and hand its name down to posterity.

3

Club Membership

"He who has made a friend, may be said to have doubled his mental resources."   Robert Hall.

Many pet owners graduate to the status of breeder and exhibitor and wish to compete in either conformation and/or obedience.

To learn more about the Collie and to associate with other Collie advocates you may apply for membership in an obedience club, specialty club (for one particular breed) or an all-breed club. The latter is just what the name implies as the membership is comprised of breeders of various breeds of dogs.

The specialty club is undoubtedly the best initial source from which to gain knowledge and share the camaraderie of other Collie fanciers. Educational programs and the sponsorship of one or two specialty shows annually to help promote the Collie as a desired companion to the public are the primary purposes of the club. Club membership is your opportunity to become an integral part of the dog world as you advance from membership to participation as a committee member or an elected officer.

Membership is also available in the Collie Club of America, the parent club for the Collie. Although the name implies that membership is limited to the continental United States, some of the 3,000-plus reside in Japan, Canada, South America, England and Europe. District Directors are elected from the membership residing in each state. Membership applications are available from a district director or from the secretary of the Collie Club of America. You must have signatures of two sponsors and the district director. The application is processed through the office of the second vice president (membership chairman). Via a monthly communique issued by the secretary, every director and elected officer is requested to vote upon the applicants.

Dahlis

27

Three publications, *The Bulletin, Newsletter* and *Yearbook,* are included in your dues and disseminate information regarding specialty show dates, educational articles, and act as an outlet for advertising by member breeder/exhibitors. The *Yearbook,* published annually, is a complete record, pictorially and statistically, of the previous year's shows. There are many committees needed to keep a club this size moving along smoothly to accomplish the many goals set to preserve and promote the Collie.

The big event of the year is the Collie Club of America Specialty which can be compared to the World Series or the Olympics of the Collie world. Here, on display, breeders exhibit everything from the year's hopeful youngsters through the mature classes and on to the lovely champions assembled to select the best Collie in the show. The show rotates around the country, each year being held in one of six designated geographical zones, under the auspices of the Collie Club of America.

THE AMERICAN KENNEL CLUB

This organization is not open to individual membership nor does it have "branch offices." The American Kennel Club (AKC), founded on September 17, 1884, is an independent organization devoted to the advancement of purebred **28** dogs. Its office is at 51 Madison Avenue, New York, New York 10010.

The AKC makes rules and regulations for registration, dog shows, obedience and field trials, approves dog show judges and provides many other services to police the purebred dog world. Information on clubs in your area can be obtained upon request.

Pure Bred Dogs/American Kennel Gazette is published monthly by the AKC and contains columns from various breed clubs and numerous articles pertinent to the canine fancy. The "Secretary's Page" contains all the actions taken by the club's board of directors, which includes listing all those applying for the privilege of judging one breed or additional breeds. The GAZETTE is one of a trio and the EVENTS CALENDAR is a supplement which lists approved shows, obedience and field trials, tracking and hunting tests. The third publication

is the American Kennel Club AWARDS, which reports show results of all dog events, lists those who have acquired titles and degrees.

Besides the *Gazette,* AKC produces the *Stud Book,* an ancestry record of every dog that has been registered since AKC's inception, which is followed by the *Stud Book Register,* a monthly publication which lists the sire and dam of each dog that has sired or whelped a litter if not previously published.

The Complete Dog Book is available from The American Kennel Club and contains the standards for every breed eligible for show competition. It depicts the standard pictorially and includes the history of each breed plus information gleaned from authorities concerning breeding, care and feeding, basic obedience and training of dogs.

Federations

These organizations are more sophisticated in their approach and aims in the purebred fancy. Situations have necessitated a diligent and dedicated force to protect the interest of the purebred canine devotees. The primary purpose has been to advance the best interest of purebred dogs and many state federations were instigated when fanciers realized that legislation was being proposed which would eliminate or harass dog breeders and exhibitors.

Currently eighteen states have federations: Virginia, Illinois, Utah, New Hampshire, North Carolina, Montana, Ohio, California, New York, Colorado, Maryland, New Jersey, Minnesota, Pennsylvania, Iowa, Connecticut, Michigan, and Florida. Memberships are open to individuals and to clubs throughout the state.

Federations sponsor seminars, publish booklets on "How to Buy a Purebred Dog," prepare listings of reliable breeders for referrals, and assist veterinary schools of medicine in many ways including solicitation of funds for research.

The legislative aspect has perhaps been the most important component of the federation's formation. Fanciers are continually on the alert for any adverse legislation and ready to combat any lobbying or proposals by groups or individuals that would arbitrarily restrict the freedom to pursue a hobby for conscientious breeder/ exhibitors.

Whichever club you choose to join initially, you will expand your knowledge and interest and will undoubtedly find a host of friends, challenges and an insatiable desire to learn all you can about your favorite breed, complete obedience titles, receive that Championship Certificate from the AKC, or support and assist in fair legislation to assure that we may all follow what we enjoy—a hobby where we can own and breed a Collie that fulfills our needs and desires!

Visitors to New York City are welcome to visit AKC's headquarters of purebred dogdom to view one of the most complete library collections (more than 12,000 volumes) on the dog and relish the many oils and famous prints by modern artists and old masters. The library is open for reference purposes Mondays through Fridays.

AKC also provides an information service available to dispense assistance to prospective dog owners concerning any of the 130 recognized breeds which are currently registerable in the *Stud Book*, and can supply booklets explaining the rules pertaining to dog shows or obedience trials, as well as all registration or transfer forms, show entries, or other official documents.

29

30

Fig. 1. Ch. Wayside After the Gold Rush a sable merle of exceptional virtue. Winners Bitch and Best of Winners at 1981 Collie Club of America National Specialty.

4

The Collie Standard

"It is reasonable to have perfection in our eye that we may always advance towards it . . ." Johnson

There are 130 purebred breeds eligible for American Kennel Club registration. Each breed has a "standard," or ultimate pattern of perfection to which each breeder aspires to produce an animal which closely approximates what has been defined as the ultimate individual. It is difficult to attain such a feat when you are working, as an artist, with flesh, blood, genes and chromosomes, but there have been a few dogs that have very nearly fulfilled this goal.

The official AKC Collie Standard, revised in 1977, follows.

OFFICIAL STANDARD FOR THE COLLIE
Rough

General Character — The Collie is a lithe, strong, responsive, active dog, carrying no useless timber, standing naturally straight and firm. The deep, moderately wide chest shows strength, the sloping shoulders and well-bent hocks indicate speed and grace and the face shows high intelligence. The Collie presents an impressive, proud picture of true balance, each part being in harmonious proportion to every other part and to the whole. Except for the technical description that is essential to this Standard and without which no Standard for the guidance of breeders and judges is adequate, it could be stated simply that no part of the Collie ever seems to be out of proportion to any other part. Timidity, frailness, sullenness, viciousness, lack of animation, cumbersome appearance and lack of overall balance impair the general character.

Head — The head properties are of great importance. When considered in proportion to the size of the dog the head is inclined to lightness and never appears massive. A heavy-headed dog lacks the necessary bright, alert, full-of-sense look that contributes so greatly to expression.

Dahlis

Both in front and profile view the head bears a general resemblance to a well blunted lean wedge, being smooth and clean in outline and nicely balanced in proportion. On the sides it tapers gradually and smoothly from the ears to the end of the black nose, without being flared out in backskull (cheeky) or pinched in muzzle (snipey). In profile view the top of the backskull and the top of the muzzle lie in two approximately parallel, straight planes of equal length, divided by a very slight but perceptible stop or break.

A midpoint between the inside corners of the eyes (which is the center of a correctly placed stop) is the center of balance in length of head.

The end of the smooth, well rounded muzzle is blunt but not square. The underjaw is strong, cleancut and the depth of skull from the brow to the under part of the jaw is not excessive.

The teeth are of good size, meeting in a scissors bite. *Overshot or undershot jaws are undesirable, the latter being more severely penalized.*

There is a very slight prominence of the eyebrows. The backskull is flat, without receding either laterally or backward and the occipital bone is not highly peaked. The proper width of backskull necessarily depends upon the combined length of skull and muzzle and the width of the backskull is less than its length. Thus, the correct width varies with the individual and is dependent upon the extent to which it is supported by length of muzzle.

Because of the importance of the head characteristics, *prominent head faults are severely penalized.*

Eyes — Because of the combination of the flat skull, the arched eyebrows, the slight stop and the rounded muzzle, the foreface must be chiseled to form a receptacle for the eyes and they are necessarily placed obliquely to give them the required forward outlook. Except for the blue merles they are required to be matched in color. They are almond-shaped, of medium size and never properly appear to be large or prominent. The color is dark and the eye does not show a yellow ring or a sufficiently prominent haw to affect the dog's expression.

The eyes have a clear, bright appearance, expressing intelligent inquisitiveness, particularly when the ears are drawn up and the dog is on the alert.

In blue merles, dark brown eyes are preferable, but either or both eyes may be merle or china in color without specific penalty.

A large, round, full eye seriously detracts from the desired "sweet" expression. *Eye faults are heavily penalized.*

Ears — The ears are in proportion to the size of the head and, if they are carried properly and unquestionably "break" naturally, are seldom too small. Large ears usually cannot be lifted correctly off the head and even if lifted they will be out of proportion to the size of the head. When in repose the ears are folded lengthwise and thrown back into the frill. On the alert they are drawn well up on the backskull and are carried about three-quarters erect, with about one-fourth of the ear tipping or "breaking" forward. *A dog with prick ears or low ears cannot show true expression and is penalized accordingly.*

Neck — The neck is firm, clean, muscular, sinewy, and heavily frilled. It is fairly long, is carried upright with a slight arch at the nape and imparts a proud, upstanding appearance showing off the frill.

Body — The body is firm, hard and muscular, a trifle long in proportion to the height. The ribs are well-rounded behind the well-sloped shoulders and the chest is deep, extending to the elbows. The back is strong and level, supported by powerful hips and thighs and the croup is sloped to give a well-rounded finish. The loin is powerful and slightly arched. *Noticeably fat dogs, or dogs in poor flesh, or with skin disease, or with no undercoat are out of condition and are moderately penalized accordingly.* In grown males, the monorchid or cryptorchid are disqualified.

Legs — The forelegs are straight and muscular, with a fair amount of bone considering the size of the dog. A cumbersome appearance is undesirable. *Both narrow and wide placement are penalized.* The forearm is moderately fleshy and the pasterns are flexible, but without weakness. The hind legs are less fleshy, are muscular at the thighs, very sinewy and the hocks and stifles are well bent. *A cow-hocked dog or a dog with straight stifles is penalized.* The comparatively small feet are approximately oval in shape. The soles are well padded and tough and the toes are well arched and close together. When the Collie is not in motion, the legs and feet are judged by allowing the dog to come to a natural stop in a standing position so that both the forelegs and the hind legs are placed well apart, with the feet extending straight forward. Excessive "posing" is undesirable.

Gait — Gait is sound. When the dog is moved at a slow trot toward an observer, its straight front legs track comparatively close together at the ground. The front legs are not out at the elbows, do not "cross over," nor does the Collie move with a choppy, pacing or rolling gait. When viewed from the rear, the hind legs are straight, tracking comparatively close together at the ground. At a moderate trot the hind legs are powerful and propelling. Viewed from the side the reasonably long, "reaching" stride is smooth and even, keeping the back line firm and level.

As the speed of the gait is increased the Collie single tracks, bringing the front legs inward in a straight line from the shoulder toward the center line of the body and the hind legs inward in a straight line from the hip toward the center line of the body. The gait suggests effortless speed combined with the dog's herding heritage, requiring it to be capable of changing its direction of travel almost instantaneously.

Tail — The tail is moderately long, the bone reaching to the hock joint or below. It is carried low when the dog is quiet, the end having an upward twist or "swirl." When gaited or when the dog is excited it is carried gaily, but not over the back.

Coat — The well-fitting, proper-textured coat is the crowning glory of the Rough Variety of Collie. It is abundant except on the head and legs. The outer coat is straight and harsh to the touch. *A soft, open outer coat or a curly outer coat, regardless of quantity, is penalized.* The under coat, however, is soft, furry and so close together that it is difficult to see the skin when the hair is parted. The coat is very abundant on the mane and frill. The face or mask is smooth. The forelegs are smooth and well-feathered to the back of the pasterns. The hind legs are smooth below the hock joints. Any feathering below the hocks is removed for the show ring. The hair on the tail is very profuse and on the hips it is long and bushy. The texture, quantity and the extent to which the coat "fits the dog" are important points.

Color — The four recognized colors are sable and white, tricolor, blue merle, and white. There is no preference among them. The sable and white is predominantly sable (a fawn, sable color of varying shades from light gold to dark mahogany) with white markings usually on the chest, neck, legs, feet and tip of the tail. A blaze may appear on the foreface or backskull or both. The tricolor is predominantly black, carrying white markings as in a sable and white and has tan shadings on and about the head and legs. The blue merle is a mottled or "marbled" color, predominantly blue-grey and black with white markings as in the sable and white and usually has tan shadings as in the tri-color. The white is predominantly white, with sable, tricolor or blue merle markings.

Size — Dogs are from 24 to 26 inches at the shoulder and weigh from 60 to 75 pounds. Bitches are from 22 to 24 inches at the shoulder, weighing from 50 to 65 pounds. *An undersize or an oversize Collie is penalized according to the extent to which the dog appears to be undersize or oversize.*

Expression — Expression is one of the most important points in considering the relative value of Collies. "Expression," like the term "character," is difficult to define in words. It is not a fixed point as in color, weight or height and it is something the uninitiated can properly understand only by optical illustration. In general, however, it may be said to be the combined product of the shape and balance of the skull and muzzle, the placement, size, shape and color of the eyes, and the position, size and carriage of the ears. An expression that shows sullenness or which is suggestive of any other breed is entirely foreign. The Collie cannot be judged properly until its expression has been carefully evaluated.

Smooth Collie

The Smooth Variety of Collie is judged by the same Standard as the Rough Variety, except that the references to the quantity and distribution of the coat are not applicable to the Smooth Variety, which has a short, hard, dense, flat coat of good texture, with an abundance of undercoat.

Lorraine Still, a resident of Oregon state, prepared this illustrated standard of the Collie for the Collie Club of America. It is one of the most complete and comprehensive artistic studies of a breed standard, and is reprinted here, with permission, in its entirety.

34

Fig. 1. Ch. Kanebriar Prime Minister.

IDEAL TYPE MALE COLLIE
(Full profile view)

35

IDEAL TYPE FEMALE COLLIE
(full profile view)

CORRECT FOREQUARTER ASSEMBLY (viewed from the side)

Left: Shows the relationship of the bone structure to the outline of the forequarters. The various large bones and the groups of smaller bones are labeled with both their Latin names and the terminology in common usage.

Middle: Detail drawing of forequarter angulation. The keystone of the forequarter assembly is the **Scapula** (shoulder blade) although it has no skeletal linkage with the **Vertebrae** (back-bone) but is held in its flexible position by sheets of muscles and a few ligaments. (The dog has no collar bone.)

Approximately 67 to 70% of a Collie's weight is supported by and distributed equally between his forequarters—being directed to and concentrated on the "Vertical Center of Gravity" (shown on drawing by a solid line which intersects the axis of the shoulder and the center of the heel pad as it touches the ground when the dog is standing at ease.) When the dog moves, the blade rotates through a small arc upon an imaginary pivot or axis. (The blade does not have an actual pin upon which to rotate: the axis being that point which remains stationary when the pull of the muscles controlling the forward and backward movement is equalized.)

The **Scapula** should be set on the Collie at an angle of 45 degrees (X) to the Horizontal when viewed from the side, and should slope downward from the highest elevation (d) to the shoulder joint (a) which is the junction of the shoulder blade with the upper arm, or **Humerus**. All that is meant by the expressions, "a good layback" or "Shoulders well laid back," is that the slope of the shoulders should not be less than 45 or more than 50 degrees with reference to the Horizontal line. (Imaginary) An imaginary line extended from the top of the shoulder (d) and continuing through, or passing over, the **Olecranon** (elbow) should intersect the plane of the shoulder at 90 degrees to form angle "Y". This line is theoretical because the **Humerus** (upper arm) is not a straight bone, but the axis are parallel to each other and therefore parallel to the line shown.

The length of the **Scapula** (a-b) should equal the length of the **Humerus** (a-c). The angle of the attachment of the **Radius-ulna** (lower arm) is not important, provided the bones are straight and stand vertically as observed from either side or front. The pastern is sloped in order to place the heel pad directly under the center of gravity and to provide additional length of reach of foreleg and increase the gripping power and leverage of the foot.

It is difficult to measure the value of forequarter angulation when neither the bones or angles can be seen, so the **"Visional Approximation"** of the Center of Gravity can be judged along the dotted line (d-e). The highest point of the shoulder should be in line with the rear section of the elbow joint and this line should strike the ground behind the heel pad as shown on the drawing.

in action, Collies conforming to these basic principles of forequarter angulation when observed from the side move correctly. (Assuming, of course, that the rear assembly is also correctly put together.) The reach, or stride, is long; the feet are lifted only far enough to clear the ground; and the gait smooth and even; and the ground covered with a minimum of muscular effort.

Right: Correct forequarters as observed in life.

36

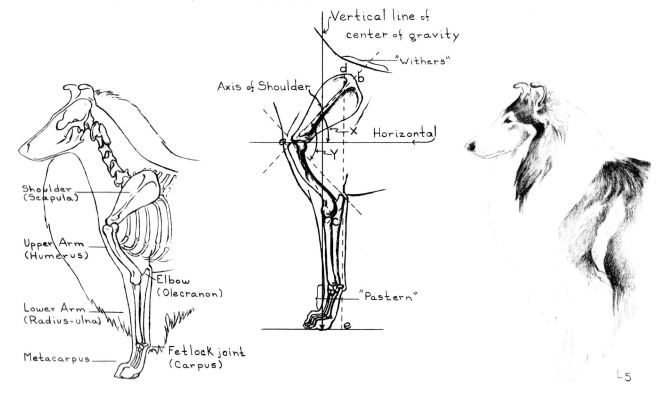

CORRECT HINDQUARTER ASSEMBLY (viewed from the side)

Left: Shows the relationship of the bone structure to the outline of the hindquarters. The various large bones and groups of smaller bones are labled with both the Latin names and the terminology in common usuage.

Middle: Detail drawing of the correct hindquarter assembly which will provide the Collie with a maximum drive, lift and power for propulsion. The mechanical efficiency depends upon several features of angulation which experience has shown to be correct for the breed.

The hind leg is firmly attached to the skeletal framework through an articulated attachment to the **Illium** (pelvis). The pelvis should be sloped at an angle of 30 degrees (Angle X) to the Horizontal as shown on the line (a-b). The axis of the **Femur** (thigh or upper leg) should intersect the pelvic slope at 90 degrees (Angle Y) as indicated by the typical axis line (c-d). The stifle, consisting of two bones, the **Tibia** and the **Fibula,** is articulated with the **Femur** and should be distinctly angled at the "stifle joint." (This is referred to as "Good bend of stifle".) At the lower end, where it meets the hock "joint", the line of the stifle (o-f) should intersect the vertical line of the Hock-Metatarsus (g-h) at an angle of 45 to 50 degrees. (Angle Z). The overall length of the stifle should at least equal the length of the thigh bone, and preferably should exceed it. ("Hocks well let down" is indicated by the shortness of the hock—i.e., close to the ground—in relation to the long stifle bone.)

Leverage exerted by the stifle and a short, straight hock, in action with the tendons and muscles, produces lifting action and, with the **Femur,** the power to move the Collie smoothly and without wasted muscular effort. (Assuming, of course, that the front quarters are also correctly "angulated".) When moving at a fast trot the combined forces reach maximum thrust along line "A" and not over the Center of Gravity "B" as might be supposed.

Line "A" dropped vertically from the **Ischium** (buttock) should parallel the inside of the hock and bisect the foot. This is the position assumed when the Collie stands "four square" at attention. When at ease, a Collie will often shift one or both feet up to the normal center of gravity. This is not to be confused with a bent or "sickle" hock which is an anatomical defect due to an abnormal curvature of the **Metarsal** bones below the **Os Calcis,** or "hock joint". A "Sickle Hock can not be straightened by the dog when in action and is faulty because it opposes the principles of leverage.

Right: Correct Hindquarters as observed in life.

An easy way to check rear angulation is to lift the hock (os calcis) up to the buttock (ischium). If the os calcis comes right up to the ischium you have a well-angulated dog. *Roos*

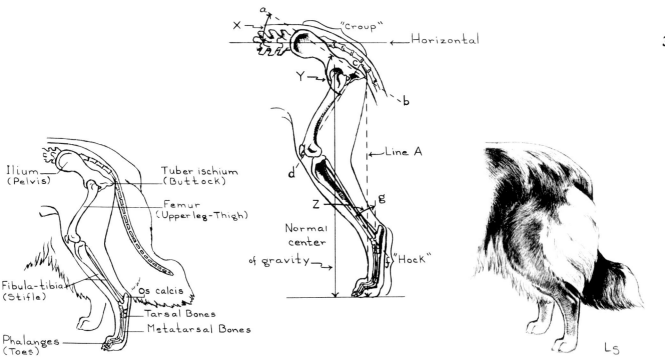

 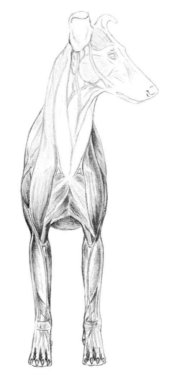 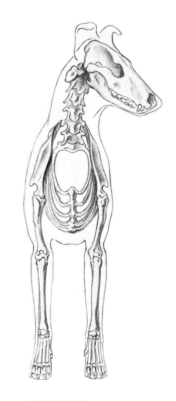

CORRECT FRONT - SUPERFICIAL MUSCLES OF FRONT - SKELETON

38

 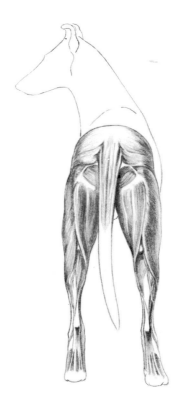 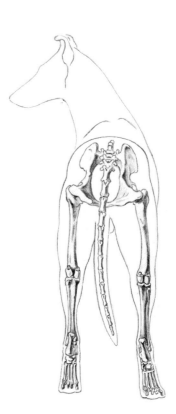

CORRECT REAR - SUPERFICIAL MUSCLES OF REAR - SKELETON

CORRECT FRONT

NARROW FRONT

FRONT TOO WIDE

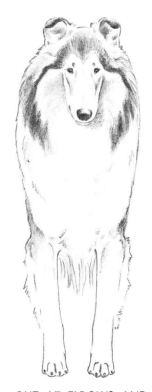

OUT AT ELBOWS AND
TOES IN

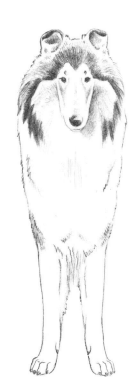

"EAST-WEST" FRONT.

Narrow and pinched at elbows
and chest; feet turn out.

"FIDDLE-FRONT".

Legs give bowed, weak effect
above pasterns, turn out
below. Weak, flat feet.

39

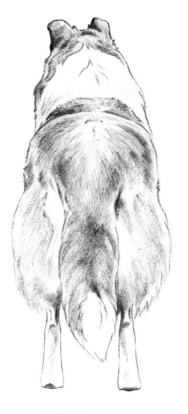

CORRECT HOCKS

"SPRADDLE" or BOWED HOCKS

40

"COW-HOCKS"

NARROW, WEAK REAR

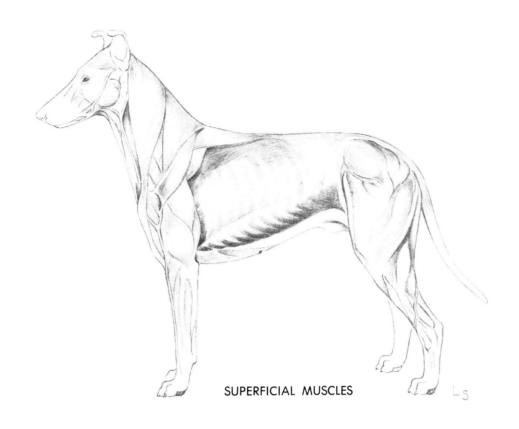

SUPERFICIAL MUSCLES

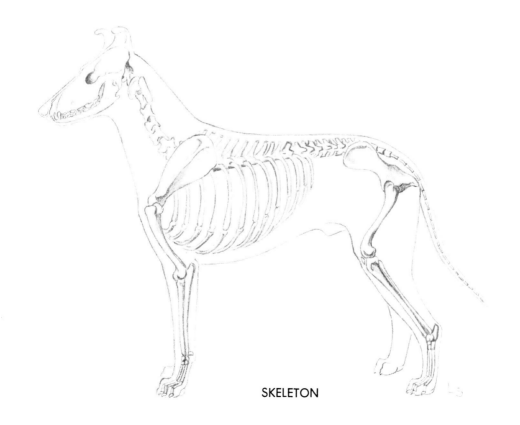

SKELETON

42

-Lorraine-

HEADSTUDY of
IDEAL TYPE COLLIE
(profile view)

DETAIL DRAWING
OF "SCISSORS BITE"

CORRECT "SCISSORS BITE"

The upper front incisors slightly overlap the lower front incisors, and the inner surface of the upper incisors touch the outer surface of the lower incisors.

EVEN BITE (Incorrect)

In this bite the upper and lower incisors fit evenly one atop the other. This type of bite causes the incisors to wear down — in older dogs they may be clear to the gums.

UNDERSHOT BITE (Incorrect)

In this bite the **lower** front incisors project beyond the upper front incisors. Also, note that the alignment of all of the teeth may be affected. In counting the teeth in this diagram you might feel that one tooth is missing in the lower jaw — however in the specimen used as model for this drawing all teeth were present, but the teeth are so out of line that the first molar is hidden from view by the upper canine tooth.

This type bite is most often found in connection with a "Roman" head or a "Roman" nose.

43

OVERSHOT BITE (Incorrect)

In this bite the **upper** front incisors project beyond the lower front incisors. The rest of the teeth may also be affected but usually not to the extent that they are in the "Undershot" mouth.

This type of bite is often, but not always, found in a head where the foreface is long in proportion to the rest of the head. Usually produces a "chinless" appearance.

HEAD FAULTS
(Profile view)

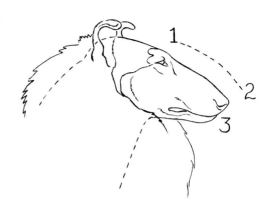

ROMAN NOSE AND UNDERSHOT JAW

1. - 2.   Shows a pronounced arch of muzzle rather than desired straight line.

3.   Jutting out of lower jaw, produced by the lowed incisors protruding beyond upper. Commonly accompanies a "Roman Nose."

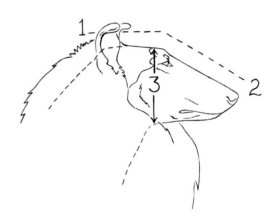

TWO-ANGLED HEAD

1. - 2.   Skull and muzzle form two lines at angles to one another instead of being approximately parallel. Also, produces a "deep through" the cheek effect (3.)

44

BORZOI-TYPE, OR FOREIGN HEAD

1. - 2.   The relation of skull to muzzle forms a curving effect throughout. Foreign to true Collie-type and reminiscent to another breed entirely.

3.   Foreface too long in relation to skull.

HEAD FAULTS
(profile view)

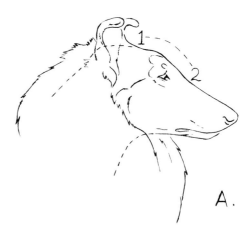

A.

HIGH OVER AND BETWEEN THE EYES

A "lump" above and between the eyes (1. - 2.) gives an "alligator" like appearance to the head. Spoils the expression as well as the planes of the profile.

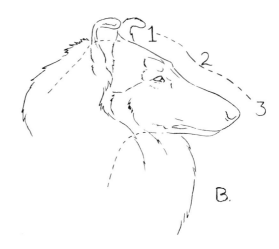

B.

WAVY PROFILE

Presents a wavy appearance rather than the desired straight line of skull, slight drop at "stop", then straight line of muzzle. Caused mostly by long "stop" (2.), and a "drop-off" at the end of muzzle (3.)

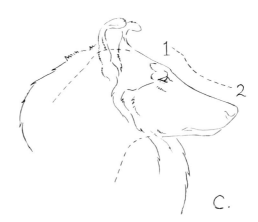

C.

DISH FACE

Here the muzzle presents a scooped or "dished" effect (1. - 2.) rather than the desired straight line.

HEAD FAULTS
(profile view)

"DROP-OFF"

A very acceptable head except for "drop-off" at the end of muzzle (1.)

"SHARK JAW"

Here a lack of chin (2.) give a weak, "shark-jawed" effect to this head. Bite may be correct and fault lie in absence of chin, or it may accompany an over-shot bite.

"SLACK JAW"

Here the lower jaw gives a slack and hanging effect (1.) In the correct jaw line the lower lip should fit tightly over the teeth and meet the upper lip. The "slack" lipped appearance often comes with old age.

HEAD FAULTS
(profile view)

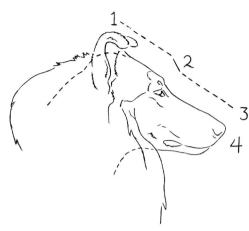

"FARM SHEPHERD TYPE"
    The head presents a "common" appearance. Too much "stop" (2.) and a short, blunt muzzle (3. - 4.)

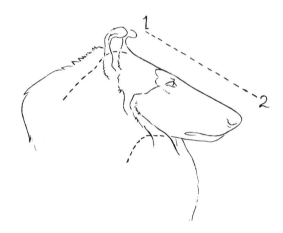

STRAIGHT LINE PROFILE (No "Stop")
    At first glance this appears to be a good type head, but close inspection reveals total absence of "stop". (1. - 2.) The "stop" on a collie is slight, but it should be there, nonetheless.

47

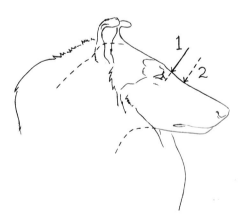

LONG "STOP"
    The "stop" on this head is too far down the muzzle (dotted line 2.) Correct location of "stop" should be at solid line (1.)

Fig. 8. Ch. Arrowhill Oklahoma Tribute. Note how smoothly the foreface blends into the stop area to form a receptacle for the eye and help form what many refer to as a "three-cornered eye." *Eva photo.*

5

Interpreting the Standard

"I hold myself indebted to anyone from whose enlightened understanding another ray of knowledge communicates to mine." Junius.

Learning, or acquiring the ability, to recognize a good specimen of the breed, will be achieved by participating in the club of your choice and personally associating with experienced breeders. It is not a matter of rote as a person must have some latent artistic ability which can be nurtured. The term "artist's eye" is used frequently to describe those that have a natural endowment or capacity to plan breedings and then select the most promising puppies that best represent the breed standard.

Many times a novice will observe a class of dogs at a show and, from ringside, select the best representative without the technical experience and background of having studied, or even read, the Standard. It is said that these people "have an eye" for a dog. This means that without becoming embroiled in the mechanism of ferreting out each sentence or paragraph of what a committee or artist depicted as the ideal Collie, this person bases their selection on balance and harmony.

These people have a high degree of awareness in evaluating proportion and emphasis (center of interest). There is a comparative choice (Fig. 1) for any observer as Collies are not all "peas in a pod." There is a variance as to type. Mrs. Robert Hamilton stated it aptly when she wrote in 1965, "Experience gives a person a perspective of the breed. By this, I mean that one can come to see how two or more types of Collies can fit comfortably under the umbrella of the Standard."

A breed standard is a "design" in which balance and proportion (Figs. 2 and 3a) are stressed. It is a *scale* with one part harmonious to another, conveying unity.

The coat on the Rough Variety is surface interest but also follows the principle of good design in balance and proportion, and creates harmony almost through a "flowing rhythm."

Dahlis

Color has an impact on the observer; a rich deep black, a silver blue merle, a burnished dark mahogany or a brilliant golden sable are very appealing. If the color itself is attractive, flashy white markings are not a major criteria for acceptable "design." Many of the most excellent examples of the breed have not had a full white collar.

We must first understand scale and harmony, then there is no need for rulers, calipers, or measuring tapes. Consider how the words "balance" and "balanced" are used in the Standard to describe the head.

The head must suit the entire dog and will differ with individuals. With the variance in substance (which the Samoyed Standard defines as "that sufficiency of bone and muscle which rounds out to a balance with the frame") and size, we can expect heads that vary in length and width without being either too heavy and coarse or too refined and light (Fig. 4). Scale has to do with the relationship of one part to another.

Harmony conveys unity (Fig. 5). Rhythm suggests a flowing movement in appraising the dog as the eye glides from head to tail (Fig. 6). In assessing the dog at a distance, you have balance, proportion, *and* a silhouette (Figs. 7 and 8).

This outline can be enhanced or destroyed in a Rough Collie by improper grooming of the coat. The contour of both varieties can be altered, detrimentally, if a handler poses or baits the dog in such a manner that an unattractive position is assumed by the dog. Placing the collar and lead behind the ears or further toward the shoulder will be just as important as how high or low you offer the bait to bring the dog to attention and create the most pleasing symbol of the standard to the ringside observer or the judge.

Fig. 1. Comparative choice is a good method in studying the design of articles used in everyday living. It becomes a personal choice.

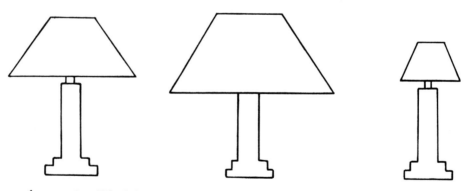

Fig. 2. Balance and proportion. Which lamp would you choose? The shade and lamp should be in relation to each other.

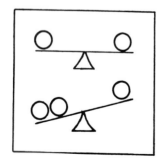

Fig. 3. Balance produces a feeling of rest.

Fig. 4. Scale has to do with the relationship of one part to another as the size of pieces of furniture in relation to each other and to the room.

50

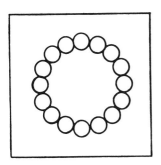

Fig. 5. Harmony conveys unity throughout a design.

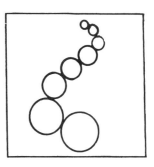

Fig. 6. Rhythm suggests motion relationship.

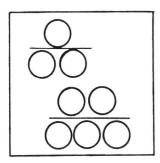

Fig. 7. Proportion gives pleasing space division.

Fig. 8. Silhouette is the outline of the shape, an outstanding feature of this vase.

Fig. 9. Ch. Stoneykirk Reflection. During his show career on the East Coast, "Reflection" cornered the breed wins, including the National Specialty and Best in Show All-Breeds. He particularly depicts the round, firm muzzle that is desirable in a male and was typical of his Sterling ancestry of the older master, Edwin L. Pickhardt. *Tauskey photo.*

51

THE SKULL

There are three types of head. Dolichocephalic (long-headed, Collie/ Borzoi), mesocephalic (intermediate, Setter/Beagle) and the brachycephalic (short-headed, Bulldog/Pekingese). It is the dolichocephalic skull which stamps our breed type. Pictured is the skull of an adult female Collie. It is more refined and lighter than the male skull. The variation of the Collie skull within the breed depends upon the personal interpretation of the standard and the vagaries of genetics. At birth there is very little contrast in breeds. The younger the puppy the greater the similarity even among different breeds—Collie, Bloodhound, Sheltie, Spaniels. If you were handed a two hour old puppy, forget markings, you might find it nearly impossible to identify the breed.

The skull has approximately forty six bones, most of which are fused.

Factors which contribute to skull variations include the curvature of the zygomatic arch (the arch is located just above the zygomatic process of the malar bone) which influences eye placement. Refer to the photo of the Collie skull. On the right you see, marked by arrow, the malar bone and the zygomatic process of the malar bone. The bone is flat and elongated and when we feel this on the side of the head we remark, "the dog is smooth in cheek." The frontal crest and frontal bone (nasal bones) determine whether or not the "stop" will influence the type of head.

Central ridging on the adult back skull is a *highly developed* sagittal crest. On either side of the parietal, or sagittal crest, are depressed areas which are filled with tissue and cutaneous facial (temporal) muscles.

Nature does not usually produce something without a purpose. The crest is the attachment points for the powerful temporal muscles which power the lower jaw (mandible). Skulls, from the prehistoric age to more contemporary times, show the evolution of hominids (human like species) of which humans are the sole surviving branch of a more luxuriant evolutionary tree.

If you study primate skulls, particularly gorillas or skulls of other breeds with various jaw and snout formations, you will notice a difference in the sagittal crest and become acutely aware of the difference between species which fed on tough grasses and nuts and the more refined, small toothed relations which had a diet of fruits and meat (small animals).

The opportunity to study and learn the intricacies of the Collie skull has been bequethed to the fancy by Dot Gerth (also refer to her work on coat color and genetics, chapter 14) through her collection of skulls. From birth to aged champions the Collie skulls are positive proof that we had many illusions about the head which have proved to be fallacies. Patti Merril donated two infant skulls and an intriguing loan was made by Dr. Jim Corbin of an archeological find in Kentucky of a canid specie skull estimated to be 6,000 years old!

At birth the back *skull* is *round* and *smooth*, much like an apple or orange. Zigzag fissure lines are visible and this allows for growth and the changes expected. The malar bone appears to "fuse" at about five to seven years of age. The fissure is located at the arrow, *zygomatic process of malar bone.* This undoubtedly explains what does occur when some puppies finish titles at an early age then do not re-appear in competition because the head flares and widens, developing into a farm-shepherd type skull.

The use of muscles can be seen when evaluating "expression" as the dog manipulates the eye brows to show interest and pulls the ears up tighter on the skull. The latter is very easy to see on the Smooth Collie as the wrinkles appear on the posterior area of the skull.

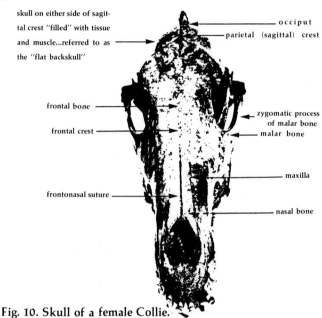

Fig. 10. Skull of a female Collie.

Dentition

We may become so engrossed in checking the eruption and alignment on the incisors that the premolars and molars are forgotten. The late Mrs. William H. Long, Jr., Noranda Collies, who was one of the breed's forerunners, became concerned over the malocclusion of the carnasial molars (the back molars will fit on the inside of the lower molars). In humans it is a cusp to cusp occlusion for chewing. This fault of malocclusion is not even mentioned in the Standard, where there is only reference to overshot or undershot bites being penalized.

However, this blemish can cause different degrees of changes in appearance, depending upon whether the inverted bite is on one side or both. In studying the skull, you can see that if

52

the upper molar is not in the correct position, you can have a fall-off under the eye area. If both sides are affected, the muzzle will be a tubular type, lacking the nice round firmness that is desirable, particularly in a male.

For fifteen years I have checked the molar occlusion when judging and from personal observation I am speculating that the inverted molar(s) is not entirely hereditary but can be an acquired oral problem due to deciduous teeth retained. The undesirable change is made when a permanent tooth erupts alongside a deciduous tooth. The permanent carnasial molar deviates from the normal eruptive pathway. Breeders should have deciduous teeth extracted if they are interfering with correct alignment. It has even been suggested that our dogs need more "chewing" such as bones which will not shatter.

"Wry mouth" is a term used by breeders to describe different malocclusions. Correctly, it refers to the *unequal* growth of the two halves of the lower jaw. This causes one half of the head to be elongated. Genetically, it is a form of prognathism (undershot jaw) or brachygnathism (overshot jaw) and affects *only* the left or right side of the head.

One of the skulls in the Gerth collection is of a "roman head." This is a fault that was more prevalent twenty years ago. A football type curvature to the skull and undershot by at least three quarters of an inch, therefore causing misalignment of all teeth and chewing appears to be impossible. An interesting observation, which could also contribute to eating difficulty, is that the sagittal crest is barely noticeable and since that is the attachment point for the temporal muscles which power the lower jaw (mandible) it perhaps is another contributing factor that the dog experienced extreme eating and chewing difficulties.

Overshot or undershot jaws are undesirable, but the Collie Standard does not explicitly penalize a level bite, and I surely do not mentally dismiss a dog from competition because of a level bite. I am well aware of the challenge a breeder has in maintaining a well-rounded muzzle with adequate underjaw to give the blunt finish required. Often it seems that in achieving this full, round muzzle with a complimentary underjaw, a level bite results, even though the Standard requests the full muzzle with a scissors bite.

Many herding dogs are allowed a level bite, including both varieties of Corgis, Old English Sheepdogs, and all three Belgian breeds. The explanation given is that when a herding dog nips at livestock they would "pinch" the flesh for discipline and a scissors bite could inflict a wound. Whether a Collie steps out of character and punishes a wayward cow or sheep with a nip is immaterial. What we do have to admit is that we are having a tug of war with nature and minor deviations from the Standard can be tolerated as we attempt to meet our goal in succeeding generations.

Some underjaws lack strength and when the mouth is closed the lips are slack and the teeth visible. This is undesirable.

EXPRESSION

The outward countenance of the Collie is one of the most difficult attributes to define. "Expression" is the most elusive characteristic. It seems to defy analysis or at least one that is universally satisfying. It is such a nebulous plus factor to clarify.

One euphemism that has been attached to this external appearance is the "look of eagles." To me, this is one of the most repulsive analogies! Perhaps it is not divined for us to fully understand this characteristic and it will remain a perplexing enigma of our Standard. As Antoine Rivarol wrote, "It is the dim haze of mystery that adds enchantment to pursuit."

The expression varies among a blue, tricolor, or sable specimen of the breed. In the sable, a very dark masking can alter the appearance, as can the complete lack of masking which occurs in many "pure for sable" dogs.

It is even more hazardous when one attempts to translate expression into such components as: ear set and placement; muzzle and how it blends into the cheeks; and foreface and whether it is overly filled, too flat, or too wide.

Expression is an angelic look in both dogs and bitches without feminizing the male. We could be idyllic and rhapsodize lyrically and after many paragraphs and debates we could summarize it so simply. This vestment borders on the occult—is it the outward communication of a soul?

Fig. 12. Ch. Jorie's Mr. G. This proud, inquisitve posture complements the expression. "Mr. G." was a double grandson of Ch. Cherrivale Checkmate. "Checkmate" and "G" were the talk of the breed when they appeared on the show scene. Breeders clustered around the dogs to revel in the "the look."

54

MOVEMENT

Effortless movement of the Collie should be as rewarding to the observer as is the head and expression. The Collie is often described as a "head" breed, but we should not tolerate severe structural faults which would impede its function as a working dog.

You hear a Collie described as "typey." It is the exemplification of the envisioned breed Standard with the harmonious characteristics relevant, one part to another, to present the symbol of the *complete* Collie. One part does not take rank over another. You *cannot* divorce body movement from head and expression nor can you accept the opposite.

Fig. 11. Ch. High Man of Arrowhill. Note similarity to Mr. G at seven months (small inset below). Again the ethereal sweetness and an almost angelic look.

When you study the illustrated Standard, the artist's epitome of the male or female would move out gracefully, achieving distance with conservation of energy. It has been said that some Collies would appear to flow along, or "float," with the absence of bobbing up and down so that a tea cup could be placed on the shoulder blades and nary a drop would be spilled.

Fig. 13. Correct gait from the rear.

I feel that the written Standard, although revised, still has inadequacies in the gait section and fails to convey what the observer should see in correct "single tracking," particularly when gait is observed from the rear.

Another fallacy which should be exploded is that if a dog is brought to a natural stop and is judged in this position that the dog will remain with "the forelegs and the hind legs placed well apart, with the feet extending straight forward." All dogs will stand slightly cowhocked. It is the undesirable excessive "posing" which leads many of us to believe a Collie will naturally stand, for a length of time, with legs well apart and feet forward. No matter how a handler poses (static balance) or trains a dog, the evaluation of correct structure can be made on movement (kinetic balance).

While the Collie is standing still, the head should rest at about eleven on the face of a clock. As the dog moves out at a normal trot, the head should drop to about ten o'clock. This would be the average pace that a working dog maintains. If a dog is structurally correct this trot can be sustained for hours.

The shoulder blade, or scapula (refer to correct forequarter assembly of Illustrated Standard), is "well laid back." As authorities study movement more closely we are informed that the desirable angle is more than the forty-five degrees which has been accepted for so many years.

When examining the adult Collie, the width of two to two-and-one-half fingers should be easily felt between the shoulder blades, at the point referred to as the "withers."

Most of the dog's weight is supported by the front legs, which act as the "shock absorbers." Therefore, the pasterns should be flexible to absorb the jar of the dog's actions but should not indicate weakness, especially when viewed from the side.

A well sprung rib cage with depth and extension of chest houses the thoracic cavity which accommodates the heart and lungs, an important component for endurance.

Propulsion comes from the rear (refer to correct hindquarters assembly of the Illustrated Standard). While the flexibility of the front allows the Collie to make sharp turns and change direction rapidly, it is the rear which gives that needed drive to thrust the dog forward (see photos of Collies herding goats).

"Well let down hocks" and "turn or bend of stifle" are two descriptive terms you will hear repeatedly. The area of the tarsal bones and metatarsal bones is the "rear pastern" or "hock." The closer the os calcis (hock joint) is to the ground and the desired angle achieved by the femur (upper thigh) and the fibula/tibia, the

Fig. 14. Side movement. This dog is not capable of great reach due to a slightly straighter shoulder setting. Caught in this photo at his maximum stride, one can see that he does not fully extend in reach or drive.

more likely the Collie will have the vigorous force needed for a sudden directional change and the stamina for hours of trotting.

You can check your dog's gait by having another person move him at various speeds. Paw prints in fresh snow, on wet sand (beaches), or by soaking the feet and then trotting the dog on dry cement will let you know if your Collie is single tracking correctly. The pads of the rear feet should be visible as the dog is going away (Fig. 20.)

Fig. 17. Moving at a fast speed, the dog is crabbing (sidewinding) or moving his rear to the side to avoid overstepping his front.

55

Fig. 15. The same dog approaching you. Note that his weight is going to be dropped on the leg after it comes back underneath the dog.

Fig. 16. Because this dog has more angulation in rear than in front, he must move his front legs out of the way of the rear and is doing so by throwing out his front.

Fig. 18. Although the coat partially covers the legs, note that this dog's feet are landing along a center of gravity without wasted motion.

Fig. 19. The leg is fully extended, yet close to the ground and ready to accept the weight of the body.

Fig. 20. Going away, this dog maintains the center line as his gravity point.

Fig. 21. The rear legs are driving as one can see by the extension of the rear.

56

6

The Collie Eye and Expression

"The eye is the window of the soul."   Hiram Power

It is impossible to dissect the head properties and pick out one physical feature which is the epitome of the sweet, gentle and inquisitive Collie countenance. All points being nearly equal, I penalize any exhibit in final consideration that lacks fill in muzzle and a nice finish. Many times as I move back ten to twenty steps for a final evaluation in judging I am mentally calculating the virtues and faults for final placings. Recalling the movement and structure, then assessing the head, everything is tabulated as to which faults are more easily corrected and which virtues can be so evasive to capture, much less retain. At a distance the overall picture of symmetry, balance and a majestic bearing can have admirable influence upon which dog is given the final nod; but I doubt that many specialty judges—or educated multiple breed judges—can deny the impact that a good eye contributes to "Collie expression."

The almond derives its name from the Hebrew word, shakad, which means awakening (opening, rising, realizing) yet the Shar-Pei standard describes an almond eye, "extremely small." The "almond" is mentioned no less than 73 times in the Old Testament.

Of 125 breeds of dogs 31 standards request an almond eye. There are many varieties of almonds, about 50, including the valancia, barbary and jordan. One of the best all purpose almonds is the non-pareil developed during the gold rush days. Is it the *all purpose*, non-pareil variety, that standard authors were envisioning when this descriptive phrase was used to describe the eye of the Irish Setter, Afghan, German Shepherd, Scottish Terrier, Pomeranian, Siberian Husky, Basenji, Komondor and Rottweiler? The latter standard states, "medium size, almond shaped." Then we see that some breeds describing an almond eye want it to be "moderate size" (Chow-Chow), "rims should be almond shaped" (Anatolean Shepherd). A number of breeds described *slightly* almond shaped (Belgian Sheepdog, Malinois and Tervuren) and

Dahlis

the additional adjective of "obliquely" and "slanted" can add to the confusion.

Is the term "almond shaped" more fanciful and poetic than correct?

There has been a tendency in the past decade for some breeders to accept the eye that veers too far from the acceptable oblique angle. The proper oblique angle is a slanting position which does not lean toward the perpendicular or horizontal. Too many Collies have been accepted as correct when the eye was closer to a perpendicular slant without the structural tissue surrounding the lids, thus presenting a sinister, wicked, or foreign appearance. This objectionable placement of the eye has been accepted and perpetuated because many novices were never tutored properly nor were they exposed to the correctly place eye.

An eye that is placed too far towards the "12" position of perpendicular (see Fig. 3) gives a very sly, squinty or piggish expression. Study the standards of the various breeds in the Working Group and you will learn that a majority require an "almond shaped eye" and request that the eye be "placed obliquely," "somewhat obliquely," "slightly obliquely," or a "trifle obliquely."

The definition of oblique is having a slanting position or direction neither perpendicular nor horizontal. As defined in the American Kennel Club's *Complete Dog Book*, the almond eye is "the eye *set in surrounding tissue of an almond shape.*"

The Collie head is very unique because of the length, a barely perceptible stop, and smooth cheek bones which form a coffin-shaped head. Yet, the eye must look forward, so the eyeball, which is round, is recessed and it is the top and bottom lids which give an elliptical look (like the longitudinal section of an egg) to the Collie eye.

The oblique eye, leaning slightly towards horizontal, is surely not a major fault any more than an eye that is "slightly light" or as some judges would critique—"I'd like a darker eye;" but it is objectionable when it detracts from the expression.

Refer to the skull (Chapter 5, Figs. 6a and 6b) and you can see that the orofice for the eye presents a receptacle for the eyeball, which is round. The eyeball is recessed. The shape of the eye is determined by multiple factors such as the curve and extension of the malar bone, frontal bone and frontal crest (referred to as the stop area).

Figure 1 shows the artist's conception of the eye in pen and ink. Just a few strokes can indicate how influential the skin, tissue and muscle can alter what we determine as eye shape.

Almond eye, head on.

58

Front view of the almond eye on a sable. Note the triangular illusion created as the eye is "chiseled" into the head with the darker hairs perpendicular to the frontal crest up to the eyebrow.

Front view of almond eye on a sable. When the tissue and hair line is absent, there is a sinister or wicked look even though the eyes are of correct shape.

Fig. 1. The correct almond eye.

Almond eye, profile

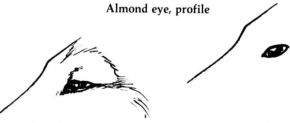

Almond eye (on a sable) set in the head. Note dark rim and dark hair in inside corner of the eye which creates an illusion of a triangular, or three-cornered eye, thusly altering the almond shape.

On a tri-color, the perpendicular line of tissue and hairs sweeping up to the eyebrow combined with the dark pigmentation of the eye rims gives the desired illusion of the triangle or three-cornered eye. If you closely examine a Collie eye, you will be aware that the eye rims should have an elliptical shape. Eyebrows are an exclamation point which give vitality and personality to each individual.

In Figure 3, close scrutiny reveals the set of the eye enveloped by the eye rim and how the frontal crest assists in giving the "three-cornered look." Eyebrows are exclamation points which give vitality and personality to each individual. Use a magnifying glass to amplify the virtues on both the Smooth and Rough Collie (Figs. 5 and 6).

When we appreciate the myriad aspects contributing to expression, perhaps we can better understand the displeasure exhibitors have when judges, lacking the intimate exposure and knowledge of a Collie head, continually select Collies that have a "common" look.

The eye, ear size, placement and carriage, plus the correct length of head to complement body structure and substance all blend to complete an individual that elevates it above the average—a Collie excelling in that elusive, mysterious communication of a soul.

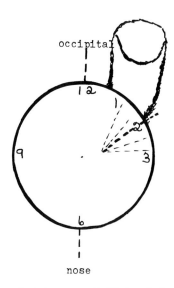

Fig. 2. Using a clock to cover a Collie head, the occipital crest will be at noon and the nose at six. The correctly placed eye will have the lower lid slanting toward an imaginary point approximating the outside base of the ear, which should be about at the number two.

59

Fig. 3. Alandale Parader. This photo captures the correct angle from which to photograph the Collie eye. *Hassel photo.*

Fig. 4. Elmhill Roderick. This sideview shows an almond shape of the eye. If the photo were taken head on, the illusion of a three-cornered eye would be given. *Hassel photo.*

Ch. Merrill's Messiah, WD, BOW, CCA '77.

Fig. 5. Ch. Kanebriar Briquette exhibits correct eye and expression.

60

Chelsea Castles In The Sky.

Fig. 6. Ch. Kings Valley's Tender Escort. Nice eye on a Smooth.

7

The Obedience Collie

"Obedience alone gives the right to command."   Emerson

A Collie responding with enthusiasm in the obedience ring will make more of an impression on the average person at a dog show than the Collies waiting for examination in the conformation ring. The activity and performance is associated with the intelligence of the Collie and the dog's original purpose—taking care of livestock and receiving and obeying commands.

Many of the current Collies are being shown in both conformation and obedience. The transformation from one to the other is commendable. It does prove that not all obedience Collies are rejects from the Standard nor are the conformation classes filled with stupid Collies that could not function where intellect and reasoning prevails. Owners are justifiably proud of Collies that hold titles in both breed and obedience classes. To witness a beautiful specimen, nicely groomed, and reveling in a performance gratifies those who have selected a Collie as a family companion and show dog.

Libby Zink-Welch has been one of these devotees of both the breed and conformation ring. Illustrating this chapter are photographs taken from ringside when her Ch. Shenmoor's Dreamer's Choice completed her Utility Dog title.

As a proponent of obedience training for show specimens, Libby has surely been vindicated, along with many other defenders of this policy, when you witness Collies functioning proudly in both rings.

Libby presents her methods and ideas with the following information:

Dahlis

WHAT ABOUT OBEDIENCE TRAINING?

by Libby Zink-Welch

Those of you who have lived with a Collie are likely to comment that you and your Collie get along perfectly well without any conscious effort on your part to train him. I will not disagree with you. A Collie by his very heredity adapts extremely well. A Collie will pick up your signals even though you may be unaware of giving any. However, like frosting a cake, obedience training can make a good thing better. Your Collie's understanding of basic obedience commands will make him even more of a joy to live with—whether he be for pet or show, living in your house or outside in a kennel run.

Through training your Collie you will increase your knowledge of him as an individual—his motivation, his interests, his mental and physical capabilities. This knowledge should improve your understanding of the individual you are training. In turn, this understanding will deepen your total 'dog knowledge.'

In addition to improving your relationship with your Collie, and adding to your total 'dog knowledge,' obedience training offers more rewards. As each new exercise is learned, both the confidence of the dog and the trainer grows. An opportunity to enhance this feeling of accomplishment is offered by formal obedience competition. The qualifying score, the earning of a title, the placement in the class all serve to reinforce your confidence. The challenge of competition is there to take on at whatever level you choose—first against yourself to improve your scores, second against others in earning class placing scores. Actually, the challenges can be limitless and always changing, but are taken on at your own pace. The people are great. Since all competitors can earn a qualifying score, you will find everyone pulling for each other. A degree of comradeship can be provided by obedience competition which would be difficult to develop in other sports, even in other dog-related sports. So if you are 'in dogs' or just have one Collie as a companion, do both you and your Collie a favor and obedience train him. You will not only reap immediate rewards in a better behaved dog, you may also discover a rewarding hobby.

What Can You Expect From Your Collie?

Whenever one makes generalizations, someone can always produce an exception to the rule. Nevertheless, when one takes a breed of dog as a whole, there are certain characteristics which set that breed apart from other breeds. It is interesting to compare the characteristics of today's dog with the characteristics for which the breed was originally developed. Being familiar with the origin and development of the breed will give you many clues as to what to expect from your Collie. You can expect your Collie to evidence characteristics for which his sheep herding forebearers were selected. Traits such as quick adaptability, dependability, willingness to work, and a steady temperament will probably be found in your Collie. Due to their willingness to work, Collies usually are quick learners. Collies do have a tendency to become bored, so a trainer must always keep ahead of his Collie, making every training session challenging and rewarding. Collies are known in obedience circles for their reliable, steady performances. Unfortunately, they also have a reputation in some areas for slow, unspectacular performances. The latter is usually an indication of a bored Collie and the blame should be placed on the trainer rather than the Collie. In short, you can expect as much and probably a bit more from your Collie than you put into him.

What Does It Take To Be A Trainer?

Not everyone should train a dog. There are certain characteristics which trainers must have in order to make training a rewarding experience for both dog and trainer. A person must have complete control of his temper, for even one uncontrolled outburst may be enough to sour a sensitive Collie for life. Patience, consistency, and self-discipline are also required. It is necessary, particularly in the early stages, to train often—every day is best, repeating exercises until the dog understands what is wanted of him. A trainer must be able to command authority while being able to give praise each time it is earned. A trainer must be willing to give forethought to every action; look at every exercise from both the mental and physical perspective of the dog.

62

A trainer must not let his enthusiasm gain control. He must remember that training is a building block process. Each command the dog masters prepares him for the next. It is important not to confuse your Collie with too much at once. In fact, this confusion can bear the blame for the old dog myth, "Obedience ruins a dog for the breed ring." A dog which has been properly trained for both breed and obedience rings will not sit in the breed ring. However, a dog which has been rushed through his training may become confused and under the strain of showing try performing his entire repertoire in an attempt to please his handler. As indicated before, training is a great experience for both you and your Collie, providing you are willing to invest the required time and maintain the proper attitude.

The Basics

It should be pointed out that entire books have been devoted to training in general as well as in specialized areas. It would be presumptuous to expect to present all of the techniques involved, and address all of the problems which may arise, with respect to the training process in a chapter. What follows should be considered merely an introduction and by no means a complete discussion.

In today's mobile and crowded world it is imperative that every dog be housebroken. "Housebroken" refers not only to toilet-trained but also to such domesticated behavior as chewing only on his own toys and keeping quiet when

Fig. 1. The proper way to place the choke collar on the dog.

told to do so. Such training will make your dog's stay at the vet as well as his stay in motels a happier experience, not to mention his home situation. Housebreaking can begin as soon as your pup leaves his littermates. You should find your Collie very easy to toilet-train as most Collies are very fastidious. If you do not have a fenced yard, your Collie should first be leash broken. To leash break your Collie, begin by placing the collar on his neck (Fig. 1). After your Collie has had a chance to get used to this, attach a small length of cord to the collar. The next step is to attach the leash and let your Collie lead you. Finally, begin encouraging your Collie to follow the direction you pull on the leash (this can be done with lots of verbal praise and physical pats). Within a week, your Collie should be used to the leash, providing you have taken the time to give him several short practice sessions each day.

If you have a small area in which to confine your Collie, toilet training should progress rapidly. Your Collie, being fastidious in nature, will not want to soil his sleeping quarters. You should take advantage of this tendency while confining him to a small area such as a utility or bath room. Your Collie will learn to adjust to your schedule (or it may be the other way around) and wait until you take him for a walk or place him in his yard. Once the schedule has been worked out, you no longer need to confine him to his small room. However, if for some reason you won't be there at the usual time, you should place him in his room which he will most likely try to keep clean until you come to his rescue.

To teach your Collie to chew only on his own toys you must, of course, have a stock of chew toys—biscuits and rawhide bones are best. When your Collie begins to chew on something other than his own, tell him, "no," and give him his own toy. He should learn that it is less aggravating to play with his own toys.

To teach your Collie to stop barking when he is told to, you must be totally consistent. Each time your Collie barks without good reason, you should verbally reprimand him. Often, however, this is not enough and you must hold his muzzle shut while telling him, "Quiet." Another approach and often the most successful is to keep a spray bottle, adjusted to shoot a steady spray of water, nearby. Whenever your Collie opens his

63

mouth to bark, shoot a stream of water into his mouth, while telling him, "Quiet."

Training for the conformation ring can begin when the pup is three weeks old or any time thereafter. The pup is first taught to remain composed while being physically examined. This is accomplished by sheer repetition and verbal encouragement. Along with this training he can be taught to stand still for grooming. After he is leash trained (discussed earlier) you can begin to teach your pup to "show." While natural showmanship should be encouraged, not every dog will demonstrate it all of the time. That is why show training is so important. Begin by training your pup to look at your hand for a tasty reward. Once you have his attention, you can work on increasing its span. Keep training sessions short and happy, striving for a better performance each time.

Obedience Basics

The basics for a dog which will later go into obedience competition consist of: heeling; the come and finish; and stays in the standing, sitting, and down positions. This training can begin when your Collie is six weeks old, but it is best if he is first leash broken.

The sit-stay is generally the first exercise taught. Beginning with your leash trained Collie, gather up the leash in your right hand, while telling your Collie to "sit," push down on his rump or pull down on his upper left thigh with your left hand (Figs. 2 and 3). Once he is in the sitting position, tell him he is a good dog and to "stay" (Fig. 4). Have your Collie hold that position for gradually longer periods, while also increasing your distance from him (Fig. 5). The goal at this point is for your Collie to stay one minute with you six feet away.

64 Fig. 2. Teaching the dog to sit by pushing on his upper thigh. Pushing on the dog's rear may be just as effective.

Fig. 3. Pressure is kept up as the dog starts sitting.

Fig. 4. The proper sit at the heel position.

Fig. 5. Having the dog sit-stay as the distance between is lengthened.

Once he has learned the sit, your Collie can learn to heel on leash. The goal is to have your Collie walk by your left side with his shoulder keeping pace with your left leg and to sit quickly and neatly each time you stop. Each time you practice the heeling exercise, you should begin with the dog sitting in the proper heel position. Call his name and give the "heel" command as you start walking on your left foot. If he lags or forges give a sharp jerk to the leash (chain collars and six-foot leads are preferred for training) and verbally correct him. Be sure your Collie sits promptly with each halt. You may have to fall back to physically sitting him until he puts the sit together with the heel exercise.

Once your Collie has mastered the sit-stay and the proper heel position, he can progress to the come and finish. With your dog in a sit-stay position at the end of the leash, call him to you while running backwards. As soon as your Collie reaches you, physically position him in the sitting position directly in front of you. Repeat this as often as necessary while progressing to the point where you can remain stationary, about thirty-five feet from your Collie, and he will come quickly on command and sit smartly in front of you. At the same time you are polishing the come portion of the exercise, you can be training your dog to finish. With your Collie sitting squarely in front of you, tell him to heel and with your lead guide him into the proper heel position (Fig. 6). It may be necessary to take a step back to accomplish this. Depending on whether you want your Collie to finish to the right or to the left, you will use the lead in either your right or your left hand, respectively, to guide your dog. With a little practice your Collie should soon be going and sitting squarely in heel position without needing physical guidance.

65

Fig. 6. Teaching the come and finish. The dog sits directly in front of the handler. To teach him to finish, use the leash to pull him around to the proper heel position for sitting.

The down-stay is taught the same way the sit-stay was taught but, of course, the dog should be in the down position. Standing in front of your sitting dog, give him the down command and quickly pull down the lead in your right hand and push down on his shoulders with your left (Fig. 7). If this does not work, you might try grabbing a front leg in the elbow region in each hand and pulling down (Fig. 8). Once the dog is in the down position, give him the stay command and proceed as discussed for the sit-stay.

The stand-stay not only involves staying in the stand position, but a brief physical examination. As you are heeling your Collie, give the stand command and quickly turn towards him so that you can slip your left arm under his belly while holding the leash taut in your right hand (Fig. 9). Keep practicing this command until your Collie will stop and stand on command without any physical manipulation. Once he has mastered the position, teach him to stay in that position just as you did for the sit and the down. When he is staying reliably, teach him to remain in the stand position while first you, and later other people, touch him on his head, midback, and rump (Fig. 10). With some Collies, their friendliness may make this one of the most difficult exercises to learn. Their wagging tail seems to make them

Fig. 7. Teaching the down by pressing weight on the shoulders.

66

Fig. 8. Teaching the down by pulling out the dog's front legs at the elbows.

move out of the stand position. However, with enough patience and practice, even these enthusiastic Collies will master the exercise.

Tricks

Children (and many adults) often enjoy training their Collies to do tricks like "Lassie." If you break down any desired action to simple, consecutive steps in terms that your Collie can understand, you can teach him almost anything. For instance, to teach your Collie to shake hands, place your dog in the sitting position. While telling him to shake, take his right paw in your right hand and shake. Repetition will likely lead to a Collie eager to shake whenever given the chance.

Teaching him to play dead is only a matter of taking the down-stay one step further. With the dog in the down position, tell him 'play dead' and roll him on his side. By improving this with each session, your Collie may progress to the point where you can even pick him up and put him back down while he still "plays dead." Collies like to "think" and love to please, so an imaginative owner can spend what might otherwise be boring time working with his Collie. Both Collie and owner will be the happier for it.

Fig. 9. Make the dog stand by placing a hand under his stomach when you stop.

67

Fig. 10. Acquaint the dog with the stand for examination by touching him.

The Challenge of Competition

The American Kennel Club offers six obedience titles which can be earned by each registered dog. These titles are: Companion Dog (C.D.), Companion Dog Excellent (C.D.X.), Utility Dog (U.D.), Tracking Dog (T.D.), Tracking Dog Excellent (T.D.X.), and Obedience Title Champion (O.T. Ch.). The regular classes, in which a qualifying score for the first three titles mentioned can be earned, are offered at a large number of all breed and a few breed specialty shows as well as at obedience specialty shows. Non-regular classes such as Graduate Novice, Brace, Veterans, Versatility, and Team are generally only offered in conjunction with the obedience specialty. No titles are associated with the non-regular classes. Tracking competitions require large, isolated tracts of land and, therefore, are generally held as separate events.

For the dedicated obedience buff, nothing beats the obedience specialty, for it is at these events that large numbers of fellow enthusiasts gather from dawn to dusk to exhibit and talk about training dogs. Not only does an obedience specialty offer a greater concentration of obedience enthusiasts, it also generally offers a greater wealth of trophies and cash awards to be won by the better working dogs and handlers. Special trophies for the Highest Scoring Collie in Trial are not unusual at these events. Of course, you need not win any trophy to earn a leg toward the title you are seeking. Conceivably, everyone can come away from an obedience trial as a winner.

Dogs competing for the Companion Dog, Companion Dog Excellent, or Utility Dog title must earn a total of three qualifying scores (legs) under three different judges. A qualifying score is comprised of more than 50 percent of the available points designated to each exercise in each class and a final score of 170 or more points of the 200 points available. Dogs compete in the Novice class for legs towards their Companion Dog title. The exercises which make up this class are: the heel on leash (including figure eight); the stand for examination (the dog stands off lead six feet from the handler while the judge touches the dog's head, body and hindquarters); the heel free; the recall and finish (the dog comes from a sitting position 35 feet from the handler, sits in front and goes to heel position on command); the long sit (the dog sits along with the other entries on one side of the ring while his handler stands at the other for one minute); and the long down (the dog goes to down position and stays as in the long sit but for a total of three minutes).

Dogs entered in the non-regular classes of Brace or Veterans perform the Novice routine. The Brace class is for two dogs of the same breed working in unison with one handler. The Veterans class is open to any dog eight years or older which has earned an obedience title.

68

Fig. 11. Selecting the dumbbell scented by the handler.

Dogs compete in the Open classes to earn legs towards their Companion Dog Excellent title. The required exercises are: the heel free (excluding the figure eight); the drop on recall (similar to the Novice recall, however, at a designated point the dog must respond to the handler's command to drop and remain down until again called by the handler); the retrieve on flat (a wooden dumbell of appropriate size is thrown a reasonable distance by the handler, and on command the dog must go out, pick up the dumbell, return as in the recall, wait for the handler to take the dumbell from the dog while the dog is sitting in front of the handler, and go to the heel position); retrieve over high jump (similar to the retrieve on flat but the dog must jump a hurdle 1½ times his height both going out and coming back); broad jump (the dog must clear a broad jump a distance equal to twice the height of the high jump); the long sit and the long down (performed as in the Novice class; however, the handlers leave the ring and go out of the sight of their dogs).

In the non-regular Team class, a group of four dogs and four handlers simultaneously perform all the exercises of the Novice class with the exception that the Open drop on recall is substituted for the Novice recall. The non-regular Graduate Novice class combines the following exercises from the Novice and Open classes: heel on leash (no figure eight); stand for examination; Open heel free; drop on recall; and the Open long sit and long down.

Dogs compete in the Utility class for legs toward their Utility Dog title. The required exercises are: signal (the dog performs an off-lead heeling routine with only signal—no verbal commands; during the heeling exercise the dog is given a signal to stand and stay, the handler proceeds to the other end of the ring and gives the following signals: down, sit, come, and finish); scent descrimination (the dog must select and retrieve a metal and a leather object which the handler has scented from among eight similar but unscented objects); directed retrieve (three gloves are placed across the ring, the dog must be

Fig. 12. **Ch. Shenmoor's Dreamer's Choice, U.D., and Libby Zink-Welch performing the heel off-lead.**

Fig. 13. **Returning to the handler with the glove on the directed retrieve.**

directed to and retrieve the one designated by the judge); directed jumping (the dog is told to go and sit at the side of the ring opposite his handler, then directed to take either a high jump or a bar jump, 1½ times the dog's height, and return to the handler; the exercise is then repeated with the dog taking the remaining jump); and the group examination (the competing dogs all remain in the standing position while their handlers go and wait at the other side of the ring until the judge has physically examined each dog).

Handlers whose dogs are to compete in the non-regular, Versatility class, draw from a set of cards on which six exercises are written, two from each of the three regular classes, with the exception that the group exercises are omitted. The handler and dog must then perform these six exercises. This class is open to any dog capable of performing at the Utility level.

In order to progress from Novice to Open to Utility, the dog must earn the titles in sequence. However, dogs may compete for the Tracking Dog title at any stage of their training. As training usually requires getting up at the crack of dawn and working on fairly large tracts of land, there are fewer people training in tracking. The

70

Fig. 14. Ch. Kings Valley's Hallelujah, C.D., taking the broad jump.

Collie tends to air scent rather than follow the trail close to the ground. This characteristic tends to complicate the training process, as it is difficult for the handler to tell if his Collie is actually on the trail. But with perseverance, Collies can be trained to track. Once your Collie has demonstrated its ability, he may be of public service in locating lost children or strayed livestock. Once the dog has been certified by an AKC tracking authority to be capable of competing at a tracking test, he may be entered in a test. The test is performed with the dog on leash and in harness with the handler following no closer than 20 feet. A track of between 440 and 500 yards is laid by a stranger a half hour to two hours in advance and an article is dropped at the end. The dog must follow the track with no guidance from his handler and indicate the location of the article. Two judges officiate at each test. If, in their opinion, the dog performs to satisfaction, he is awarded the Tracking Dog title.

As if all of the foregoing tests are not enough, obedience enthusiasts are always coming up with new challenges. One such, which is gaining in popularity, is scent hurdle racing. While not an official AKC competition, enthusiasts are developing scent hurdle racing into a challenging and enjoyable sport. In these races, a team of handlers and dogs compete relay style with other teams. The dogs must go out over a set of jumps, select his own dumbell, and retrieve it back over the jumps. Obedience enthusiasts will continue to develop more challenges and competitions. You will find you and your Collie can spend countless hours in working to meet these challenges. Of course you may find a Companion Dog title is challenge enough and that is all well and good. For obedience training is a hobby which you can tackle at your own pace with the full satisfaction of knowing you have truly accomplished something due to your own (and your Collie's) work and perseverance.

Good Advice and Where To Get It

If your appetite for obedience competition or training has been whetted by the preceeding discussion, the best thing to do is to join an obedience training club. Many local organizations sponsor "training classes" which are okay for the purpose they are intended—to teach you to train your dog to be a good "citizen." However, if you are interested in competition, you should try to affiliate yourself with a group which sponsors at least one annual obedience trial. This group will provide you with the incentive for daily training, the advice of veteran trainers, and the co-enthusiasts to share your ups and downs. If such a club is not located in your area, try to attend an obedience symposium. These symposiums, presented by the nation's top obedience authorities, will serve as a crash course in obedience training. Your contact with others interested in the hobby can be increased by a subscription to one of the several obedience oriented periodicals. You might also visit your library, local pet or book store, or the novelty stands prevalent at any large dog show to acquire books on just about any phase of obedience training in which your interest lies. The American Kennel Club publishes a comprehensive guide on obedience regulations. It may be purchased for a nominal charge and contains a wealth of information.

Updates

In March, 1980, the AKC instituted yet another title for obedience dogs to attain, Tracking Dog Excellent (T.D.X.). The testing for the T.D.X. title is even more difficult, demanding and complicated than the test for the Tracking Dog. Full particulars on the requirements can be found in the obedience regulations booklet obtainable from the AKC.

The final jewel in the crown of an obedience dog is the new Obedience Trial Champion (O.T. Ch.). To garner this title one must start with a dog that already has his Utility Dog title. The dog must acquire 100 points in obedience competition determined by chart in Figure 18. The points are received by placing either first or second in a class, but there is a restriction that at least three first placements must have been won, one in Open B and the other in Utility, with the third in either class. After a dog has earned enough points to gain his Obedience Trial Championship, he may continue to compete and win points although he will receive no further title.

Obedience Championship Points

OPEN B CLASS

NUMBER COMPETING	POINTS FOR FIRST PLACE	POINTS FOR SECOND PLACE
6-10	2	0
11-15	4	1
16-20	6	2
21-25	10	3
26-30	14	4
31-35	18	5
36-40	22	7
41-45	26	9
46-50	30	11
51-56	34	13

UTILITY CLASS

NUMBER COMPETING	POINTS FOR FIRST PLACE	POINTS FOR SECOND PLACE
3- 5	2	0
6- 9	4	1
10-14	6	2
15-19	10	3
20-24	14	4
25-29	18	5
30-34	22	7
35-39	26	9
40-44	30	11
45-48	34	13

Dahlis

8

The Working Collie

"We enjoy ourselves only in our work . . . our best doing is our best enjoyment."　　　Jacobi

If there is a sense of pride and exhaltation upon completing titles in conformation and obedience, we can only surmise how the fanciers feel who work their Collies with livestock. Even a cynic has to admit that the emergence of the herding instinct that has been dormant for several generations is a heartwarming experience.

If the opportunity is provided, many Collies pass the test for native herding tendency. Monica Mattiucci in Florida and Mary McDonnell of Colorado are two Collie owners who vow that the modern Collie has not lost the instinct for herding and working with various kinds of animals. Sheep and goats have been the easiest choice, plus a few ducks.

Mary McDonnell is working with a group of working dog enthusiasts which includes owners of Australian Cattle Dogs, Australian Shepherds, Bearded Collies, Border Collies, Samoyeds and Shetland Sheepdogs. They feel that the instinct to herd can be preserved even though a majority of owners cannot live on a working farm or ranch.

While facilities for city owners are uncommon, through organized groups, space can be made available for club members and visitors to test their dogs to see if the innate proclivity exists before applying for membership. If it does not, another dog may be acquired which displays the aptitude desired.

A group such as the Stock Dog Fanciers of Colorado, organized in 1972, can be instrumental in encouraging owners to cultivate the herding instinct in their working dogs. Ducks can be taken home by club members who want to give their dogs everyday exposure to livestock. The ducks present a minimal problem in a residential neighborhood and will usually bring out the herding instinct with many dogs that just are not interested in sheep.

Dahlis

The accompanying photos of the McDonnell Collie working sheep is indicative of the "lithe" movement called for in the breed Standard. Miss McDonnell's adult Collies are from the Wind Call Collies of Glen Twiford, who has been such an ardent exponent of the working Collie. Miss McDonnell is adamant in making the point that because a puppy's parents are excellent herders, it does not guarantee they will follow in their parent's paw prints.

But when the Collie does have the natural ability, training to herd can be a lot of fun. A trainer

Fig. 1. The Collie comes forward to turn the sheep back.

74

should never put a dog with livestock that it cannot outrun. Figure 1 shows the Collie coming forward to turn the sheep back. Her aggression is quite positive, but she will occasionally grab a top knot of wool above the eyes if a ewe decides to charge her or give her trouble. The ewe will then do as the Collie wishes. It was found in this Collie's early training that her instinct was to work too close, and she would on occasion turn the lead sheep with a good bump on the shoulder while she was air borne.

Certainly you have seen your Collie tease while assuming the pose shown in Figure 2. When a dog has very "sticky" sheep he will tease one out rather than wearing himself down physically by trying to push it away from a fence or corner. Usually one ewe will move forward, stamping her hooves to challenge the dog. As the ewe makes her move, the rest of the flock will start to follow her out. Then the dog will run around behind to keep them moving.

In Figure 3 the sheep are penned and the Collie will keep them there. The photograph captured the dog changing directions. The Standard describes an agile, free-moving dog with good extension of forelegs and powerful drive in the rear. It is quite obvious in watching any Collie work livestock that it is necessary for him to be well-structured.

A true herding dog does not "chase" the livestock but will attempt to circle and hold them in a

Fig. 2. Teasing one of the lead sheep out of the herd to draw the herd away from the fence.

Fig. 3. The herd is "penned." The agile Collie is shown shifting weight in her efforts to have the sheep remain where they are supposed to be.

cluster or pen them. The Smooth Collies belonging to Monica Mattiucci of Florida are shown herding goats. Note the agility of the sable Smooth and the strong, powerful rear drive propelling him. Figure 7 shows how the dog can shift all his weight to the rear, freeing the front for a flying shift to the left or right. There is definitely an extra sparkle and good muscle tone evi-

dent in these working dogs which Mrs. Mattiucci feels gives them an added advantage in the show ring.

While the Collie may lack the opportunity to use his inherited traits with animals in our urban society, he frequently transfers these caring and protective traits to children and the family, making him a real dog hero.

Fig. 4. Smooth Collies belonging to Monica Mattiucci herd goats.

Fig. 5. Dogs circle goats to hold them.

Fig. 6. Note that the Collie does not chase the stock.

Fig. 7. Quick turns are necessary as the dog "heads" the goats.

75

ˉFig. 8. A gentle nudge causes the baby to return to his mother.

Fig. 9. A firmer approach is needed for this older goat.

76

Fig. 10. Monument erected in New Zealand by the runholders of MacKenzie County. The quotation on the monument is Gaelic. Freely translated it means "Blessing on the Collie dog."

9

Collie Care

"If there be any kindness I can show, or any good thing . . . let me do it now."   Penn

Since a majority of present day fanciers are limited as to the number of dogs kept for breeding and exhibiting, facilities are improvised and could seldom be termed "kennels." A garage, a section of a basement, or one corner of a back yard are often utilized for confinement.

"Space" is grossly exaggerated when the public has the opinion that a Collie must have a farm and large acreage upon which to run free. Collies are content in a limited area as household companions as long as they receive controlled exercise. Cities and counties are enforcing leash laws, but dogs can be supervised in certain areas for free running.

SANITATION

Sanitation, odor and parasite control are of the utmost importance for the well being of your Collie and also to avoid discontented neighbors. Prompt removal of stools will help control flies and odors. There are commercial disposal units available. If there is enough land space, dig a deep pit in which to bury the droppings. Cover with powdered agricultural lime, then with dirt.

Odormute, a granular powder, dissolved in water according to directions is excellent to control odors, especially if you are using a garage or basement to house your dogs. *Super C-D,* a concentrated deodorizer, is good for indoor or outdoor use. Two drops will eliminate odors in a 2,000 cubic foot area. A household bleach is a good disinfectant and deodorizer for wooden floors, beams, and cement. A good froth suds applied, rinsed, then rinsed again with a diluted bleach leaves a run clean and sweet smelling.

Dahlis

A portable flame thrower is very useful for parasite and bacteria control. The temperature of the flame is well over 1,000 degrees Fahrenheit and this intense heat helps destroy worm larvae. If fecal matter gets down into the lower layer of gravel, the flame thrower will help eliminate maggots.

Unless a grass enclosure is quite large it can become worn down quickly, resulting in a quagmire during heavy rains. So, if you are planning a run for your dog, use the various kinds of rock (pea gravel, small rock) or cement. A gentle slope will allow run-off to eliminate puddles in either a rock or cement run.

Preparation of the soil prior to the laying of gravel is important in odor and parasite control. Powdered agricultural lime and rock salt should be worked into the soil. Mix laundry bleach according to directions and pour over the lime and salt mixture, then layer blue stone or course gravel followed by smaller rock or pea gravel. The salt and lime mixture can be applied on the top of gravel and raked in as a periodic sanitation treatment.

Cement should be rough textured for solid footing. Do not smooth it out as the dogs will slip, and this can cause splayed feet, weak pasterns and cow hocks. Slick cement is also hazardous for janitorial duties.

To control hookworm in the soil mix 2¾ pounds of coarse salt in one gallon of water and apply to 100 square feet of run. A monthly application should suffice for normal circumstances, but it can be more frequent if a severe infestation exists. Be cautious with the salt solution if trees, shrubs, and flowers are close because the salt will kill foliage.

HOUSING

Security fencing can be of chain link or woven galvanized wire. Gates should have good catches or locks to prevent escape.

Noise abatement can be helped by stockade or board fencing, plus a thick row of trees to muffle the sound of barking dogs. Many owners are now having dogs surgically de-barked.

Housing can be either a single dog house or a small building that can accommodate several dogs. Guillotine doors or plastic or rubber flaps, will allow the dog to enter and leave at will. A wooden pallet, about 27 × 54 inches, gives the Collie an elevated place to rest.

Shade and fresh water are two essential items that are of utmost importance for the comfort and welfare of the dogs. If trees or shrubs do not furnish a natural shade, the run may be covered with green corrugated fiberglass sections. This also helps prevent sunburned coats.

Water buckets should be anchored to prevent spilling. A hose can be allowed to drip slowly into a bucket for fresh water, or there are "lick it" nozzles which eliminate buckets.

Rodent and pest control makes for healthier dogs and happier neighbors. Spilled feeds can attract mice. Keep kibble and meals in galvanized covered cans.

CONTROLLING EXTERNAL PARASITES

Fleas, ticks and lice are external parasites that can contribute to skin problems. Insecticides available in sprays, powders and shampoos eradicate these pests. Adult fleas live on the dog but leave the ambulatory host to lay eggs on the ground, floor, or carpets. All kinds of powders are available. An inexpensive substitute is *Sevin* (registered trademark of Union Carbide Corporation for carbaryl insecticide), a garden insecticide which is effective against fleas and ticks. This may be sprinkled on the dog every two weeks, or more frequently if the situation is acute. Sprinkle the powder around areas where the dog sleeps or rests, too.

Concentrated dips such as *Zema*® dip are effective, as is *Mycodex*® with Lindane. The latter is available from a veterinarian. There is a wide selection from which to choose, but follow all directions carefully.

James K. Page, writing an editorial for *The Smithsonian* magazine, including the saga of the research instigated (and he humorously added "at no cost to the taxpayer") to determine the best defense against fleas which had infested an aged German Shepherd. (This dog had traveled from head waters to the mouth of the Amazon on a raft along with one mop-shaped dog and one game three-legged cat as part of the crew gathering material for *Exploring The Amazon,* National Geographic Book.) They went through every commercial dip, bath, spray, powder, soap, tag and collar. Mr. Page volunteered that there is room for desparation in science and a researcher was dispatched to a health food store for penny royal oil. The oil was not available, but the clerk recommended Brewer's Yeast. Sixty grains was administered to each of the dogs (thirty grains for the cat) daily and soon there was no sign of a flea. Five months later they were still free of the scourge.

If the condition gets beyond you, check with your local County Extension Agent for helpful pamphlets. The U.S. Department of Agriculture has several bulletins available. Pharmaceutical companies encourage a supply of brochures at veterinary clinics, and the large feed companies publish periodicals and leaflets with updated information and helpful hints for dog owners, whether one dog or more are housed.

INTERNAL PARASITES

Fleas are more than just an external problem as they may also lead to internal parasites. When the dog ingests fleas, tapeworms can result. Your veterinarian may recommend a variety of anthelmintics, some of which purge only certain types of worms, some of which are broad spectrum and eliminate round, hook and whip worms as well. Self-diagnoses should not be practiced. If you suspect worms, take a sample of your dog's feces to your veterinarian for a microscopic examination, then a specific vermifuge can be prescribed. Fatalities from treatment have occurred even under veterinary supervision, so you can understand why it is foolish to diagnose and purchase "off the shelf" wormers. The tolerance level varies with the individual; there can be unexpected, unpredictable reactions.

Tapeworm segments can be seen in the anal area. These segments cling to the long hair on

the Collie and resemble a grain of rice when dried. *Scolaban* is an efficient eliminator of the entire tapeworm, including the head. Do not expect to see the dead worms expelled in the feces after treatment.

Roundworms are quite common and are visible in the stools. They can be treated by safe, gentle vermifuges and can be seen when expelled after treatment.

Hookworms can be extremely debilitating to older dogs or puppies. Young puppies can succumb to anemia if untreated. One excellent treatment for hook, specifically, is *Canopar*. It is not recommended for puppies less than ten pounds. We use *Nemex* and/or *Vermiplex* for the younger Collies. All of these medications are dispensed by a veterinarian with explicit directions. Caution must be exercised with any worming medicine.

Two good general purpose wormers are *Task* (*dichlorvos*) and *Telmintic. Task* is dispensed as small pellets for the control of roundworms, hookworms, and whip worms. Because there can be adverse reaction if the dog has undetected heartworm, it is important that it be used under veterinary supervision. The use of chemical external parasite controls can also cause adverse reaction if used in conjunction with *Task. Telmintic* is fed for three to five days and is an easy, safe, multipurpose wormer if the dog will eat each of the meals that include the worming agent.

Heartworm, once a problem in warm, damp areas, is becoming a national problem. The worms are spread by mosquitoes, and infestation eventually results in death due to heart failure. Treatment is difficult and expensive, so prevention is the best policy. Some breeders screen the run areas. The best preventative is daily medication prescribed by your veterinarian. A blood test must be conducted first to make sure the dog is free of microfilaria when treatment is begun.

COAT CARE

A healthy dog, free of parasites, will normally boast a thick, shining coat. But keeping a coat in top condition, especially on the Rough Collie, requires regular maintenance. Keeping the coat clean is as important to the Collie's appearance as it is to his comfort, so an occasional bath is necessary.

If your Collie is free of external parasites and only a cleansing agent is needed, you can make your own inexpensive shampoo. Rinse an empty plastic gallon container and mix the following:

6-8 ounces of *Ivory Liquid* or similar detergent
4 ounces of glycerin
4 ounces white vinegar
fill container with water.

Some may prefer the ration of 16 parts liquid detergent to 16 parts water.

To enhance the white section of the coat, pour a cup of the mixed shampoo into a separate container and mix a tablespoon or more of *Miracle White,* a detergent booster for clothing, and work into a good lather. Allow to remain on the coat while you shampoo the rest of the dog, and then rinse thoroughly with clear water.

We also use a rinse of slightly diluted apple cider vinegar. The coat, especially on tricolor and dark mahogany sables, will gleam and glisten.

When the Collie starts his annual shedding, remove the loose hair with a steel comb and rake, then shampoo. The dog is more comfortable and it prevents a trail of dog hairs. If the loose, wooly undercoat is not removed, "hot spots" can break out, particularly when humidity is high. These lesions can be caused by various irritants; fleas, lice, ticks, or pollens and dust. The itching makes the dog scratch and chew until an open sore exists. Several home remedies can be kept on hand to start treatment immediately until you can get your Collie to the vet. Trim the hair around the lesion to expose it to the air. Cleanse with hydrogen peroxide, tincture of green soap, or a good bacterial agent. Allow to dry. *Maalox*® can be poured or patted on with a cotton ball. This seems to relieve the itching. *Sulfodene*® and *Happy Jack*® *Mange Medicine* also are beneficial and seem to have excellent healing power. A medicated talc may also be used as a drying agent on the lesion.

Allergies can be vexing when some people want to have a dog but are allergic to dog dander and hair. I do not know the source, but for dog lovers this treatment may be the solution: bathe the dog in a good, no-tears protein shampoo. Rinse with a solution of ten percent white vinegar or lemon juice in water. Rinse well with plain water and blot dry. Then pour over the dog a solution of one part fabric softener (the kind for the rinse cycle, not the wash) to six parts water. Let it soak in and dry the dog. Repeat every three to 10 weeks, as the allergic reaction indicates.

CONDITIONING FOR SHOW

Bringing the Collie into full show bloom is a continuation of nutrition, climate, kenneling and fulfilling the need for external care. Abundance and length of coat is established through hereditary factors. The most judicious use of food and brushing will not bring forth a coat that has not existed in the ancestry.

Condition is just as apparent in a smooth coated dog, as "condition" also refers to skin and muscle tone. At one of the tattoo clinics the technician wielding the needle commented, "It is much easier to tattoo the dogs that are in good condition."

Ch. Stoneypoint Sun Country Flyr.

Nutrition plays such an important role in the condition of skin and coat. Economy is a consideration at all times. For the inclusion of milk in the diet (see Ch. 20) for growing pups, in-whelp and lactating bitches, use any of the powdered milk replacers or the products at feed stores provided for orphaned foals and calves. Some breeders complain about diarrhea with the inclusion of milk in the diet. To avoid this, sprinkle the milk powder over meal and allow to soak. Do not dilute as directions indicate for drinking; rather, serve it as a supplement.

A dried meat mixture from Buffalo, New York, is an excellent source of protein (60%—one cup of dried meat equals three cups of fresh meat). An analysis in a veterinary magazine of this product was excellent. Fresh meats, if available, are surely desirable but you can substitute dairy products such as cottage cheese, sour cream, yogurt, cooked eggs, canned fish, or chicken necks and backs cooked in a pressure cooker.

If your dog is too thin and is worm free and free of digestive system problems, try noodles, macaroni and oatmeal supplements. Rice and breast of lamb are also very good for the lean ones. If you have a fence runner, confine him to a small pen and regulate his exercise.

As for vitamin supplements it is, again, wise to consult your veterinarian. After using an excellent powdered vitamin for many years, we abstained for about four years. Now we have decided we prefer to use vitamins. During the **81** interim, in-whelp bitches always had supplements as did young puppies. Some of our older dogs are on "maintenance" diets, a rather spartan diet when compared to an expectant bitch, stud dog, or one we are bringing into full show bloom. An additive we recommended many years ago and which continues to be a favorite after experimenting with others is *Linatone*. A more economical oil additive would be peanut, safflower or soy oils (see Ch. 20). The diet is important, but one can be economical.

Some climates can be very hard on Collie coats. Air conditioning is an asset. Dogs exercised in early morning and later evening and kept air conditioned during the hottest portion of the day will have better appetites and their coats will be thicker. If you want to show your dog, forego the pleasure of having them as constant house companions as the central heating will not encourage good coat growth.

As for the external care of the coat, another type of oil is very beneficial—elbow grease! Brushing stimulates circulation, and while you are brushing you can keep a wary eye for any skin disorder. We have been pleased with a coat dressing mix of *Alpha-Kerri* (a bath oil) and water. In a spray bottle pour two to three capfuls of *Alpha-Kerri,* then fill the spray bottle with water. Part the coat down to the skin about one-half to one-inch apart. Spray right down to the skin and undercoat. Brush *hard* from skin out. Twice a week is excellent. You can use this up to one week prior to a show. It is also wise to use it after a show weekend to prevent coat from becoming brittle and breaking due to the use of harsh laquers and sprays.

As sophisticated as we have become with our ingenious methods and products, many of our "old fashioned" remedies can be used successfully and are less expensive. We have experimented with oiling several of our dogs completely. One young pup was doused with a bottle of *Mazola* oil and worked into the coat. I read in a poodle magazine of an oil treatment I thought would be interesting. Mix one part each of olive oil, coconut oil, and safflower oil. Massage into coat thoroughly, parting the coat and getting the mixture right down to the skin. This oiling takes several months to absorb. The *Mazola* oil was absorbed in less time, but we used it on a shorter puppy coat. Allow plenty of time if you wish to experiment with this type of oiling. After using a good diet and this oil treatment, I did feel the dog's skin and coat were in good condition. The coat was initially softer than desired; but, when absorption was complete and after numerous brushings, I was pleased with the new growth and sheen. This is a drastic treatment, and should be reserved for a dog that you did not intend to show for at least four to six months.

Another oil treatment from a 1957 issue of *Collie Cues* came from the files of a respected old timer, Florence Cleveland. "For itchy, scaly, dry, hairless skin and some forms of mange, mix 1 quart *new* light-weight engine oil, 1 cup kerosene, 1 cup coconut oil, 1 cup castor oil. Put it in a can or bucket and warm over hot water. Heat water to boiling point BEFORE heating the oil. Remove

82

the bucket from heat, set can of oil in hot water, then stir in enough flowers of sulphur to make a thin hot cake batter consistency. When warm, stand dog on table and scrub all spots with a brush dipped in the mixture. Let dog rub and roll as much as he likes. Repeat until the skin will not absorb any more. This is ALSO a marvelous coat grower."

Still another hint was extracted from a *Collie Review* article about twenty years ago, and I believe the author was Ada Shirley. The advice given to hasten shedding was to add one tablespoon of flaxseed meal to the dog's daily dinner. When the old coat is nearly out, the addition of a tablespoon of olive oil to the diet will really bring the dog into its prime.

Dahlis

EXERCISE

Exercise makes so much difference in your dog's attitude and health. Our puppies and older dogs have a better appetite and are kept in better physical condition due to adequate exercise. If dogs are confined in a small run, they limit their exercise to brief trips to the water bucket, feed pan, and a place to defecate. A 4-foot by 18- or 24-foot run is preferable for a Collie.

A free run is a stimulant to the dogs and is surely needed for your stud dogs and brood bitches. Firm muscles give your Collie power and drive essential to a bitch when whelping puppies. Supervised free exercise can be a run in a wooded area, on a long leash or rope behind a car on a secluded road, beside a bicycle, or jogging along with the owner. We have never felt that trotting on a hard surface was detrimental to feet, pasterns or rear quarters.

Chasing a ball or a frisbee is excellent sport, too. We throw an empty bleach jug which the dogs can carry by the handle.

Treadmill type machines are surely one of the best forms of exercise in our diminishing suburbia, but the cost is prohibitive and currently limited to large kennels and a few of the professional handlers.

Exercise can be a form of comaraderie for owner and Collie. Brisk walks, jogging, chasing sticks and balls are far more beneficial than languishing in a confined kennel run.

WHERE OH WHERE HAS MY LITTLE DOG GONE?

It is a traumatic situation when the family pet disappears. Besides the affectionate bond between dog and owner, it may be a great financial loss when a valuable animal wanders away or is stolen.

If your Collie disappears, act swiftly and calmly. Canvas the neighborhood. Ask the residents and particularly the children if they have seen the dog. Contact the postman, garbage collectors, and regular delivery men. Call the dog pound or animal shelter, veterinarians (the dog may have been injured), and ask help with announcements over local radio stations. Place an advertisement in the local newspaper, offering a reward. In it, describe your dog, omitting the obvious identifying details since this will help you tell if a caller has really found your dog. DO NOT GIVE THE DOG'S NAME. By revealing the name, it gives the "finder" more control over *your* dog. If the animal's name is being used, he may not feel "lost" and will accept his new environment more easily.

Additional advice to locate a lost or strayed dog is to post a photograph of the dog on neighborhood bulletin boards and in public places such as grocery stores, laundromats, and schools. Be persistent by returning to previous contacts and canvas the animal shelters personally. Do not rely on telephone calls.

A loss or theft can many times be avoided by using common sense and obeying local restraint and confinement regulations. Most dogs are picked up while wandering loose. Escape can be accidental from a gate left open or a door slightly ajar.

If you value your dog, the wisest protection is a simple tattoo. If your dog is tattooed, you may register it in the United States with the National Dog Registry for a modest one-time fee, giving your Social Security Number. The National Dog Registry works through veterinarians, humane societies, laboratories, and other organizations and has a high record of returning lost dogs to their owners.

Most clubs and individuals across the country offer painless tattooing through a clinic or on an individual basis. Check with your local dog club or humane society.

Tommy and Nancy Mantlo, Collie breeders of Richmond, Virginia, travel about forty weekends a year and have tattooed some 10,000 dogs in a radius of six states. Their genuine concern is to help dogs and their owners stay together. According to Mrs. Mantlo, a dog license or rabies tag is *not* adequate protection as these can be easily removed. The best type of permanent identification is tattooing with the owner's social security number. Mrs. Mantlo stresses the fact the "dognappers" do not care to get involved with animals carrying tattoos. This type of stolen property is too easily identified.

The tattoo should be placed on the inside right thigh or on the stomach. The abdomen area is preferred on the Rough Collie as the tattoo is more easily seen through the long hair without having to keep the area clipped. Ear, lip, and tail tattoos are useless as well as distracting, and they may be amputated or snipped off.

The Mantlo's use a simple, painless procedure to tattoo the dog. While the dog is held as still as possible, a vibrator type machine is used to apply the numbers permanently on the dog. The vibrating needle penetrates the skin just enough to put the special tattoo pigment under the upper layer of the skin. In addition to the owner's social security number, which enables anyone to identify and locate the owner easily, the dog's registration number may be used.

Dogs are personal property and identification marks such as tattoos are generally court accepted proof of ownership. It is recommended that tattoos on the thigh of a long-coated breed be kept closely clipped or shaved for visibility.

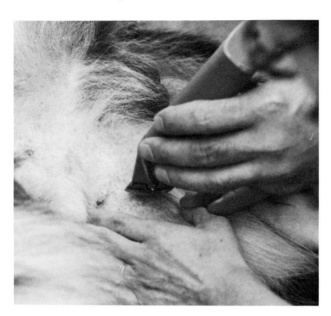

Fig. 1. To prepare for tattooing, all hair is clipped from the area.

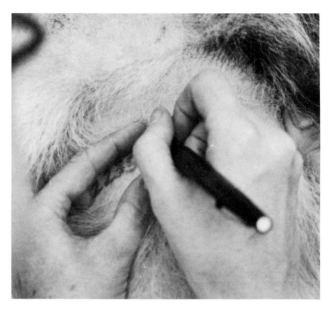

Fig. 2. The numbers to be tattooed are first penciled in to assure accuracy.

84

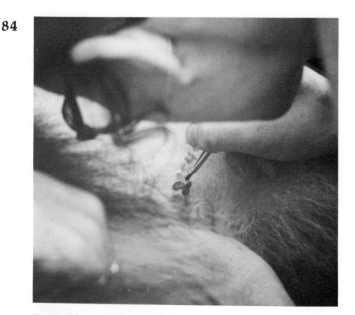

Fig. 3. The actual tattooing is done with a vibrating needle.

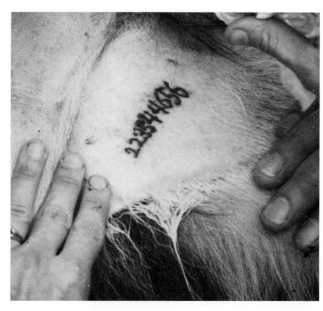

Fig. 4. The completed tattoo. The numbers are distorted here as the skin is being held taut.

Fig. 5. Another angle of the tattooing looking over Mrs. Mantlo's shoulder.

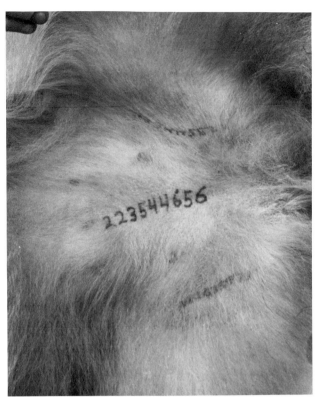

Fig. 6. Experimenting with various size numbers and placement. Note that the stomach tattoo is more visible than the number covered by the more profuse thigh hair.

Fig. 7. A dog that is so cooperative that restraint was hardly necessary as the owners observe the Mantlos putting the finishing touches on the tattoo.

86

Fig. 8. Ch. Clarion the Platinum Minx, Best Puppy 1983 Collie Club of America.

10

Nutrition

"The building of a perfect body . . . is at once the greatest problem and the grandest hope." Dio Lewis

We in the United States are in a state of nutritional neuroticism—"science diets," "all you add is love," "there is a difference in the stools." How do you cope with what you read and feed?

Ninety-nine percent of us start out in this hobby backwards! We get a dog and *then* attempt to learn veterinary medicine, nutrition, the art and science of genetics and, at the bottom of the totem pole, the Standard. The continually successful breeders are those who use an abundance of common sense as they continually learn and in the quest for knowledge accept and adjust to change. As progress is made you can have the old props knocked right out from under you.

The *science* of genetics can leave you clear out in left field if you are unable to apply the *art* of genetics. Slide rule those x-chromosomes all you want. But, if you lack the "eye" or "feel," then success will be a long time coming, or it can be a brief fling if ever encountered.

Like genetics, nutrition is a science and an art—the "eye" and the "feel." At one judging assignment, two dogs from the same kennel (not littermates) had the same drab coats. Not blowing or shedding, the hair resembled an old bale of straw—dull and lifeless. The feel was harsh and brittle. One can tell if this is due to grooming aids. As the sunlight reflected on the coats, these two remained lusterless while several others literally shimmered with glints of gold on the sable guard hairs.

87

Dahlis

―――――

*This chapter on nutrition is offered as observations by the author and is not meant to replace the professional service and advice of your veterinarian.

When a dog's coat is said to be "in condition," the observer refers not only to the amount of coat but also the appearance. The color, gleam and radiance of the coat reflects the physical and mental health of the dog. If a dog is receiving needed nutrients, it is mirrored in his coat, skin, and demeanor. Nutrition and adequate exercise produces muscle tone which in turn not only affects the external appearance but has an obvious consequence on gait.

Basically, nutrition is the sum of the process by which the dog utilizes food to supply his bodily functions and energy. A wide variety of proteins, carbohydrates, fats, vitamins and minerals are required by the dog and must be supplied in properly balanced ratios. We will not try to cover all these in detail in this chapter because, on the whole, they are included in any type of commercial dog food labeled "complete" or "balanced nutrition." If you would like to study further, one of the best books on feeding is *The Collins Guide to Dog Nutrition* by Donald R. Collins, D.V.M. You will find a kindred spirit as the author recognizes the needs and variations that a breeder experiences with show, breeding and working stock.

The efficiency of a diet can vary in individual dogs. It is my personal observation that it also can differ in breeds due to factors such as haircoat, activity, and so on. A biological individuality is very evident when you see one dog that appears to thrive on a diet of kibble without supplements, while another dog on the same diet has problems with reproduction, skin and coat.

SOME ESSENTIAL NUTRIENTS

Protein, which we usually associate with meat, can also come from plants or vegetables. Proteins are composed of amino acids, of which twenty-two are known. (Some authorities quote twenty-three.) Excellent sources of protein are eggs, fresh milk, yogurt, powdered milk, cheese, soybeans, buttermilk, powdered yeast, meats, fish and fowl. Brewer's yeast, powdered skim milk, and wheat germ are inexpensive but excellent sources of protein.

A new breakthrough in the search for a protein alternative is alfalfa. Richard Edwards, a U.S. Department of Agriculture official at Berkeley,

California, has outlined a process whereby alfalfa can be squeezed into pure white powder which is almost all protein. It may be years, however, before the FDA approves this for human consumption. Many years ago, before the advent of our current assortment of commercial feeds, some breeders purchased alfalfa meal for inclusion in kennel diets. Some manufacturers then started using it in their dog foods. Alfalfa not only is a good source of protein, but also of vitamins A and B 2 (Riboflavin). Leon F. Whitney, D.V.M. asserts that vitamins A and D are the most important ones in reproduction. Some horse breeders have felt that alfalfa rations increased in a mare's feed prior to breeding helped solve some reproductive problems.

B-Complex vitamins are most essential. Natural sources include wheat germ, rice bran, and unprocessed brewer's yeast. Raw wheat germ is an economical source of calcium, some B vitamins, and phosphorous. It tastes a bit like green grass and should be refrigerated after opening.

Liver, a potent source of vitamins A, K, B 1, B 6, and B 12, is now available in tablets and powdered form called "dessicated" liver. The price of beef and pork liver has escalated along with everything else so the purchase of dessicated liver seems to be an economical and convenient source. Most dogs do not seem to care for raw liver and unless it is mixed very thoroughly with feed they will either eat around it or choose to leave the hunks of red gold lying in a heap!

Vitamin K, the anti-hemorrhagic vitamin, has been recommended by many veterinarians to be included in a bitch's diet the last ten days of gestation. Following whelping our bitches routinely receive a shot of Coagsol (hemostatic) or K5 (menadione, sodium bisulfite) as directed by our veterinarian.

Calcium and phosphorus must be provided in exact balanced ratios. Most commercial feeds do this very conscientiously and supplementation is generally not required.

Iron is important for red blood cell production and a lack of iron can cause anemia. Our forebearers used molasses as a source of iron, along with liver and egg yolks. The black strap molasses was also an excellent source of calcium and magnesium for in-whelp bitches and growing puppies.

Essential Fatty Acids In The Dog's Diet

A dry, dull, hair coat can be the result of internal parasites, a vitamin-mineral deficiency, and also lack of proper fats in the diet. But *what* kind of fat supplement is important. If you have a practiced or experienced eye, you can almost pinpoint a problem and make a quick diagnosis. Veterinary consultation will be of great help, so refrain from going overboard on any supplement.

An eroded area can appear anywhere on the body. If you are sure this is not a fungus or "hot spot," you may want to check your dog's diet more closely. Hot spots or fungus can appear on a healthy dog with a glossy coat, but the eroded areas we are speaking about usually accompany a very dull, lifeless coat and a scaly skin, resembling dandruff.

You want to be sure your dog is receiving an adequate (not excessive) amount of essential fatty acids. A dog has a rather wide tolerance for fat and some can get along nicely on a diet that has as high as forty percent fat. Some dogs do better on a lower ratio of ten percent or less. You must be observant and cautious that your nutritional balance of protein, minerals and vitamins is in accord with the fat content.

So we speak of "fatty acids," adding "fat;" then we run into various kinds of "fats." The chemical terms of saturated and unsaturated (polyunsaturated) refers to the hydrogen content of these

Dahlis

acids. Fats that are solid are predominantly saturated, i.e., margarines, tallow, butter, lard, and fats from all meats (animal fats). The unsaturated fats are liquids such as fish and vegetable oils.

The following description of saturated and polyunsaturated fats is taken from the "Dietary Management of Hyperlipoproteinemia—Type II Diet," National Heart and Lung Institute, Bethesda, Maryland, Revised and Reprinted January, 1971:

> Saturated fat is present in such foods as butter, cream, whole milk, and cheese made from whole milk and cream. Among the few vegetable fats which are saturated are coconut oil and palm oil (used in non-dairy cream substitutes, some frozen desserts, etc.) and cocoa butter (the fat in chocolate).

Polyunsaturated fats are fats of plain origin. Vegetable oils vary in the degree of unsaturation. Safflower oil is, for example, more unsaturated than olive oil.

Three fatty acids, linoleic, linolenic and arachidonic (a dressed-up word for peanuts) can be obtained from vegetable oil. Peanut, safflower and soy oils are among the best sources of these three fatty acids. Cornell researchers in canine nutrition *(Laboratory Report,* Series 2, No. 3, March, 1973) report that linoleic acid is *the only essential fatty acid* required in a dog's diet.

Fats are needed for the proper assimilation and absorption of the fat soluble vitamins A, D, E, and K. The B vitamins are water soluble.

Rancid fats can induce serious vitamin deficiencies, particularly of vitamin E, which has been stressed as the "fertility vitamin." (Some experts have stated that vitamins A and D are equally as important as E for reproduction.) Any opened bottle of oil should be refrigerated. If you collect bacon or animal fat drippings, be sure they are refrigerated, as well as wheat germ (bran type as well as oil). Animal fats and oils should never be kept in a copper container as the copper acts as a catalyst, causing the fats to become rancid.

When you add oil, remember you are adding calories, so you must use caution if your dog has a tendency to obesity. About a tablespoon daily is sufficient for the average Collie.

Economical sources of the essential fatty acids are available on the grocery shelf—the corn oils (*Mazola,* etc.), peanut and safflower oil. If you want the highest content of linoleic acid, purchase safflower, which has 10 grams of linoleic acid per tablespoon. Then following, each with seven grams per tablespoon, would be corn, cottonseed and soybean. Olive and peanut oil are much lower in linoleic acid. Butter has even less (three grams per tablespoon), as does margarine.

Butter and margarine are very palatable to dogs. Occasionally for one meal, instead of mixing a pan of feed for four to six-month old puppies, I will melt several sticks of margarine and pour it over a pan of kibble or chow. The pups will curl around a bowl munching contentedly away like they had a Saturday matinee box of popcorn. It keeps them occupied and helps appease the urge to chew when teething. I would not use this as my only source of fat supplement nor would I, myself, use this as the only type of meal.

SUPPLEMENTS

It may seem incongruous that we use time and energy concocting special diets for our show dogs when it is so simple to feed the dry "complete" kibbles that are available. I have seen dogs in apparently superb condition on such diets. I have also talked to breeders who abandoned this method either for the entire kennel or for several of the dogs when they became aware that flesh and coat were not flourishing as expected.

Nutrition is a complex field that should be studied before attempting to radically correct a problem by overdosing. It must be realized, too, that the addition of certain vitamins and minerals to a diet can cause such an imbalance as to destroy other essential vitamins and minerals. Some of the better, safer supplements are listed below.

Milk

We have advocated the use of milk for many years—for adults as well as puppies. Check a dog food label and you will find that whey (the clear, watery substance that remains after milk coagulates) is included in the list of ingredients.

The common complaint that milk causes loose stools generally occurs when milk is given as a liquid substitute for water and the dog is allowed to drink a large amount at one time. We use warm water with powdered milk mixed right in with the meat and kibble. We have divided litters through the critical growth period when a puppy needs the best nutrition and kept the ones we were watching as show potentials on a diet which included powdered milk added to the mixed feed. As the pups approached nine to twelve months of age, those that had received milk through the critical stage of physical development carried better flesh and weight. Coat and skin appeared to be in better condition. There was seldom a stool problem—only if we were overly generous with the milk or oil, or changed the type of meat, and added too much initially.

Consumers can now purchase a new type milk in the dairy department of supermarkets, either regular or low-fat milk with acidophilus added. Dr. Dennis Westhoff, professor of food science at the University of Maryland, states he is a "believer" in the benefits of acidophilus milk simply because it is a simple way to introduce beneficial bacteria into the intestinal tract where they help aid digestion. Dr. Marvin L. Speck, a North Carolina State University professor (microbiology) figured out a way to keep milk sweet when adding the bacteria. Previously it has had a sour taste. This supplement is not meant to be medicinal. It is allowing some people to enjoy drinking milk for the first time in years. Dr. Speck is furthering his research to determine if lactobacillus acidophilus (lactobacilli—bacteria which feed on milk; acidophilus—formed of the acid) somehow affects the enzymes, too. An estimated 30 million Americans, including a majority of blacks, find it difficult to drink milk because they suffer from a deficiency in the enzyme *lactase,* which is necessary to break down the *lactose* in milk products.

Dr. M. Reed Lambert, a leader in the nutrition section of Foremost Research and Development Center, wrote on "Milk and Milk By-Products In The Pet Food Industry" when he advocated that milk be included at low, recommended levels:

The low levels of dietary lactose have been found to greatly benefit the dog in three distinct areas. Numerous studies have been conducted to substantiate the fact that lactose markedly improves mineral metabolism. In some studies, it has been found that calcium absorption was increased over fifty percent by including low levels into the diet. Two well-known universities have recently found that low levels of milk products significantly increase the digestion coefficient of all dietary protein and fat. In some controlled studies, the digestion coefficient of all dietary protein and fat was increased more than ten percent, saving in feed cost and/or improved performance of the animals on the same volume of feed.

Dr. B. E. Sheffy of Cornell University spoke before the Dog Fanciers Club in New York. Dr. Sheffy remarked that some dogs did need supplementation. When queried as to what would be a safe and effective supplement, Sheffy suggested *milk,* which he described as an "excellent supplement to provide high quality protein balanced with minerals and vitamins."

Store brands of powdered milk are available as are the milk products at feed stores which are used for orphan foals and calves. Instant soy milk powder is available at health food stores and the brand that we have used costs approximately nine cents a quart.

Friends who have goats feel they have a real advantage over their city slicker cohorts as they are full of praise for the beneficial results of goats milk.

Lactobacillus Acidophilus

The previous material offered on the value of lactose (milk sugar) in the canine diet included mention of lactobacillus acidophilus. This is a beneficial bacteria which helps digest food, acts in opposition to the harmful or putrefactive bacteria in the digestive tract, and helps maintain a better acid balance essential to good elimination.

Before we became so ultra-sophisticated in our saran wrapped world of foods and goods, our predecessors learned to work with Mother Nature. As a youngster growing up around livestock, I can recall mention of vinegar, honey, milk products and apple sauce being used to correct or alleviate certain conditions in animals.

Such milk products as whey, yogurt and buttermilk help promote the growth of the "good" intestinal flora. Now lactobacillus acidophilus and other strains of lactobacilli are cultivated in various media such as soy bean milk, whey and milk. These cultures are dried and put into capsule form and are available at health food stores.

Some breeders have found this product very helpful in the treatment of *some* cases of diarrhea. A few breeders who are operating on a breeding scale large enough to evaluate valid results feel they are getting preliminary favorable results in giving this to bitches that have had reproductive problems, such as not conceiving or losing puppies the first few days (which can be caused by a myriad of problems, so be cautious with self-diagnosis). But there does seem to be a correlation in human and canine between an infection known as *fungus monilia albicans,* which can develop in the intestines and vaginal tract and is perhaps due to the decline of the desirable bacteria.

Oral antibiotics are known to destroy the intestinal flora needed for good health, so it is wise to be cautious in using them. Never overlook the assistance of antibiotic therapy as these miracle drugs have eased the heartaches and disappointments of infections, debilitating illnesses and losses in the past years.

Our predecessors used natural sources to maintain the optimum level of nutrients ... brewer's yeast, wheat germ, milk products. If the intestinal flora is adequate, the B vitamins can be synthesized in the intestines, so that it would appear that *promiscuous use* of antibiotics could cause a chain reaction deleterious to health and reproduction. This surely DOES NOT MEAN that you delete antibiotics, particularly for whelping bitches.

Check the health food stores for an economical source of the acidophilus capsules (i.e., yogurt tablets). If you wish to give these to puppies, you may break a capsule, which dissolves rapidly, into a small amount of formula or honey-water and administer with an eye dropper or add to the formula when tube or bottle feeding.

Vinegar

One tablespoon daily of apple cider vinegar helps to create an acid environment. It is interesting to note that this, along with a natural source of lactobacillus acidophilus (buttermilk, yogurt, milk or whey), was used by breeders to help create a better environment in the urinary tract and probably as a help in reducing reproductive tract infections. Initially, breeders who were adding the vinegar felt it was an appetite stimulant. Again, the old time breeders and "farm folk" used apple cider vinegar for a number of reasons, such as increasing milk supply in lactating animals and reducing intestinal infections due to this acid environment.

D. C. Jarvis, M.D., has written a fascinating book, *Folk Medicine,* a doctor's guide to folk medicine practices. Dr. Jarvis' own experiments with dairy herds is intriguing. One side effect of the vinegar additive was the fact that flies did not bother the cattle that were receiving vinegar in their daily feed and the cattle's arthritic symptoms disappeared.

A Siberian Husky breeder wrote in that breed's *News Bulletin* (January, 1974) that she had used vinegar for six years to control fleas—one tablespoon daily mixed in the feed, or one fourth cup per gallon of water in the drinking bucket. This breeder recommends the addition of iodine along with the vinegar for best flea control. Kelp tablets, readily obtainable at most drug stores and health food stores, are a good source of iodine. She offered this not as a cure-all, but as worth a try to reduce the flea population that torments dogs.

FEEDING PUPPIES

If puppies are well nourished as infants they literally learn to eat and relish a meal. They should not be sloppy fat, but should carry comfortable weight and be eager eaters.

We don't wait for puppies to be toddling about and ice skating through a pan of pablum, but hand feed them as early as two weeks. A large litter of robust puppies can be started earlier by careful hand feedings. You don't want them to aspirate food into the lungs. Start with small lumps of lean beef or strained baby meats (liver or beef). You can make your own "strained" foods more economically by using a food processor to pulverize cooked liver or beef. The handle

of a demitasse spoon is just the right size for a pup's mouth.

This early feeding has several advantages. The extra handling prevents some puppies from becoming headshy and shrinking back when someone touches them. As soon as the puppies can negotiate the meat, start diluting it with milk and pablum. It won't be long before they can be switched to a soaked kibble or meal. When their teeth are in, the pups will enjoy crunching on a crisp food.

One reason we do not keep the puppies on an all-meat diet is the nutritional imbalance that can result. Another reason is the learning process—if they get used to meat, they develop a healthy appetite for it and will ignore a pan of feed and wait for a handout of meat. In mixing the feed, we thoroughly mix the fresh or canned meat through the soggy meal so the pups cannot pick out the meat. They seem to respond more to the odor of the distributed meat product.

Something that has piqued my curiosity in observing a litter is that if there is some food left along the sides of the pan and a few pups are still eating, rather indifferently, if I stir the food out of the corners to make it more accessible, there is a renewed interest and a flurry of activity, even from those who apparently had eaten their fill and wandered away. Whether this is due to the movement, I'm not sure. It could possibly be a holdover from the wild state when the dam regurgitated food for the whelps. Later she was assisted by other members of a pack in caring for older pups who still were not hunting and had to wait to receive their share in this second-hand manner. This movement seems to be a signal for milling about with heads down, inspecting or eating the remaining food. This is a behavior pattern that is interesting to observe.

Our litters do not receive additional vitamin/mineral supplement as a group. We watch the puppies and any supplementation is done on an *individual* basis, particularly for those that are retained as show prospects.

FEEDING THE UNDERWEIGHT COLLIE

Underweight may be caused by many problems. First eliminate either internal or external parasites as a cause. Then check for glandular malfunction. Your veterinarian may suggest a blood workup and thyroid tests. Tonsil problems can cause painful swallowing. Knowledge of the dog's family tree helps. Have relatives had this trouble? Barring physical ailments, eating can be a learning process. If your veterinarian can find no physical cause, then you can start working on your own—cautiously and judiciously.

If your underweight dog is worth the effort, then use any logical method to put him into better shape, but not to the detriment of his health. Questionable drugs may give temporary good results, but could be a risk later.

Hyperactivity can burn up needed calories. A fence runner is boiling over with energy. Channel this energy into periods of controlled exercise, as some dogs won't stop until exhausted. If necessary, crate the dog or keep him in a confined area where he will not be stimulated into extra activity by other animals or neighbors. Provide a rawhide bone to alleviate boredom and a radio nearby to break the monotony.

Internal parasites can be difficult to diagnose and repeated fecal checks may be made before discovering that the dog is infested. Daily observation of the stools is necessary. Appetite, coat and weight can be affected by a small species of tapeworm (Dypylidum canicum).

Sometimes the underweight dog is simply a "finicky" eater. For this dog that has to be encouraged to eat, two small meals are better than one large meal. Competition helps. If the dogs tend to fight, separate the dogs but place the two pans on either side of a fence.

Feed companies do much research as to what odor will tempt a dog, and you may have to do the same thing—chicken, fish, liver. Supplements may have to be given by hand or even force fed if the dog picks out the tablets or capsules.

The B vitamins are helpful in stimulating appetite, especially vitamin B-12 which can be given orally or in injections. One meal a day can consist of a calorie-laden pan of cooked rice (220 calories per cup), or oats (110 calories per ounce of uncooked oats) served with canned fish. Cat food tuna, canned herring or mackerel are acceptable. The rice may be cooked in a broth or bouillon. Chicken necks and backs cooked in a pressure cooker can be fed and the broth used to prepare

rice, noodles, or spaghetti. Tomato sauce appeals to many dogs. Breast of lamb is another source high in calories, and makes a good broth.

Fig. 1. Ch. Kings Valley's Blue Enchanter. *Rappaport photo.*

Cooked oats may be served with whole milk and honey or with products like "Nutrament," a naturally sweetened canned milk supplement for human use. Undiluted *Eagle Brand Sweetened Condensed Milk* can be poured over the food. *Karo Syrup* and commercial products like *Stim-U-Wate* are a source of calories. Also, check your health food store for weight gain products.

Many times if you can get a finicky eater to *start* eating, then the difficulty is solved. Try some of the high potency feeds like *Wayne's Solo, Eukanuba, Iams,* or *Science Diet Maximum Stress.*

Sour cream and yogurt can be mixed in with the feed. These not only add calories but help with the intestinal bacteria, too. We have experimented here with the addition of papaya enzymes (in tablets) and Fenugreek tablets (the seeds were not available) to see if there was any result.

You can always turn to chicken soup. The canned variety, either diluted or undiluted, does seem to appeal to a dog when other foods are ignored.

Always keep plenty of fresh water available as this is vital to the intake of food.

93

"DO IT YOURSELF" MEDICATION

Among the multitude of disappointments in breeding and exhibiting, it is difficult to assess on a scale of one to ten, the most heartbreaking. Many a tear has been shed over the young hopeful which sports a crop of hot spots or loss of hair in strategic places or who comes out on the short end of the stick in a battle with wounds on the face. We never fail to use our veterinarian—the patience this man has with some of our home remedies!

A young hopeful was discovered to have had quite a run-in with a wire from fencing. The wire had been chewed loose and had done extensive damage inside the mouth, leaving an abyss of torn tissue and blood. Our vet was concerned over the appearance this severe destruction of tissue would render to the muzzle. Through the finesse of astute needlework, the hanging shreds of tissue were gathered, tucked and folded. Now it was up to Mother Nature and the healing process. No promises, but when healed there could be a deep indentation due to the severity of the wound and the delicate area in which it was located. There was also the threat of nerve damage to the teeth resulting in the loss of some molars.

First on the agenda was reducing the immense swelling. Dimethyl Sulfoxide solution (DMSO or DOMSO) was applied topically. This medication was first brought to my attention by horse owners who use it in the stable. It is available as a liquid or ointment and is currently approved for use in dogs and horses. It is an unbelievable topical aid to reduce acute swelling due to trauma, hemotoma, fractures, sprains, surgery, and contusions, and is used as a vehicle to carry drugs to the site of injury with fantastic results. It should be applied with cotton swabs or while wearing plastic gloves. The odor is like not too fresh raw oysters. If you get some on your skin, you can taste it shortly in your mouth. Use outdoors as the odor will linger. DMSO was used in processing pulpwood in lumber camps. Some of the workers noticed reduced swelling in injuries as there was rapid permeation in the wound area.

DMSO was applied according to my vet's instructions. He called it "liquid gold"—quite expensive but worth every drop. When the DMSO application was made, I also used vitamin E, puncturing a 400 IU capsule (or two) and squeezing on with an eye dropper and swabbed across the area.

Then came the "chicken soup" treatment. A "good doer" is a blessing. Two meals a day were the best route to introduce all of my healing potions, such as vitamin A, E, and Zinc. The latter was given in tablet form of about 50 milligrams daily. Pantothenic acid is almost nature's cortisone and like Zinc I feel has healing properties, although I would depend more on Zinc. At this time of stress, I felt that resistance would be questionable, so vitamin C was started at 1,000 mg. daily, then reduced to 500 mg., plus Brewer's Yeast for my B-Complex (Pantothenic Acid is one of the B vitamins).

We do not have an adequate source of quality fresh meat to feed 30 dogs, so the special cases receive the ground meat mixed with kibble and powdered milk. This supplies the source of good protein needed for the manufacture of new tissue. The powdered milk assists the assimilation of the protein and promotes better intestinal flora.

When it came time to remove the sutures, the vet commented on the remarkable healing. The combination of excellent surgery and a good diet prevented the loss of a champion. The dog used in Chapter 14 for the grooming demonstration was the puppy involved. Four years later there is still no sign of nerve damage or loss of teeth.

With the exception of the DMSO, the procedure used was the same as in previous bouts with battle scars and undiagnosed encounters with bald spots appearing, primarily on the the eye, cheeks, muzzle and lips).

Although my veterinarian had prescribed administering vitamin C during times of extreme stress, it had never occurred to me to use it for skin conditions until Barbara Schwartz (Impromptu Collies) related her experiences with vitamin C. I also had the opportunity to hear Dr. Bellfield, who spoke of his work with hip dysplasia and high doses of vitamin C along this line of study.

It stands to reason that teething is a time of stress for pups and that is when we noticed pups with bald sports appearing, primarily on the head. Scrapings and various tests ruled out demodectic mange, so some years ago we instigated our own regimen on this troublesome problem. We supplement with 1,000 mg. of vitamin C daily and topically apply vitamin E (200 or 400 IU capsules). We also use *Maalox, Sulfodene* and *Happy Jack Mange Medicine.* If applied around the eyes, we first put an ophthalmic ointment in the eye for protection. The topical application is made twice daily.

Time and further research will undoubtedly reveal much more about nutrition and its effect on the dog. Judging from the vocal complaints of Collie breeders, we seem to have a high incidence of reproductive difficulties and conditioning problems in the breed. The answers may well lie in nutrition. Funding for such research has been scarce and much experimentation has been done in breeder's back yards. Some correlation can be made between the dog and studies done on other animals such as beef and dairy cattle, swine or mink. Even in human research, the effect of over and under supplementation with various nutrients is indefinite and research continues. Until such time that more concrete evidence is available, we can read, study, and try safe, natural supplements in moderation and with veterinary supervision.

Fig. 1. Am. Can. Ch. Wickmere Chimney Sweep, by Ch. Wickmere War Dance out of a Ch. Wickmere Reveille daughter, shown winning the Collie Club of American National Specialty Show in Louisville, Kentucky.

"Sweeper" is being presented a blanket of twelve dozen red roses made up by the same florist who does the Kentucky Derby blanket, and the sterling silver loving cup donated in the early twenties by J. Pierpont Morgan. This perpetual trophy is valued at $4,000.00 and is held by the winner for one year. Each winner's name is engraved on the cup and the owner of the Best of Breed must be a member of the CC of A to receive custody of the trophy.

"Sweeper's daughter, Ch. Wickmere Golden Chimes, was Sweepstakes winner in an entry of just under two hundred puppies that same day. This was the first time in the history of the breed that the Best Puppy was sired by Best of Breed and both owned by the same person.

Ch. Barksdale Early Light, Best of Opposite Sex, 1981 Collie Club of America.

11

Now 'Ear This!'

"Beauty is the first present nature gives . . . and the first it takes away." Mèrè

Nothing is more desirable or more beautiful to the trained eye of a "Collieite" than a pair of correctly carried ears, but they are difficult to get and get naturally. This may sound like an exaggerated statement, but if you think so I suggest that you experiment for a period of five years, breed any way you wish and see if you can breed a perfect tulip ear on every pup in the litter. My own experience is that it can be done only occasionally. This, I think, is the experience of others, too. A perfectly eared Collie, ears that never have to be touched in any way, is a gift of the gods.

—Charles Wernsman

So many inquiries request "naturally tipped ears" on a show prospect puppy and some pet owners become alarmed when their pups ears start waving around like semaphore flags, and they seek help and advice. Some breeders have taken too much credit for having produced a dog with naturally tipped ears when they were actually blessed by nature.

We are tackling a job that has been overly simplified. Leon Whitney, D.V.M., *(How to Breed Dogs)* points out that some characteristics are governed by so many genes as to make a Mendelian prediction impossible. He does not consider body length, head length, or ear length a simple matter.

Marca Burns *(The Genetics of the Dog)*, reports on comprehensive research by Iljin (1937), Kelley (1951), and Marchlewski (1930), some of which she felt over-simplified the situation. Stockard (1941) reached the conclusion that the German Shepherd erect ear was due to multiple factors and that in certain crosses ear carriage is independent of ear size.

Dahlis

You will notice *natural* ears can be of different sizes, texture and placement although a shorter, broader head is usually accompanied by heavier, more pendulous ears or those larger ears with a break almost at the halfway mark. I have not been able to make any definite conclusions that a naturally tipped ear automatically accompanies a certain head type.

When conversing with many knowledgeable breeders, no one wanted to make a positive statement as to just how many genes would be involved to produce a natural ear. One breeder remarked that it would not be unreasonable to presume that over thirty genes could be implicated as we would have to consider not only the ear but accompanying characteristics such as head shape (length and width).

We can assume that correct ears would depend upon poly-genetic factors, environment and the human element which would give an assist when necessary for better placement and tipping.

Study wildlife and observe how nature has developed ears in animals living in varied climates. The Polar Bear has very small ears. This is actually conservation of body heat. Then there are the large extremities of the Western Jack Rabbit, the Kit Fox (North American desert) and the Fennec (Sahara desert). The large ears of these arid area inhabitants serve two purposes: they aid dissipation of body heat and catch sounds efficiently.

98   As breeders, we do not want to leave ear set up to nature and try to control many physical aspects regardless of what area or climate we live in. If we are not successful genetically, we can

intervene by many methods to either bring the ears up from a low position or encourage a proper tip.

The natural placement of the ear allows the inside corner to be placed on the skull in a position so that if a straight line was drawn from the innermost side of the ear straight down it would create a direct line through the center of the eye (Fig. 1).

Please refer to the skull photo (Ch. 5) and you will be aware that the ears' foundation is not on a bone portion of the skull but on tissue (cartilage) and muscle.

Whether your Collie has low, pendulous ears or high ears with a tendency towards prick, there are numerous products and solutions to aid in correcting ear set. You can choose whichever method you prefer and can cope with easily.

HIGH EARS

Adhesive Tape—*Curity* wet-proof adhesive tape. Cut into a strip, rull BB shot into one end. Roll up, leaving a small end of tape exposed, place on inside tip of ear to weight over.

Jiffy Sew® and Speed Sew® are Canadian products used to mend fabrics and are available on order through breed magazines and some clubs have fund raising 'ways and means' committees which sell the products. Squeeze a small amount on tip of ear, fold ear over and press firmly until liquid dries. Why the Canadian product holds and the American made counterpart does not is a mystery. We experimented with many U.S. brands of liquid fabric menders and none bonded.

Skin Bond® is also a liquid and the ingredients are natural rubber and Hexane. It is used to hold large bandages in place. To remove use Uni-Solve®. These two products are available through medical supply houses or a pharmacist. Paint thinner and finger nail polish remover can also be used to remove the adhesives. Skin Bond is applied in the same method as the two fabric menders.

Antiphlogistine®—A medicated poultice obtained at a drug store. It comes in a jar or tube. Place this on the inside tip of the ear, enough to weight the ear over easily. The problem with *Antiphlogistine* is that a dog can flip if off by merely shaking the head vigorously. To avoid this, work very fine sand, pumice, or powder into the *Antiphlogis-*

Fig. 1. Illustration of proper ear carriage so that the inside edge of ear is in a straight line with the center of the eye.

tine. It is wise to also lubricate the fold of the ear where it breaks with an oil such as a very good lanolin-based hand lotion, or vitamin E from a capsule punctured and squeezed. A small piece of torn paper towel or newspaper may also be placed over the *Antiphlogistine* to keep it from getting too messy.

Other emollients which will help soften the ear are:

Neatsfoot oil—Available at drug stores, leather good stores, or tack shops as this compound softens and preserves leather. Highly emulsified, it does help to keep the ear pliable.

Bag Balm—This is used on cows' udders and teats to help heal chafing, windburn, sunburn and some injuries.

Vitamin A and D Ointment (Reg. T.M.)—This is used on human infants for diaper rash. Usually sold in a tube. Squeeze onto fold of ear and rub in gently to encourage tipping.

You will notice that these ointments have a petrolatum-lanolin base. Pure lanolin is very difficult to use. It is wiser to purchase the highly emulsified products.

For ears that need only slight assistance in tipping, there are many excellent hand and skin lotions at cosmetic counters including the old reliable glycerin.

Insect and fly bites can play havoc with ears. If you are oiling to keep the ears tipped, add a drop or two of oil of citronella daily or use any of the spray and wipe products recommended for cattle and horses.

LOW EARS

There are several methods used to elevate low ears and to bring the ear placement up on the head to give a more pleasing expression.

Assemble the following materials:

Scissors

Alcohol or ether—to remove the natural oils from the skin. The latter is purchased as "Starting Fluid" in an aerosol spray can at automotive supply stores and service stations. This product should be used with caution as it is extremely flammable and highly volatile.

Dr. Scholl's Molefoam No. 39

Dr. Scholl's Moleskin (Kurotex) No. 814 or Mole-

skin available in strips seven inches by ten inches.

Yarn

Half-inch adhesive tape

Silver electrical (duct) tape

Heavy duty double-faced foam tape (used to hang pictures)

Trim excessive long hairs from inside part of ear. Using a cotton ball, clean the ear from the canal to the tip with alcohol or ether. While the ears dry, cut your forms to fit inside ear.

It depends on the amount of support needed whether you wish to use the *Molefoam,* which is heavier, or the lighter weight *Moleskin.*

If you plan to use the support with the half-inch adhesive tape, use the support in the bottom of Figure 2. Spray the adhesive side of the foam or moleskin lightly with the ether to increase adhesion and press firmly into the ear (Fig. 3).

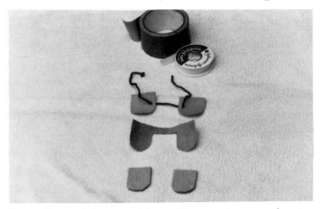

Fig. 2. Some of the materials used in propping ears, showing three different forms for props.

Fig. 3. Place prop in ear with the top just below where you want the ear to tip.

Cut a strip of the half-inch adhesive to go around each ear separately. Spray lightly with ether and wrap around the base of each ear (Fig. 4). Be sure no hairs are caught under the tape. You can use a toothpick or hairpin to pluck out any hairs that are caught.

Cut a longer strip of half-inch adhesive. Spray lightly with ether, and press the end of the tape firmly into the left ear where the support and previous short piece of tape are (Fig. 5). Cross over the backskull and press tape firmly onto the half-inch tape and support in right ear (Fig. 6). At this time you are pulling the ears up tight on the head to improve the placement. Circle around the right ear and across the skull to the back of the left ear. Bring the end of the tape around to the front of the left ear and, again press firmly into place (Fig. 7).

Now you want to bring the ear tip over. Cut a strip of silver electrical tape. With sticky side out, make a circle. Place this "loop" on the moleskin support (Fig. 8), pull the tip of the ear over and squeeze the ear between thumb and forefinger (Fig. 9) so that the ear tip is firmly held in place. If you have trouble with this "loop" coming loose, cut a strip of the heavy duty double-faced foam tape and insert inside the loop and press together.

Again, check to be sure hairs are not caught under the tape as this can irritate the dog and he will shake his head or scratch vigorously and all of the taping can be removed in a hurry. Figure 10 shows how the ears will look upon completion.

We use, and prefer, the use of the form second from the bottom in Figure 1. Using either the

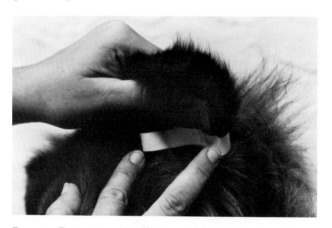

100 Fig. 4. Cut strip of adhesive tape and wrap each ear individually.

Fig. 5. Cut a long strip of adhesive tape. Press firmly onto one ear on top of prop and previous tape wrapping.

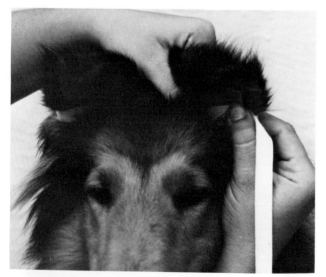

Fig. 6. Cross over and wrap other ear.

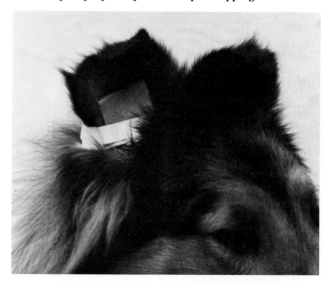

Fig. 7. Follow around the back and meet in the front.

moleskin or molefoam, cut the size and width needed. This depends on the age of the dog and size of the ear.

Clean the ear as recommended to remove natural oils. Spray the adhesive backing on the moleskin form and insert into ears. The crossbar is placed at the top of the ears and creates a one-piece bridge so that the form not only supports the ear erect, but pulls them closer together. Proceed to tip ears over as described.

The top form in Figure 1 is also the foam or moleskin, but yarn is used as the brace between the ears. Cut a small slit in each form and lace a piece of yarn through them. When the supports are placed in each ear, tie the two end pieces of yarn together to pull the ears up tighter. Adjust the yarn until the ears are positioned correctly. Tipping the ear over is the same procedure no matter which type of support is selected.

If you live in a high humidity area, you may prefer using one of the methods with no taping.

Dogs become accustomed to this "harness;" but, if it annoys them initially, check to be sure hairs are not caught under the tape. Give them a large bone to chew on to distract their attention. Check the ears daily for any skin irritation that could be caused by the tape. Some dogs have an allergic reaction. If so, there is nonallergenic tape available.

The ears should remain up for two to three weeks. When the forms begin to pull loose, remove and watch the ears for several days to see if the placement and tipping is effective.

To remove the tape, spray *very lightly* with ether and gently pull the tape away. Residue from the tape may remain. Ether on a cotton ball will remove it easily, and is particularly good if you are attempting to raise the low ear because the cold ether encourages the ear cartilage to stiffen.

If you are very concerned about tipping, the less oil you remove from the ear the better; so to remove tape residue, rub a small amout of *Lestoil,* a household cleaning agent, on the ears. Any remnants of tape will roll right off.

Fig. 8. Place the loop made of silver electrical tape on prop.

101

Fig. 9. Pinch ear tip over.

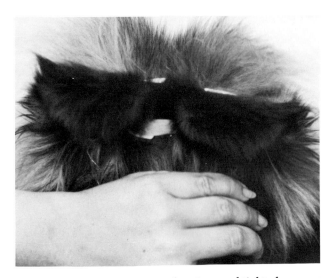

Fig. 10. Finished ear propping showing good tight placement on skull.

I would prefer to see a lower breaking tip on younger dogs as many males will have ears go up higher when being used at stud and after loosing coat. Bitches will seem to have erratic ear carriage prior to and during a season. If bred, bitches' ears usually have a tendency to go prick when they shed completely after weaning their litter.

If you wish to continue showing an older dog or bitch and the ears become capricious, keep the tip taped over at home. Use the moleskin support and the loop on the tip, pressed over to the moleskin. It is not necessary to use the brace between the ears.

Should the ear tip too low for proper expression, astute use of thinning shears to eliminate excess hair will help reduce the weight and lift up the tip.

Cold weather and high winds play havoc with ears; thusly, weather can affect the tipping just as any other aspect.

Fig. 12. Ch. Kings Valley Tender Image as a puppy.

102

Fig. 11. Male, age three months. Ears will come up and can remain like this for several weeks. As teething progresses, ear carriage will usually become erratic. It is at this age, particularly, that ear training should be persistently practiced if required. This pup did not require any artificial aids and finished as Ch. Wickmere Branding Iron.

Fig. 13. Ch. Kings Valley Carry the Torch exhibits perfect ears as a puppy.

12

Grooming

"Love of beauty is taste, the creation of beauty is art." Emerson

Could there be anything more beautiful than a Collie groomed to perfection?

What follows is an outline that will enable anyone, with practice, to present a well-groomed Collie. Grooming is an art. As in the study of painting, once one has mastered the basics an individual style will start to emerge.

In order to get the best results it is necessary that the dog be clean and in the peak of condition. Regular maintenance of the coat, teeth and nails will help guard against any trouble spots becoming too serious.

TOOLS AND EQUIPMENT

The few basic pieces of equipment shown in the illustration (Fig. 1) are all that will be necessary to follow the step-by-step instructions for preparing your dog for the show ring. By purchasing only these few items, the expense of supplying a grooming kit can be kept to the minimum. Individual tastes, experience and preference will be the ultimate factor in determining your supplies.

A good sturdy grooming table with a non-slip covering will place the dog at the right height, to eliminate back strain and enable the groomer to be more accurate in trimming.

The items required include: (top row) spray bottle, waterless shampoo (in this instance *Kote-Glo®*), and a whitening agent; (middle row) sandpaper or a product sold at kennel supplies as a "stripping stone" (available in hardware stores as foam glass), a good pinbrush, a stiff-bristled brush, and a fine-toothed comb; (bottom row) nail clippers,

Dahlis

straight-edged scissors, and single-edged thinning shears with at least 40 teeth. The use of double-edged thinning shears or those with fewer teeth may leave unsightly marks as they tend to cut the hair rather than thin.

Beyond these necessities, a few towels and a small tin to store the chalk will be all that is required to present your Collie as effectively as any professional.

Preparing for the Show Ring

Nothing will aid you more in preparing your Collie for the ring than being thoroughly knowledgeable of the standard and its application to your dog. When you have your ideal envisioned, grooming will only complement the virtues and minimize the faults your Collie possesses.

An astute judge should be able to determine the qualities of a dog no matter how he is presented. However, it is a psychological advantage to show an impeccably groomed specimen. Invariably, a well-groomed dog of lesser quality will defeat a better specimen who may not be presented to his best advantage. Each dog is thoroughly examined in the ring, but the *overall* impression weighs heavily in the final decision.

The following grooming procedures may be done in any sequence. The order in which they are described is due to personal preference.

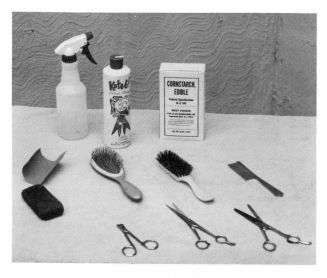

104

Fig. 1. An assortment of grooming equipment.

Fig. 2. The ungroomed dog.

Fig. 3. The untrimmed head.

CLEANING THE TEETH

Bright, white teeth are a credit to the owner and a compliment to the judge. As a puppy grows older, tartar accumulates on the teeth, revealing a greenish-brown cast that becomes progressively difficult to remove.

Soft foods hardly assist the dog to clean the teeth. Hard kibble on which to crunch and large knuckle bones that furnish hours of enjoyment can help prevent the build up of layers of unsightly plaque.

If hard deposits (calculus) occur, they may be difficult to remove except with regular dental tools. These may be ordered through some kennel supply retailers or your own dentist may be cooperative in sharing his supply. Scrape from the gum line (Figs. 4 and 5). Don't forget the premolars and molars.

To polish the teeth, use a powdered dentifrice, garlic salt or purchase plain pumice powder at the drug store. Wrap a small piece of gauze or cheesecloth around your index finger, dip into barely dampened dentifrice and rub across the teeth.

You can join the age of mechanization and use an electric or battery powered toothbrush.

The individual brushes and the vibrator power source are easily sanitized by submerging in alcohol or antiseptic solution for medical instruments. We use the electric toothbrush and the dogs have become accustomed to this type of dental care and have no objections.

It is important to start a dental health program early, as soon as the deciduous (puppy) teeth are being shed and the permanent teeth are erupting.

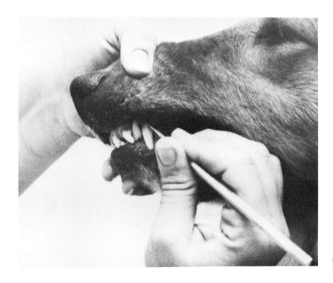

Fig. 4. Scrape the teeth with a dental tool.

105

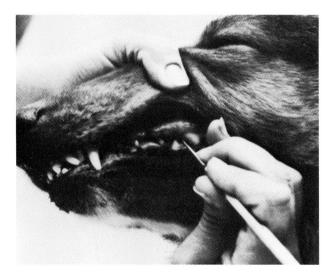

Fig. 5. Be sure to clean the back teeth, too.

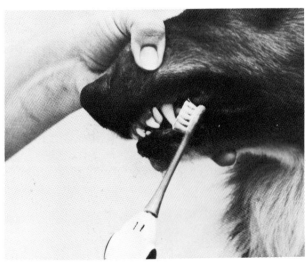

Fig. 6. Polishing the teeth with pumice and an electric toothbrush.

NAIL CLIPPING

In order to develop the appearance of a nice, tight foot, the nails must be as short as possible. Routine maintenance of the nails will keep the quick retracted. If the nail is allowed to become too long, the foot may become splayed. Nail cutting will become difficult when the nail is left too long as the quick is easily cut and effusive bleeding will result. Any time the nails are cared for, an anti-coagulant should be at hand.

Use any type of sharp nail clipper. Cut off the new growth close to the pink quick. With snipping action, the nail can be rounded off, removing the excess to leave the quick almost exposed.

The quick will pull back and will not cause any discomfort to the dog. Any uneven or ragged edges may be filed down if necessary (Fig. 7).

A rotary nail grinder may be purchased through a kennel supply. Once the dog has become accustomed to the noise of the motor, the grinder may be used quickly and painlessly to give a very neat appearance to the nails. The grinder is often preferred for its ability to expose the quick without causing bleeding and for smoothing any rough edges (Fig. 8). If you have trouble with the hair on the feet getting caught up in the grinder, pull the nails through the toe of an old nylon stocking, thus protecting the coat and pads.

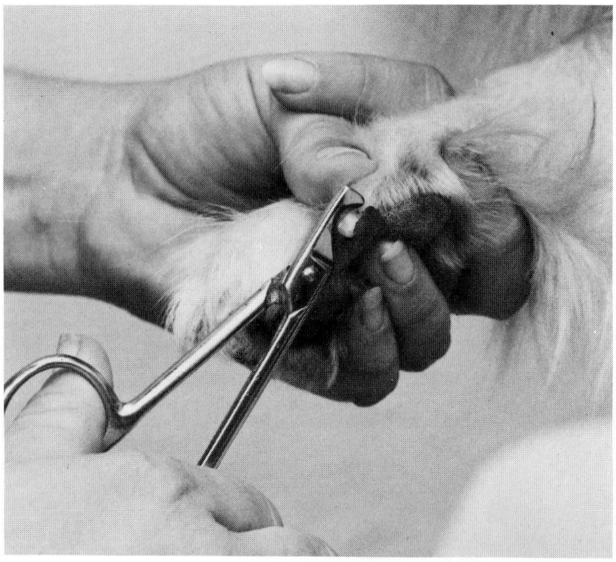

106

Fig. 7. Clip off the new growth, holding clipper at an angle.

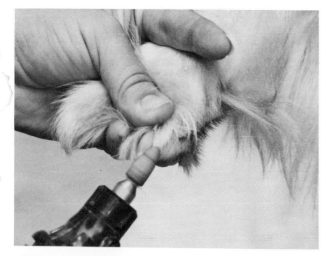

Fig. 8. Using the rotary nail grinder.

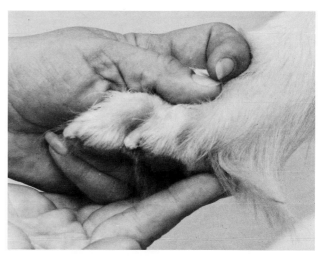

Fig. 9. Comparison of the ground nail (left) and the nail done with the clipper. Note the roundness, smoothness, and length of the nails.

TRIMMING THE FEET

You will find foot trimming much easier if the nails are kept short. Most of the trimming on the foot is done with the straight-edged scissor. Until you are confident of your trimming ability, however, you may wish to use the thinning shears when shaping the hair on the pasterns. One must remember that thinning shears actually thin out hairs that may be cosmetically necessary to create the look of bone or angulation. Always keep in mind that the effect one wishes to achieve is that stated in the Standard: "the toes are well arched and close together."

Starting with the front feet, comb out the hair on the pasterns. Lay the scissors flat against the heel of the foot and cut straight up to the digital toe. Do not cut too close. Comb out the hair again and sculpture (round out) the cutting line to follow the contour of the leg. With straight-edge scissors, trim the hair around the outside of each pad to outline individual toes (except the back of the heel). Remove all hair in the middle of the foot. Do not remove all the hair between the toes as this can make them look splayed. To shape the foot, have the dog standing. Comb the long hairs straight up and with the thinning shears trim these hairs to create the appearance of a tight, rounded foot (Fig. 12). Trimming the hair on the top of the foot back behind the nail is personal choice. From a distance, the foot will appear smaller but upon closer examination this excessive trimming will defeat the objective of trying to present a soft look all over.

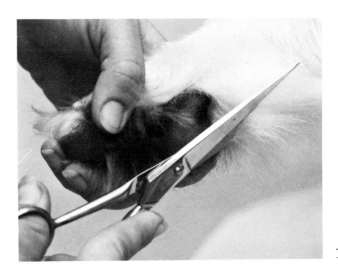

Fig. 10. Trim the hair on the front pastern from the heel to the digital.

107

Fig. 11. Outline each individual toe and remove the hair in the middle of the foot.

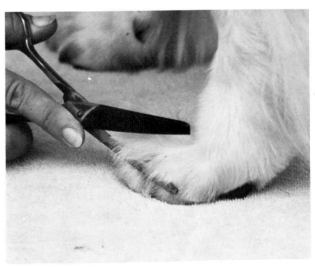

Fig. 12. Comb the long hair on the top of the foot straight up and shape the hairs with the thinning shears.

For the rear pastern, comb all the hair straight out. Using the heel as a starting point, place the scissors flat and cut at a slight angle up to the hock joint. Do not cut too close as this will give the illusion that the dog is higher on leg and lighter in bone. Comb out again. Round out and sculpture. This trimming can be cosmetic if necessary. For example, if the dog is lacking in angulation, trim the hair closer near the foot and much longer at the hock joint to give the appearance of a stronger angle. Trim the rear feet in the same manner as the front ones.

Fig. 13. The untrimmed front foot.

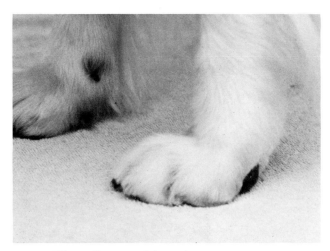

Fig. 14. The well-trimmed front foot.

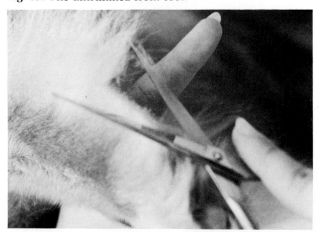

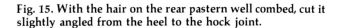

Fig. 15. With the hair on the rear pastern well combed, cut it slightly angled from the heel to the hock joint.

108

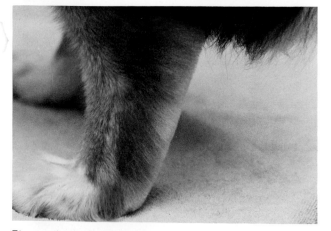

Fig. 16. A neatly presented rear pastern.

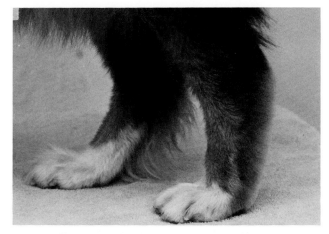

Fig. 17. The trimmed and untrimmed rear leg.

CHALKING

The application of chalk enhances the white-ness and aids in creating the appearance of more bone. There are many commercial whitening agents that may be purchased from a kennel sup-ply. A reasonably priced solution is the use of cornstarch or painter's whitening. If you find preferences in the whitening ability of one prod-uct or the "stiffness" provided by another, your own secret formula combining products may fill all your needs.

Chalk is applied to damp hair. One may either bathe the dog and apply the chalk as the dog dries; use the spray bottle to dampen down the hairs; or use a waterless shampoo (Fig. 19). Towel dry the dampened areas briskly until the

Fig. 18. Separate the ruff down to the skin and set the chalk in every few inches.

hair begins to stand apart. Apply the chalk with a stiff-bristled brush (a vegetable, manicure or cheap hair brush are good examples). *Push* the chalk into the coat generously in the direction opposite the hair growth. Chalk each leg whether or not the coat is white.

To apply the chalk to the white ruff and chest, separate the hair all the way down to the skin and generously set the chalk in every few inches.

If you are chalking at home the day before a show, you may find it easier to lay your dog on his side and use a flour sifter to apply the chalk. Separate the coat down to the skin and sift the chalk into the coat every few inches. This manner is excellent for chalking the belly coat. Chalking the stomach area will make all the lighter hairs stand out and separate to give the look of more coat and the appearance that the dog is built closer to the ground.

It is against the rules of the American Kennel Club to have foreign substances in the coat when in the ring; therefore, let the chalk "set" while grooming the rest of the dog. When thoroughly dried, it can be easily removed, still enhancing the appearance.

The chalk is removed by brushing against the grain with the same stiff-bristled brush used to put it in. The final brush stroke should be against the grain to leave the hair standing out. A vigor-ous brushing of the ruff and chest is necessary to remove all chalk in this area.

If you are very concerned about chalk landing on your tricolor, you can drape a towel over the dog's back. Just brushing the coat, however, will remove any chalk that may settle on it.

109

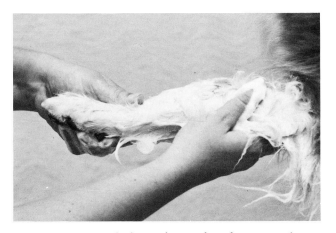

Fig. 19. Sudsing up the leg with waterless shampoo to cleanse the hair and dampen the coat before chalking.

Fig. 20. Using a stiff-bristled brush, push the chalk into the hair against the lay of the coat.

TRIMMING THE HEAD

A working knowledge of the Standard applied to your dog will aid in developing, through trimming, the best possible image. Illusions can be created of a leaner, longer head, less stop, less depth of head, and so on by deftly removing hair growth in appropriate places. Remember, trimming only creates an illusion and it will not correct a fault. We can only hope to leave the impression we wish to in the judge's eye.

Trimming on the head requires much skill in the use of scissors before it can be accomplished without leaving marks where too much hair has been removed. Remember *practice on the dog that won't be attending the shows for awhile* because once the hair is removed it will take some time to grow back.

The completed head trim should leave the dog with a soft look, devoid of harsh cutting lines. It is far better to leave too much hair in an area than to give a scalped impression!

Beyond the trimming of the whiskers and lip line with straight-edged scissors, the following procedure incorporates only the use of a fine-toothed comb, thinning shears, and sandpaper (or a stripping stone) to smooth out and remove additional hair growth. One may prefer the use of a stripping comb, *Duplex Dresser,* or more extensive equipment. However, our method is easy to master and requires little expense in purchasing additional tools.

In order to do the best possible trimming job, be sure to thoroughly comb out an area first, then comb out the excess hair after *each* snip to see what you have accomplished.

Whiskers and Lip Line—To attain the look of the attractive, well-turned out dog, the whiskers should be neatly removed. The choice of scissors to use is up to individual discretion. Remember that you are working on the head and damage can be done to the eyes or the dog can be cut should he jerk away. If regular scissors are too long for you to handle, get some snub-nose or manicure scissors.

With the left hand, firmly grasp the muzzle. Run the thumb over the whiskers and turn the nose slightly. In this manner, the whiskers will be exposed to the skin (Fig. 21). Slide the scissor point down to the base and snip, avoiding any facial hair. Trim the whiskers on the cheeks and eyebrows individually. You might find it easier to hold the end of the whisker in one hand and slide the scissors down to the base.

With straight-edged scissors, carefully outline the lip by shortening the hairs along the lip line. The purpose of this is to present a neat, tight, straight lip line.

Decreasing Depth of Head—For a cleaner throat and less depth of head, lift the dog's chin straight up and start removing, with thinning shears, the

110

Fig. 21. Run your thumb over the whiskers and turn the nose slightly to expose the whiskers to their base. Clip individually.

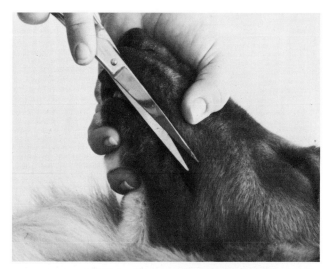

Fig. 22. Straighten the hairs around the lip to make it look straighter and tighter. Trim close to the skin.

excess hair where it starts to lengthen. This is the best place to start head trimming as one can become accustomed to handling the scissors. In fact, even straight-edged scissors may be used here as this area does not show. Blend in the trimmed area by slowly lengthening the hairs down into the ruff. If a dog is throaty, electric clippers can be used to eliminate any hair that adds to the look.

Stop—To clean out the stop, pull the hair forward and trim with thinning shears. Start just below the eyebrows and come forward toward the nose, stopping where fullness ends. Using the toothed side of shears (it acts as a stripper), comb the hairs down flat (Figs. 24, 25, and 26).

Tricolors and blue merles may have more hair removed in this area than a sable, as the sable's lighter colored undercoat will show through.

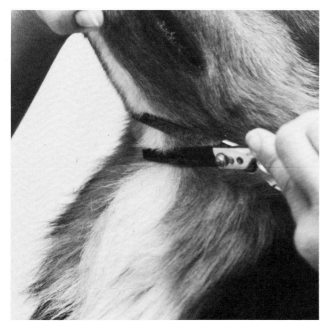

Fig. 23. Trim hairs under the throat to lessen depth of head and add length to underjaw.

Fig. 25. Thin from just below eyebrows to where fullness stops.

111

Fig. 24. Run your thumb down the stop to rough up the hair.

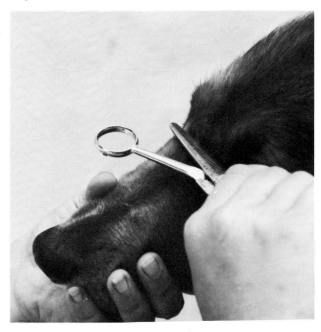

Fig. 26. Use edge of shears as a stripper.

Backskull—To enhance the flatness of the backskull, it is sometimes necessary to remove excessive hair directly behind the eyebrows. Working from the back towards the eye, snuggle the thinning shears close to the skin and make several snips as you slide the shears out. Smooth down with toothed edge of thinning shears or with coarse sandpaper (Fig. 27).

Quite often young puppies will have "puppy bumps" on their heads just behind the eyebrow. De-emphasize these bumps by thinning the hairs directly in front of these bumps. If you remove the hair directly over or behind these areas, it will only emphasize the bump.

Ears—Make an imaginary line around the base of the ear and comb all hair below it down towards the ruff. Comb the rest of the hair so that it stands up towards the tip of the ear. Hold the ear so that it falls at its natural break. With the thinning shears, trim any excessive hair above this break even with the break line (Fig. 30). Comb the hair so that it will fall naturally. This should give a nice rounded appearance to the back of the ear.

Hold the inside edge of the ear between forefinger and thumb, bringing the longer hairs on the inside and outside of the ear toward this edge (Fig. 31). With thinning shears, trim fairly close to the edge of the ear as far up as the natural tip (not beyond, as each hair is additional weight and will aid in keeping the ear tipped). On the outer edge of the ear, bring the hairs to the outside as you did before and, from the skin flaps near the base of the ear, trim up toward the natural break with thinning shears (Fig. 32). Next, turn the ear inside out and remove the lighter hairs growing inside the ear (Fig. 33). Hold the ear up on the skull in its proper placement and bring the thinning shears in from the back. Snuggle the shears to the skin and make several snips as you bring the shears out. Trim twice in this area—once having the scissors pointing towards the opposite eyebrow and then in the other direction to form an "X" pattern. Comb the excess hair out. By removing this hair, one should have formed a proper receptacle for the ear when it is held in the upright position (Fig. 34).

If the tips of the ears are rounded slightly, it will soften the expression. Great care must be taken not to take off too much weight, however.

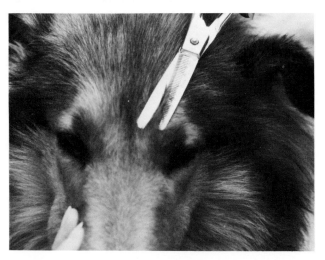

112

Fig. 27. Flatten backskull by removing hair growth just behind the eyebrows.

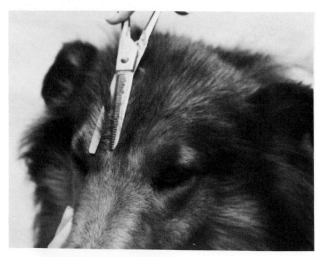

Fig. 28. Thin each side equally.

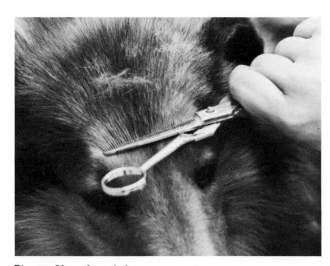

Fig. 29. Use edge of shears as a stripper.

Fig. 30. Comb hair on back of ear straight up and trim even with natural break.

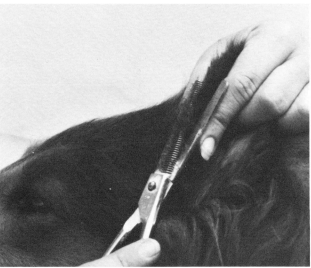

Fig. 31. Remove the hairs on the inside edge of the ear to the break.

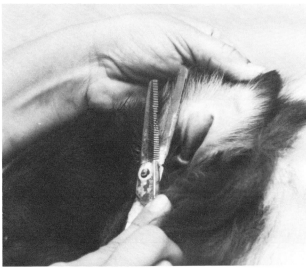

Fig. 32. Turn the ear inside out and remove lighter hair growth.

113

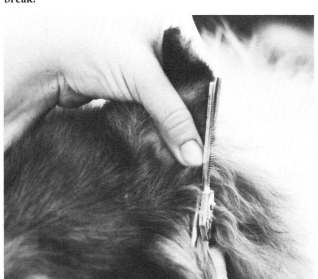

Fig. 33. Remove the hairs on the outside edge from the skin flap to the break.

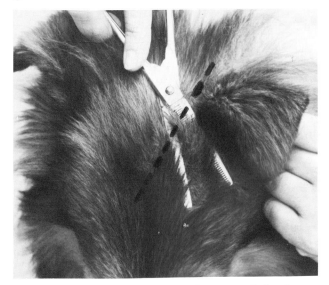

Fig. 34. The "X" pattern that forms the receptacle for the ear.

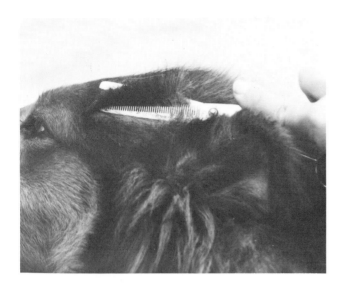

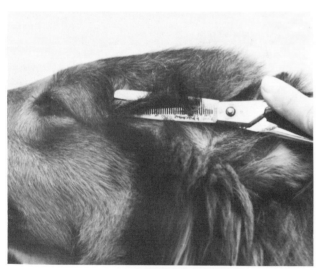

Cheeks—To smooth out and flatten cheeks and lengthen the head, start with the thinning shears just below the eyebrow level in a straight line back towards the inside corner of the ear (parallel to the backskull). Snuggle the shears to the skin and make several snips as you pull the shears out in the direction of the hair growth. Move down slightly and repeat. Follow this procedure all the way down the cheek until you come to the throat trimming (Fig. 35). Comb out the excess hair (Fig. 36) and repeat in any section that still appears rough or has too much hair. The coarse sandpaper is rubbed along the cheeks from below the eyebrows toward the ruff, thus removing any additional loose hairs (Fig. 37).

Each time a trimming procedure is done, the area should be thoroughly combed out and examined to see if it was done correctly. The ears should be held in place each time the head trim is observed to assure that you have achieved the desired effect and that each portion of the trimming complements the other.

The amount of hair removed in front of the ears will vary greatly with each individual, depending upon head qualities and the size and placement of the ears. The cheek trimming procedure has already thinned out this area, however, you may wish to return and thin it even more or take the thinning shears and softly straighten out the longer hairs.

114

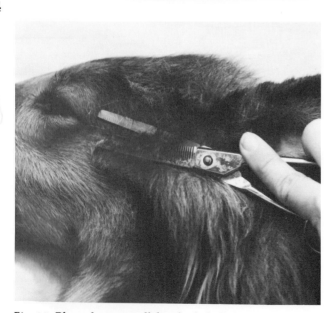

Fig. 35. Place shears parallel to backskull. With snipping action, trim hair by steps down the cheeks.

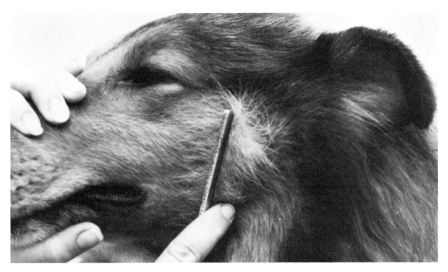

Fig. 36. Remove excess hair.

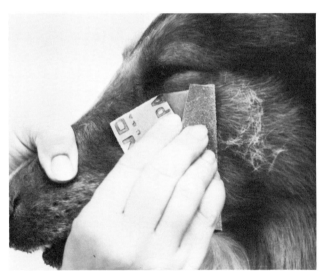

Fig. 37. Sandpaper is used to smooth down trimmed hairs.

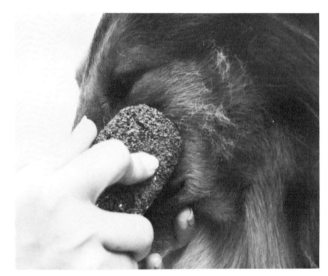

Fig. 38. Stripping stone in use.

115

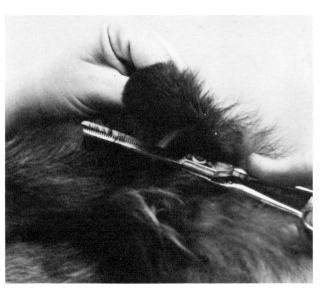

Fig. 39. Thinning hair in front of ears.

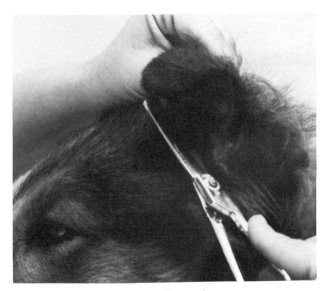

Fig. 40. Straightening hair in front of ears.

BRUSHING

The Standard says, "The well-fitting, proper-textured coat is the crowning glory of the Rough Variety of Collie."

Nothing can achieve this look better than proper brushing. It is simple, although it requires a little muscle, but it seems to be the most difficult talent to acquire. After a good brushing from the skin out, you will be surprised by the amount of coat your dog has. Brushing separates the undercoat and makes the longer hairs of the outer coat stand out individually.

Linebrushing

To insure that every square inch of your dog is well brushed, use the "linebrushing" technique. Start at one end of the dog and separate the coat down to the skin in a line. Spray with water. Then brush the hair to form another part about an inch away and spray again. You can either use your other hand to hold back the coat or use a second brush (Fig. 41). By spraying the part each time, you are thoroughly dampening the undercoat which will hold the moisture and keep the outercoat "standoffish."

Fig. 41. Separate the coat and spray with water.

116

Fig. 42. Linebrushing

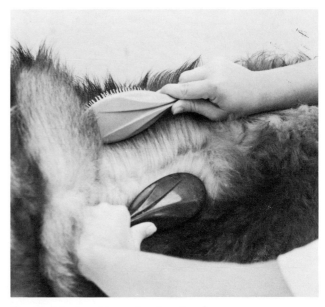

Fig. 43. Linebrushing using two brushes.

Coat Dressings

Water should be the only item necessary in your spray bottle if your dog's coat is in optimum condition and of the proper texture and you are adept at brushing. Constantly keep in mind that foreign substances are not allowed on the coat in the ring.

Special problems may necessitate the use of other products, but be aware that any harshner you add to the coat must be thoroughly brushed through so that the coat will not feel too harsh and be questioned by the judge.

A good quality whitening agent should be enough to make the white ruff harsh enough to stand up on its own. Other commonly used products are stale beer, hair spray and hair setting gels. The gels can be diluted in warm water for use in a spray bottle. Spray-on starch will keep those hairs on the leg standing out nice and crisp. Kennel suppliers will be happy to sell you a product with a fancy doggy name that will be just as effective as any of these, but are likely to be more expensive.

Brushing Technique

By following the illustrations you will be able to master a brushing technique that not only loosens and separates the undercoat but almost "back teases" the outer coat.

Go through the coat a second time. With one hand holding the coat down to the body, take the pin brush and pull some hair out from underneath your hand. The skill comes in taking the hairs the brush has picked up and flipping the brush away from the dog in order to make the hairs literally stand on end.

It is difficult to dampen the undercoat the same way you did in linebrushing, so spray the outercoat until it is well dampened and work it through to the undercoat with a quick brushing or with your fingertips. You can stop occasionally and spray the hair section by section.

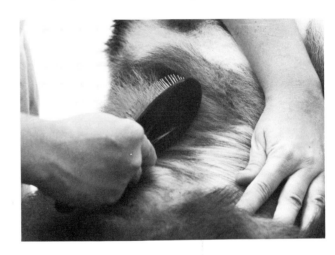

Fig. 44. Brushing technique that uses a back teasing method to make the coat stand out.

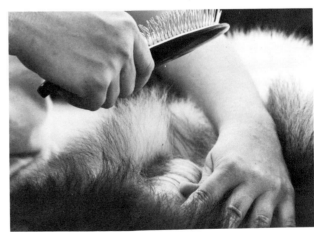

GROOMING THE SMOOTH VARIETY

Although the Smooth Collie will require less time to prepare for the ring, he should also be prepared impeccably. The white parts should be cleaned and dampened for the chalk. Because of the difference in coat texture, you may wish to also take a *French White Chalk Block* and rub over the white parts to enhance the whiteness.

In certain areas of the country, trimming is done on the Smooth in the area of the loin and pants. Trimming the fold of skin at the loin cleans and accentuates the tuck-up. The pants are trimmed somewhat to make cleaner lines.

Nothing will make the coat look prettier than shining it to the hilt. A good oil-based coat conditioner (or good quality human product) sprayed on the coat and rubbed in will intensify the natu-

ral sheen. Using a towel, rub in the direction of the hair growth until your arms ache. Then get a large horse grooming brush and go with the hair until the coat sparkles.

Finishing Touches

Before starting the final brushing, "set" your lead well into the coat. A choke chain can be nestled in by sliding it back and forth. Brush out any hairs that are caught, so there will be no interruption to the silhouette.

Again, a critical analysis of your dog will help you to contour the coat to present the best possible outline. Look at the illustrated standard (Ch. 5). This is your ultimate goal.

You must rebrush every section, and this is a good time to look for any matted hairs or dirt not previously removed.

The pants should be full. Take your hand just above the hock joint and hold the hair up against the dog. Using the brush, pull the hairs down and out, and you will achieve the effect of fullness.

Rebrush the tail against the grain as you hold it by the tip. Give it a slight shake and the hairs will fall into place.

The croup should appear slightly squared. By holding the hair back against the grain and shaping each layer with the brush, you can flatten out this area (Fig. 47). Should your dog be too high in rear, deftly remove some of the undercoat on the rump with the thinning shears. If the tail set is

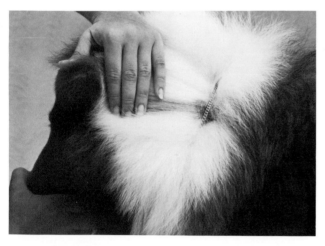

118

Fig. 45. Snuggle the choke chain close to the skin by moving it back and forth.

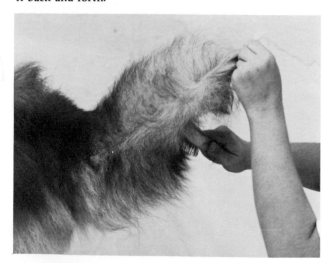

Fig. 46. Brushing the tail against the grain.

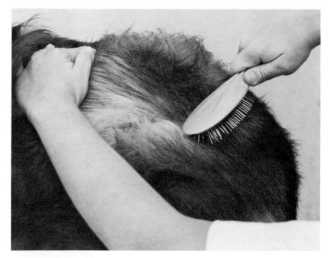

Fig. 47. Squaring off the croup.

very low and the croup too sloping, you will have to create the illusion of the squared-off croup by roughing up the undercoat and combing the longer hair over it.

A nice level topline will require no special touches except to rebrush the coat. A weak back can be improved by brushing the back hairs straight up or even doing a little teasing (back-brushing) in this area.

The ruff is always brushed up. Special attention should be paid to the soft hairs directly behind the ears. If they do not look good and separated after being thoroughly brushed or combed, a light sprinkling of baby powder may help.

Invariably your dog will shake just after you have completed shaping his coat. If your dog needs no assistance in any area, this shaking will let the hair fall naturally. To make him shake before you do your styling, blow in his ear.

Brush and rebrush each section of the coat until you are completely satisfied with it. You are now ready for the final "spit 'n polish." Make sure you have removed all remnants of chalk, especially now that the legs are well dried. Use a stiff-bristled brush, comb, or slicker brush to make the hairs on the legs really stand out and show off the excellent trimming job on the pasterns. Brush the feathering straight back. Comb the long hairs on the inside of the stifle down to accentuate the bend of stifle.

Clean out the longer hairs just in front of the eyes with the thinning shears.

A little vaseline on the nose will darken and shine it. Rub the residue of the vaseline into your palms and smooth along the head to hold down any hairs that prefer to stand up.

A final misting with the spray bottle just before you head for the ring, and you have prepared a very competitive dog. Good luck!

Fig. 48. The completed Collie looks good from any angle.

120

Fig. 49. The correctly trimmed head.

13

Showing Your Collie

"We are such stuff as dreams are made on."   Shakespeare

The prefix "Champion" has such a glorious connotation that pet buyers are impressed by the title and have boundless pride of ownership when boasting of their Collie's family tree.

If the Collie purchased as a family companion has introduced you to the show world, you will find a multifaceted experience ahead. It is wise to acquire the booklet "Rules Applying To Registration and Dog Shows" from The American Kennel Club to learn how the various types of shows are governed and managed.

SHOWS AND MATCHES

A purebred dog must be six months of age (minimum) before it can be entered at a point show. These are the shows where "points" towards a championship title are awarded to the winners. Each year the AKC establishes regional point scales based on the previous year's entries in the area. They determine the number of dogs one must defeat to garner from one to five points at each show. Every breed has their own point system, divided by sex. A dog becomes a champion when he has attained the proper number of points as stated by the AKC:

> Any dog which shall have won fifteen points shall become a Champion of Record, if six or more points shall have been won at two shows with a rating of three or more championship points each and under two different judges and some one or more of the balance of said points shall have been won under some other judge or judges than the two judges referred to above.

Dahlis

Sanction Matches are just what the name implies. A show held with the approval (sanction) of The American Kennel Club, but a win does not carry any points towards a championship title. Entries are usually restricted to dogs that have not acquired any championship points, particularly major points. Classes can be available for puppies as young as two months and, usually, there is not a limit on adults.

Fun Matches are held by many clubs and groups without the approval of The American Kennel Club. These are usually sponsored by clubs and organizations which need the expe-

rience in the rudiments of presenting a show prior to requesting recognition as a club from AKC. If you are apprehensive about entering your dog at either an all-breed or specialty point show, then sanctioned or fun matches are an excellent training ground for you to observe and gain ring experience for you and your Collie.

Contact breeders for information about area matches and shows. Some dog publications have sections devoted to lists of upcoming shows.

Entry fees at matches are usually $2 to $5 in comparison with the $10 to $18 fees for point shows.

Fig. 1. A few "benched shows" are still held. The dogs must be on the bench unless they are being groomed, exhibited, or exercised. Crates provide safe enclosure for dogs.

122

Fig. 2. Colorful tenting covers a small portion of the ring and the table where the judge and stewards keep their supplies at an outdoor show.

AMERICAN KENNEL CLUB SCHEDULE OF POINTS

The Points toward a Championship shall be awarded to the winners dog and winners bitch of each breed, which shall be based on the actual number of dogs or bitches competing in that breed.

Fig. 3. Points awarded depend upon the number of dogs of each breed entered. This varies in different regions of the country.

SCALE OF POINTS	1 POINT		2 POINTS		3 POINTS		4 POINTS		5 POINTS	
	Dogs	Bitches	Dogs	Bitches	Dogs	Bitches	Dogs	Bitches	Dogs	Bitches
Bullmastiffs	2	2	3	3	4	4	6	5	9	7
Collies (Rough)	2	2	9	10	16	19	24	27	39	41
Collies (Smooth)	2	2	3	3	4	5	5	6	7	9
Doberman Pinschers	7	6	19	20	31	34	40	46	57	67

The judges at matches may be anyone who is in good standing with The American Kennel Club. Point shows must have currently licensed judges or those approved by AKC as a provisional (who will be licensed by AKC if they exhibit knowledge of ring procedure and confidence in their interpretation of the standard during three provisional judging assignments). There are a few individuals whose livelihood depends on judging assignments, but a majority do not receive remuneration beyond actual expenses.

So you can see that matches are a training ground for more than just amateur dog owners aspiring for show experience.

OFFICIAL AMERICAN KENNEL CLUB ENTRY FORM

TIDEWATER KENNEL CLUB

March 19, 1988

I ENCLOSE $ __$14.00__ for entry fees
IMPORTANT—Read Carefully Instructions on Reverse Side Before Filling Out. Numbers in the boxes indicate sections of the instructions relevant to the information needed in that box. (PLEASE PRINT)

BREED	VARIETY [1]	SEX
Collie	Rough	Female

DOG SHOW CLASS [2] [3] Best of Variety	CLASS [3] DIVISION Weight color etc

ADDITIONAL CLASSES	OBEDIENCE TRIAL CLASS	JR. SHOWMANSHIP CLASS

NAME OF (See Back) JUNIOR HANDLER (if any)

FULL NAME OF DOG   Ch. Wickmere Tear Drops

X AKC REG NO   Enter number here   WE-108171   DATE OF BIRTH   5/16/84
☐ AKC LITTER NO
☐ I L P NO
☐ FOREIGN REG NO & COUNTRY   PLACE OF BIRTH ☒ U S A ☐ Canada ☐ Foreign   Do not print the above in catalog

BREEDER   Shelley C. Roos

SIRE   Ch. Wickmere Silver Bullet

DAM   Ch. Wickmere Swept In Time

ACTUAL OWNER(S)   Mrs. George H. Roos, Jr.
[4]   (Please Print)
OWNER'S ADDRESS   5401 Sasher Lane
CITY   Fairfax   STATE   VA   ZIP   22030

NAME OF OWNER'S AGENT (IF ANY) AT THE SHOW   Shelley C. Roos   ID #   0967-6

I CERTIFY that I am the actual owner of the dog, or that I am the duly authorized agent of the actual owner whose name I have entered above. In consideration of the acceptance of this entry, I (we) agree to abide by the rules and regulations of The American Kennel Club in effect at the time of this show or obedience trial, and by any additional rules and regulations appearing in the premium list for this show or obedience trial or both, and further agree to be bound by the "Agreement" printed on the reverse side of this entry form. I (we) certify and represent that the dog entered is not a hazard to persons or other dogs. This entry is submitted for acceptance on the foregoing representation and agreement

SIGNATURE of owner or his agent duly authorized to make this entry   *Mrs. George H. Roos Jr.*
Telephone   703-631-1597

Fig. 4. A properly completed entry blank.

123

RING 12.
   Judge - Mrs. George H. Roos, Jr. (165)
8:00 am
   5 Cardigan Welsh Corgis 1-0-4
   28 Pembroke Welsh Corgis 14-11-3

9:20 am
   54 Shetland Sheepdogs 23-27-4
12:00 Noon
   1 Smooth Collie 1-0-0
   77 Rough Collies 33-38-6

RING 13.
   Judge - Mrs. Mary E. Wiggins (46)
8:00 am
   46 Novice A Class Entries
      (010 - 056)

Lunch Break from 12:00 Noon to 12:30 pm

Fig. 5. Example of a judging schedule telling the judge, ring, time of judging, and entry (first the total, then dogs, bitches, and any specials entered).

THE "HOW TO'S" OF SHOWING

The Obedience Chapter can be helpful with the training of your dog and how to use the "choke" chain, which many exhibitors use in a fine link form in the show ring. You may prefer to use a martingale collar, although it affords less control over the dog.

If you feel apprehensive about entering the ring even after practice sessions at matches or training classes, for a fee you can engage the services of a professional handler who acts as an agent for your dog. The American Kennel Club terminated the licensing of professional handlers several years ago, so now anyone in good standing may accept pay and act as an agent for a dog owner.

Teach your Collie to gait on a loose lead on your left side. Practice the gaiting patterns. The patterns illustrated here are the ones usually requested by the judge. The "triangle," the "L," the "T," and the "down-and-back," are concluded with a full circle around to the end of the line of the other dogs in the class. Some exhibitors, when gaiting the "T" or "L," will switch the dog to their right side so that the dog is always visible and on the same side as the judge. Practice before attempting this maneuver in the ring so that your Collie is used to being switched to your right side.

Gaiting is always counter clockwise. Each judge sets his own ring pattern so try to watch a class or two, if possible, to acquaint yourself with the ring procedure.

Fig. 6. Rosslane Ruffian O'Bar-Morel at eighteen months being selected Winners Bitch at an outdoor show.

124

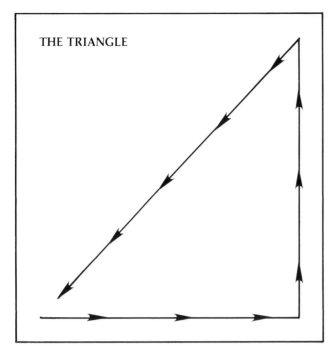

THE TRIANGLE

The most commonly used gaiting pattern is the triangle. This means leaving the judge, turning to the left, and returning to the judge on the diagonal. It is most used because it enables the judge to view the dog's rear, side, and front movement with no awkward turns.

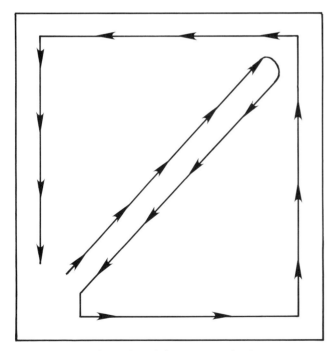

The judge may have the exhibits gait on the diagonal or any direction—away and return ("straight down and back"). He may then ask them to gait around ringside to the end of the line.

Fig. 7. Gaiting patterns.

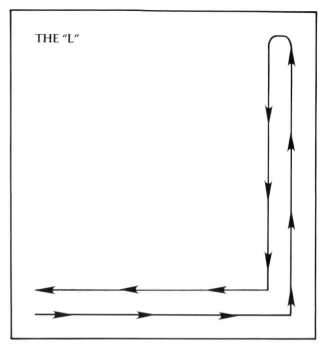

THE "L"

The "L" pattern requires some practice to properly execute. Leave the judge, turning to the left at the end of the ring. At the far edge of the ring, you must reverse in such a manner as to not destroy the dog's stride. Keep the dog between yourself and the judge if it does not affect his gait to change side. Return to the corner of the ring, turn right and return to the judge.

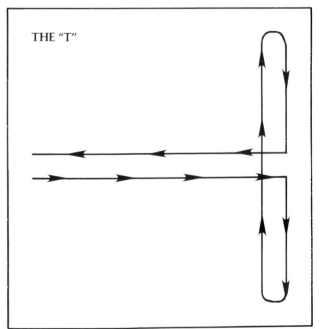

THE "T"

125

The "T" is difficult to maneuver. It is also difficult for the judge to see good side movement, since the dog has little time to recuperate from the turns. Leave the judge, turning in the direction he instructed. At the edge of the ring, reverse and go to the opposite of the ring. Reverse again and return to center or aligned with the judge's position and return to him.

PERSONAL APPEARANCE AND RINGSIDE ETIQUETTE

Consider your own appearance as well as that of your Collie! Wear light colored clothing for contrast if you are showing a dark colored dog (tricolor or deep mahogany sable) or dark shades if exhibiting a white or light sable. Shows are becoming more casual and many men are wearing leisure suits with open neck shirts; but the sport coat, shirt with tie and slacks are still very popular. Women are wearing dresses, pant suits, and coordinated skirts and blouses. Pockets are helpful as storage for tidbits (boiled liver, etc.) to bait your Collie and a small brush if a grooming touch-up is needed in the ring. Comfortable shoes are a must as you will be standing and walking for hours on all kinds of terrain and flooring. Crepe or rubber soles are recommended to give you firm footing. You do not want to worry about slipping.

Grooming coats, aprons, or smocks can be worn to protect your clothes from being soiled while grooming. A clothes brush or the roller tape is a handy item to include in your tack box to remove any dog hairs from your clothing. Being comfortable and confident in your own appearance is vital to concentration on presenting your Collie.

Your Collie will be judged on how he looks the day he is shown. If he is penalized as a puppy for lacking fill in skull, be aware that the judge cannot adjudicate the puppy, visualizing how he should look as a mature dog. Accept your placing with a polite thank you. If you wish to question the judge, wait until your breed's judging is concluded, then request a critique. Please do not preface your remarks with, "What was it you didn't like about my dog?" Evidently, if you place second or lower, or not at all, there must have been attributes on the other entries that the judge preferred.

Most judges are very willing to confer with a novice, and you can probably gain excellent advice on presentation or quality. If your Collie is a promising prospect, don't get discouraged. The late Edwin L. Pickhardt (Sterling Kennels) remarked that if you could win two out of three times you had a good dog.

Competition has become very keen with more professional handlers appearing in the Collie ring and larger entries at most specialty shows. Exhibitors are taking advantage of the "circuits," from a three-show weekend to nine or 12 shows held

Fig. 7. Mr. John Giuliano of Bellbrooke Collies examines a young exhibitor's Collie. *Kernan photo.*

Fig. 8. Mr. Giuliano goes over the head while the exhibitor stands to one side. *Kernan photo.*

Fig. 9. The neck and shoulders come under the scrutiny of the judge as he assesses the Collie's body for faults and virtues. *Kernan photo.*

126

within a particular geographical area. These are conducive to exposure to various judges and, thusly, larger entries and a better opportunity for the major points needed for the championship title.

It takes patience and perseverance and a large financial investment to attain that coveted title. If your Collie is a good specimen and you just could not win, re-evaluate the situation. Seek advice from one whom you respect. Was your dog in good condition? Weight? Coat? Trained sufficiently with proper ring decorum? Too young? Too old? How was your selection of judges? If you have been showing a blue merle under five judges who prefer sables and tris, you wasted five entry fees. Conversely, it is an equal error of judgment to enter your sable under a judge who has the reputation of always looking for a "good blue."

It is never a disgrace to be defeated by a good Collie. You just have to learn your strategy and believe in your Collie.

Fig. 10. Mrs. Lorraine Still, artist of the Illustrated Standard, examines a tricolor puppy.

Fig. 11. Mrs. Roos assesses smoothness of cheeks and fill of muzzle by viewing the dog from above and slightly to the rear of his shoulder.

Fig. 12. Mrs. Roos examines shoulder placement as handler distracts dog's attention with bait.

Fig. 13. Some shows in motels are held on carpeted floors without mats. Here the author selects winner at the Kentucky Collie Club Specialty.

Fig. 14. The "Specials" (champions) class. The handler is making an inconspicuous noise to get the Collie's ears up at the crucial moment.

14

Collie Kaleidoscope

"The most delightful pleasures cloy without variety." Syrus

You have selected the Collie as your ideal companion or the breed you wish to exhibit and raise. Initially most breeders start with a sable or a tricolor Collie, and exposure, coupled with experience, leads them down the path to where they eventually wish to experiment. A little experience teaches the basics of color genetics and erases some of the prejudices, allowing them to appreciate the kaleidoscope of coat colors acceptable in the breed.

Special permission was granted by the Collie Club of America to include the following material by Dot Gerth, who originally prepared it for "The ABC's of Collie Coat Color Inheritance" for the 1969 *Collie Club of America Yearbook.*

The four basic coat colors in Collies are sable, tricolor, blue merle and white. With certain crossings of the merle factor, two other colors can be produced—sable merles and defective white merles. Deviations from the normal due to mutations or linked recessive genes in certain individuals can also result in the lethal grays, the maltese, the sable faced tricolor, the chinchillas, etc. However, it is the purpose of this article to provide the reader with a simple reference chart concerning the more common color crosses as well as some of the less common crosses involving the merle factor. Thus, we shall eliminate the rarer combinations as well as genetic technicalities. The percentage ratios (1:1, 1:2:1, etc.) of the resulting *possible* progeny are factual, but not necessarily a *positive* end result of each breeding as nature's whimsies cannot be computer programmed due to the laws of chance.

Dahlis

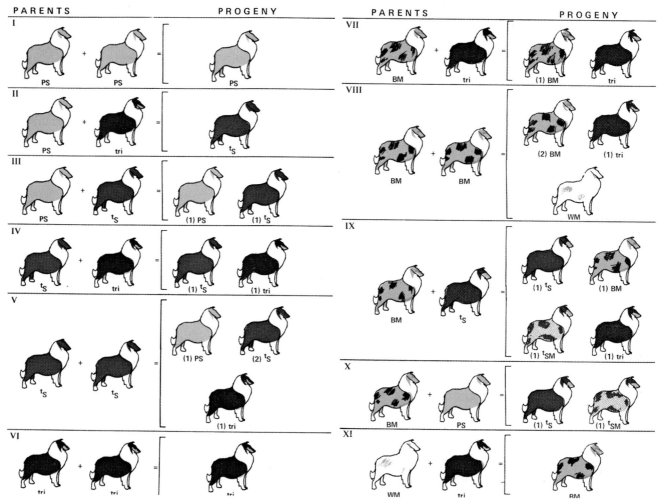

Fig. 1. Parent/Progeny Chart, part one.

130 S— SABLE. Dominant over tricolor. Shadings may run from straw through red to dark mahogany.

PS— Pure Sable. Usually a clear shade of straw or orange red with dark maskings or fringes. These individuals carry no tricolor gene and can produce only sable color regardless of what color is combines with them. (Charts I, II, III, X, XIV, XVI, XIX)

tS— Trifactored Sable. Sable Collies carrying the tricolor gene in conjunction with the dominant sable gene. Usually (but not always) a dark orange to a very dark mahogany in color with dark masking and fringes. (Charts II, III, IV, V, IX)

tri— TRICOLOR. Recessive to sable. Black Collies with white and tan markings on sides of muzzle, above the eyes, sides of cheeks, chest and inner margins oflegs. (Charts II, IV, VI, VII, XI, XII, XV, XVII)

M— MERLE. A dominant dilution gene which in combination with sable or tri genes produces merled collies.

BM— Blue Merle. Bluish gray with black splotching, carrying sable markings in the same pattern as the tricolor. Color results from the interaction of the dominant dilution gene (M) with the tricolor gene (t). (Charts, VII, VIII, IX, X, XVIII)

SM— Sable Merle. Sable spotted Collies. Color results from the interaction of the dominant dilution gene (M) on the sable color. At birth, all sable merles exhibit a bluish tinge on tail and muzzle which disappears in a few weeks. Brownish merling on body or head may or may not remain at maturity,

Fig. 2. Parent/Progeny Chart, part two.

and thus these individuals, if they have dark eyes can be mistaken for a "normal" sable. However, many sable merles inherit blue or blue flecked eyes, a sure sign of a merle.

PSM—Pure Sable Merle. Usually a light or even "washed out" sable at birth with brown merliang. At maturity, quite often these Collies lose their merling and coat color becomes a clearer red. No tricolor gene is present in their makeup. (Chart XV)

tSM— Trifactored Sable Merle. Usually a darker sable color than the PSM with dark brown merling which quite frequently is still visible at maturity. The tricolor gene is present in conjunction with the sable and merle gene.(Charts XIIl, XIII, XIV)

w— WHITE. These collies are the result of a cross between either two white parents or white factored parents. Color is carried on a recessive gene (w) and is inherited INDEPENDENTLY of sable, tri or blue merle and may occur in combination with ANY of them. A blue headed white is just as sound and normal a Collie as the tri or sable headed white. These are not to be confused with the white merle whose 'white" color results from the double dominant dilution merle gene, whereas the white color of a blue headed white results from the recessive gene (ww) and its blue color from the normal interaction of the merle gene with tricolor. (Charts XVI, XVIII)

w^f— White factored. Colored dogs usually with large white frill, heavy white tail tip, possibly a body splash of white hairs and white extending upward from

131

hind feet over stifle to meet the white underbody. (Charts XVII, XVIII)

non   Non white factored. Regular colored Collies NOT carrying the recessive white factor. (Chart XIX)

WM—White Merle. DEFECTIVE WHITES, resulting from the combination of two merled parents. These Collies inherit the dominant dilution gene (M) from both parents. Thus, color is diminished almost to the vanishing point by the gene in duplex. They are almost white in appearance and may or may not have a few merling spots. Eyes, IF present, are pale blue; skin, including the eyelids, lips, nose and pads are pigmentless except within an area of merling; hearing and sight severely impaired. These are commonly destroyed at birth. (Ed. note. since this treatise was prepared in 1969 it has been learned that the white merles are not necessarily defective and many have sight and hearing. This information is expanded in continuation of chapter by the author.) If a white merle is raised to maturity and is from a BM to BM cross, it can be bred to a tricolor and will produce 100% blue merles. (Charts VIII,

XI) This is not true of white merles carrying the PS genes or the ^tS genes when bred to a tri.

It is important that we should be aware and understand that there is a variation in the genetic color inheritance factor in various breeds and other species. When it is understood how the color pattern produces, then our tolerance level increases.

A rare commodity is an open mind and the willingness to try the unfamiliar and take a calculated risk, if necessary, to produce quality if the virtues are present in the prospective pair, regardless of color. Dedicated breeders who are interested in the welfare and progress of a breed do not want to see a radical, convulsive revolution; but I have never understood the stigma attached to sable/blue merle breeding or a blue to blue. We are bridled and restrained by heresay, but years of experience and exposure encourages some fanciers to delve into the more mysterious unions that require depth of thought and planning. A sable merle can unfold a prismatic combination, all in one package.

If several daring breeders had not tried the unconventional unions decades ago, we would not have had some of the outstanding specimens. It might have been many more years before we learned that a sable to blue merle breeding can produce an attractive silvery blue. The gamble in the sable to blue merle breeding is that a sable merle can have blue eyes. If

132

Fig. 3. Ch. Robel Jason, a shaded sable CC of A winner.

Fig. 4. Ch. Glocamora Evermore of Emboy, dam of twelve champions, a golden sable Smooth.

you are an adventurous sort, there is nothing in the Standard to prevent exhibition of a blue-eyed sable merle. Your dog may be penalized and thusly top awards may be elusive, but there is not a disqualification. The only disqualifications are the American Kennel Club rules for all breeds for the presence of monorchidism or cryptorchidism.

Many fanciers have questioned whether the Standard could be changed to accept sable merles as an additional color rather than reading as four colors, and to possibly allow blue eyes, eliminating any discrimination. This could possibly come to pass within a few years.

A few daring breeders have gambled and kept "defective whites" from a blue merle to blue merle union and learned, to the amazement of many, that they are NOT impaired in sight or hearing. This couragous experiment by a few breeders has been a progressive step in several ways. We have learned that not all white merles are "defective," having passed an ophthalmic examination, with sometimes, better visual acuity ratings than other colored members of the breed and the bonus is, blue merles have increased in popularity with exhibitors and the pet buying public. For those wanting to increase the probable percentage of blue merles in a litter there are white merles of quality to incorporate into a color/breeding program. An interesting side light to this color situation is that in some instances the sable/merles and white/merles are the select *quality* individuals in a litter. Is nature conveying a subtle message to breeders?

The Standard explicity allows four colors but prejudice prevails. It is a wise exhibitor who knows which judges to avoid and where to invest the entry fee when a particular color is the judge's favorite.

True Collie expression is inevitable regardless of color because of the head properties. You should see and feel the same sense of awareness that the Collie has a unique countenance whether it is a tri, blue, sable or white.

Fig. 5. Ch. The Pied Piper of Kings Valley, blue merle, as a puppy.

Fig. 6. The Pied Piper at nine months.

Fig. 7. Puppies from a blue merle to a sable breeding. The female, far right, is heavily merled at birth. Puppy in the center has slight merling.

Fig. 8. Heavily merled puppy (far right above) at four months. Spots have almost disappeared. Some dark masking is apparent. Very dark eyes with deep pigmentation of eye rims, lips, and nose. At this stage and as adults it is difficult to know whether a pup is pure for sable or sable merle just by appearance, especially if merling was less obvious at birth (see pup in center, above).

134

Fig. 9. Blue merle bitch puppy, seven weeks. Nice eye, round muzzle, good bone, style.

Fig. 10. Ch. Pickwick Spirit of the Wind, a tricolor Smooth.

Fig. 12. Ch Ledgedale Money Broker, a pure for sable.

Fig. 11. Ch. Rosslane Ruffian O'Bar-Morel, a shaded sable, at three months of age.

Fig. 11A. Riverhills Incredible Storm. A double dilute with hearing and an excellent eye check. For many years it was believed all double dilutes were defective until some adventureous breeders raised them to have hearing and eyes checked.

Fig. 12A. Ch. Paradice Against the Wind by Ch. Paradices Cloak 'N' Dagger ex Zirl Criban Moon. Breeder, owner, Paul and Valerie Nassetta.

Fig. 13. Ch. Starr's Blue Jeans 1982 Best of Breed and 1986 Best of Breed Collie Club of America.

Ch. Merrils Honest Abe

15

Genetics—The Building Blocks
by Timothy Garrison

"The first step to knowledge is to know that we are ignorant."   Richard Cecil

As a breeder you must be inventive, instinctive, and have a keen intuition. You will be an artist; but the tools will be genes, chromosomes, and flesh; not a chisel, spatula or clay.

To create a Collie that pleases you, personally, is of utmost importance. Then you want that Collie to be accepted and admired by judges and other breeders and exhibitors. A male will receive attention by bitch owners because they feel he will complement the bitch and in turn help perpetuate or improve certain virtues. Good bitches are the jewels in the crown of any kennel and breeder.

When the question is asked, "What has been the most difficult aspect of this hobby for you to learn?" most breeders reply "Genetics." Here we will open the door to the complex world of genes, the units of inheritance.

SOME BASICS

The basis of any successful breeding program is the ability to see, or perhaps "feel," the quality of an individual animal. If such a program is to be an ongoing one, the breeder must also possess the inherent ability to select what animals, when bred together, will produce well. In this respect, the maintenance of a kennel of high quality individuals is an art rather than a science. However, an understanding of a few genetic basics is not only desirable, but necessary for the benefit of the breed.

Genetics is the science that concerns itself with why tigers beget little tigers and not little elephants. This is because specific physical elements are transmitted from parents to offspring through the **gametes,** that is, the sperm and the egg. Thus, the distinguishing characteristics of a given species or breed are maintained generation after generation.

Dahlis

To begin with, the **gene** is the unit of inheritance. It is in turn made of deoxyribonucleic acid (DNA) of which the constituents are adenine and guanine (purines), and cytosine and thymine (pyrimidines). The purines and pyrimidines pair into base pairs, and three of these pairs in a specific order create one **amino acid.** The amino acids combine in a chain to form an **enzyme,** which is the expression of the gene. Therefore, one gene will determine one enzyme. Each gene is found on one of the dog's 39 pairs of **chromosomes,** and each chromosome contains an indeterminate number of genes. One-half of each animal's chromosomes come from each parent—39 from the sire and 39 from the dam, so each animal has a total of 78 chromosomes.

SIMPLE GENETICS

Simple genetics is also referred to as Mendelian genetics. Traits which fall into this category are controlled by one pair of genes. These genes can be either **dominant** or **recessive.** A dominant gene is one which always produces the trait which it carries, no matter what its companion gene is, such as the gene for sable coat color. A recessive gene is one which will not yield its effect unless its companion gene is the same, such as the tricolor gene. In other words, only one gene need be dominant for that trait to be displayed, but the recessive trait is produced only when both genes of the pair are identical. When both genes of a pair are identical, they are referred to as being **homozygous.** When the genes in a pair are unlike, they are referred to as **heterozygous.**

A term which will be seen in many genetics articles is **alleles.** An allele is simply the position on a chromosome which a specific gene occupies. Therefore, the gene for sable (A^y) and the gene for tricolor (a^t) are alleles.

It is fairly easy to predict the outcome of certain breedings as far as the simple genetic traits are concerned. For example, if two heterozygous sables are bred together, each parent can give either a sable gene (A^y) or a tricolor gene (a^t) to the offspring, the possible combinations of A^y and a^t are shown below and result in the possibility of one A^yA^y; two A^ya^t; one a^ta^t; or one

homozygous sable, two heterozygous sables, and one tricolor.

Fig. 1

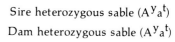
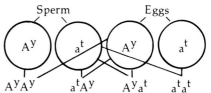

1 homozygous sable; 2 heterozygous sable; 1 tricolor

Epistasis is a genetic phenomenon which we can class with the simple genetic traits also. An epistatic gene (or genes) will cover or alter the effects of a given set of alleles. They do not take the place of the genes they cover, only mask their effect. In fact, most epistatic genes are not even on the same chromosome as the genes which they override. The merle gene in Collies is an example of an epistatic gene. One dose of the merle gene (M) will alter a tricolor to a blue merle. The **genotype** (actual genetic makeup) is a^ta^t,M^t, while the **phenotype** (what the animal looks like) is blue merle.

MORE COMPLEX GENETICS

Everything discussed so far pertains to single gene pairs. Consider the fact that the dog possesses thirty-nine pairs of chromosomes (seventy-eight individual chromosomes) and that each of the chromosomes carries hundreds—or even thousands—of genes, and see how complex even simple genetics has become!

Unfortunately, nature in its wisdom wasn't happy with simple genetics, so it complicated it a little. The next step in genetics is **polygenics,** or quantitative genetics. In these forms of inheritance it takes several pairs of genes to form one trait. If only part of the genes for a trait are present, the trait is not expressed; or it is incompletely expressed. In the Collie, many of the structures one is interested in from a conformation standpoint fall into this category, such as eye shape and placement, head structures, and ear shape and carriage. An interesting point to make is that quantitative traits become fixed or set in a line with inbreeding. Traits which fall into this category are therefore called "familial traits."

Since most breeders have their own ideas of what constitutes **inbreeding** and **linebreeding,** we will suffice it to say here that inbreeding is generally considered to be the matings of close relatives such as daughter to father or sister to brother, while linebreeding is the mating of distantly related animals such as a dog to his granddam or a bitch to her great uncle. An **outcross** is the breeding of unrelated animals.

A phenomenon related to these breeding systems is overdominance. This means that the heterozygous is more desirable than either homozygous form. In layman's terms, this is called "hybrid vigor." An example in the Collie could be the merle (if you are a merle fancier) where the heterozygous merle results in a blue merle (desirable) while the homozygous merle results in a double dilution merle which may be blind or deaf, and often times both. Hybrid vigor results from outcrossing, especially if the outcross is between two very inbred individuals.

Inbreeding, on the other hand, increases homozygosity, which is why inbred lines are more likely to produce certain traits repeatedly. This ability to reproduce traits reliably is referred to as "prepotence."

All of these things and more go into the genetic makeup of the dog. It would be nice to be able to list exactly how smooth heads, natural ears, good bodies, and other traits are inherited; but since everyone interprets the Standard a little differently, such a list would not hold true for every breeder's line, nor for that matter for individual dogs within a line.

Determining the Presence of Recessive Genes

Every breeder is curious about the presence of recessive genes in their breeding stock, be they detrimental or beneficial. The breeding of dogs, and of Collies in particular, is an art form. Yet, it is a scientific discipline as well. When we, as breeders, question our dogs' genetic makeup, we can find answers in one of two ways: probability

is a tool of many scientific fields and is defined as "the likelihood of occurrence," progeny testing, or test breeding, is a basic tool of animal husbandry.

Test breeding is the only way of being certain of an animal's genotype. Test breeding is both time consuming and expensive. It requires the housing of affected animals and/or carriers of the recessive trait. The offspring and siblings of the affected animals being tested may also be used.

The advantages of using probability are that it wastes none of the animals' productive years, is inexpensive, and does not require the production of unwanted offspring for proving an animal. One of the disadvantages is that we must have some knowledge of the genotype of the ancestors of the animals in question, for even one mistake here can change the odds.

In the past five or six years, there has been a great increase in Collie breeders, openness about their dogs' producing records concerning such things as lethal grays, CEA, PRA, epilepsy and patent ductus arteriosus. This openness is rarely found in other breeds and reflects the concern for the future of the breed that most Collie breeders possess.

Simple probability is easily understood. One of the basic concepts is that 50 percent (one-half) of an animal's genetic material is derived from each parent. The sperm or egg contains one-half of the animal's genetic material carried from the parent.

The easiest way to understand this is by example. You wish to breed Dog A to Bitch A, but you are concerned that xx will appear. Dog A's sire produced xx puppies but was "normal" in appear-

ance. Therefore, he is a carrier or heterozygote (Xx). His dam's pedigree is clear of the xx trait and we assume her genotype to be XX. Dog A could have received either an X or x gene from his sire, but only an X gene from his dam. Thus, there is a 50 percent chance that Dog A is a carrier.

Fig. 2

Dog A Sire (Xx)
       Dam (XX)

	X	x	
X	XX	Xx	2 XX = 50%
X	XX	Xx	2 Xx = 50%

Now let us look at Bitch A. We don't have any information on her sire or dam, but her paternal grandsire and her maternal great grandsire are carriers.

Fig. 3

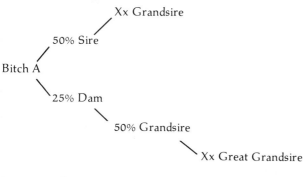

Xx Grandsire
50% Sire
Bitch A
25% Dam
50% Grandsire
Xx Great Grandsire

(50% + 25%) × .50 = 37.5%
      75% × .50 = 37.5%

Each generation removed from a carrier will decrease the chance of the recessive gene being present by 50 percent so that the chance of Bitch A being a carrier is 37.5 percent.

Fig. 4

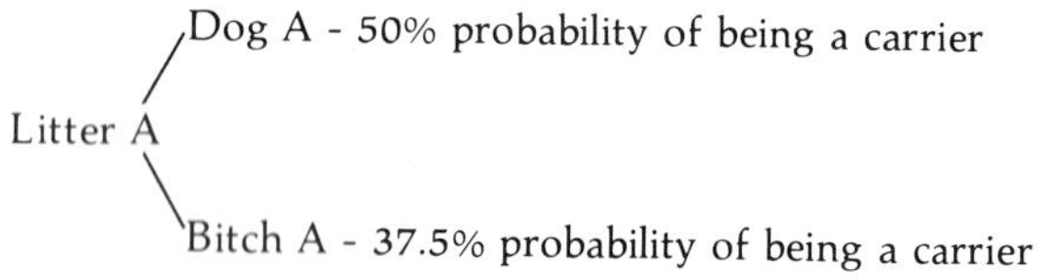

Dog A - 50% probability of being a carrier
Litter A
Bitch A - 37.5% probability of being a carrier

(50% × 37.5%) = 87.5%
87.5% × .50   = 43.75% probability of Litter A members
                         being carriers

Now we are ready to determine the probability that our breeding Dog A to Bitch A will produce offspring that carry the x gene.

We can also determine the probability that a puppy from the litter will be affected with trait xx. Since one-fourth of a litter between two carrier animals will be affected, we simply multiply the probability that a puppy in the litter will be a carrier by .25. Therefore, there is only a 10.93 percent chance that Litter A will contain a puppy displaying trait xx.

Fig. 5

	X	x	
X	XX	Xx	= ¼ XX; ½ Xx; ¼ xx
x	Xx	xx	

43.75% probability of producing a carrier
× .25   percent affected from two carriers

10.93% chance litter A will contain a puppy
          displaying trait xx

This simple method can be carried on an infinite number of generations if no known carriers are present. Let us say we own a dog whose great grandsire is a carrier. There is a 50 percent chance his grandfather is a carrier, a 25 percent chance his sire is a carrier, and a 12.5 percent chance he is a carrier (50% × ½ = 25% × ½ = 12.5%). But, should his grandsire later be found to be a carrier, the percentage increases to 25 percent that our dog is a carrier (50% × ½ = 25%).

The use of a test breeding program is the only sure way of determining an animal's genotype. This is its primary advantage, as it is both costly and time consuming. It entails the actual production of puppies from an animal whose genotype you wish to know. In order to test an animal with this method, there must be mates available which display the recessive trait (heterozygotes), are from carrier parents, or are offspring or siblings to the animal being tested.

A disadvantage is that the use of animals displaying the trait is not always possible if the gene being tested is a deleterious one such as lethal gray or patent ductus. Also, *all* the offspring from such breedings will be at least carriers. (If the trait appears, the animal being tested is a carrier.) This results in the problem of disposing of the offspring.

140

Fig. 6

Table 1. Number of Litters To Test An Animal For A Recessive Gene

Litter Size	xx Mates	Xx Mates	Mates from* Xx Parents	Offspring or Siblings as Mates
1	7	16	26	35
2	4	9	14	19
3	3	6	10	14
4	2	5	8	11
5	2	4	7	10
6	2	3	6	9
7	1	3	6	9
8	1	3	6	8
9-11	1	2	5	7
12-16	1	2	5	7
17+	1	1	5	7

Every litter in this column must be produced from a different mate in order to insure that heterozygotes (carriers) have been included among the test mates.

Table 1 shows the number of puppies and litters required to clear an animal to a ninety-nine percent confidence level.

One point which many breeders forget is that if you have accurate breeding records you may be able to clear an animal without actually test breeding yourself. For example, if we own an actively used stud dog that has bred ten daughters of Dog B, and we know Dog B was a carrier, we can check with the bitch owners to see if their bitches ever produced the trait. Now, presume that five of those bitches are known carriers. We further check to see if any puppies from our stud displayed the trait. Luckily, none have shown up, and the average litter size is six puppies. From the table preceeding, we find that with litters of six, only three litters are required to clear an animal. So we can safely say the animal is clear.

141

Fig. 7. Ch. Barksdale Bullseye

Fig. 8. A four-week old Collie Puppy.

Fig. 1. Ch. Wickmere Silver Bullet and sons, Ch. Barksdale Best Dressed and Ch. Stoney Brook Silver Saint.

16

The Stud Dog

The average layman's conception of a stud dog owner is that they accept payment for what Nature takes care of in the alley. This is a fallacy. If you want to be completely thwarted by Mother Nature, frustrated by all laws of averages, and excommunicated by protocol of genteel propriety, then own one or more male dogs placed at public stud.

Initial selection of a stud dog is based on conformation and temperament. He should have several outstanding characteristics and be an excellent overall representation of the breed with no serious faults. From that point on stud ownership involves proper training, nutrition, exercise and conditioning.

Even then, not all males will be good aggressive studs. Some males just naturally have a very low sex drive. In fact, if you study the behavior of wild members of the canine family, you will learn that not all males in a pack breed. Many are quite content to hunt and care for the young. They are psychologically castrated, eunuch without surgery. The sexual urge or instinct is non-existent.

Just as is observed in wild dogs, our domestic dogs tend to arrange themselves into a hierarchy. The most powerful and confident individual has the highest rank, and if a male, will be the most aggressive stud. The less dominant males may not be as readily inclined to mate. So we often experience breeding difficulties with our Collies that are caused by environment or possibly hereditary traits.

EXERCISE

Exercise can be one of the best aphrodisiacs for your stud dog. Some breeders have learned, much to their dismay, that it is difficult to maintain a simultaneous show and breeding career for their male dog. Lack of exercise on a show circuit, coupled with the stress of the

143

Dahlis

campaign, can create loss of sexual interest and a decline in sperm production. "Show weight" means a couple of extra pounds to carry a dog through erratic schedules and interrupted routines. If a dog is too heavy, he will tire easily, and if he is frustrated by failure in initial attempts at copulation, he may give up entirely.

NUTRITION

Until I learn otherwise, it is my opinion that most of our Collies do need supplements to achieve the optimum reproductive capability. One must be careful, however. While a small amount is vital, too much can be damaging. This is particularly true of vitamins A and D. Cornell researchers advise that intake of vitamins A and D should never exceed two times the minimum daily requirement.

Dr. Leon Whitney considers vitamin A the most important vitamin for reproduction. It is found abundantly in carrots, alfalfa, fish liver oils, egg yolk and animal liver. Vitamins E and C have also been reported to be important to fertility and the production of sperm. Several friends would take an oath that vitamin E has been highly successful in elevating a low sperm count in their stud dogs. There could be other explanations, but I don't want to hazard a guess. Vitamin E is known to affect the thyroid and pituitary glands. Yet, despite its publicity as the "fertility

144

Fig. 1. Ch. Jadene's Breeze Along

vitamin" in many species, canine and equine researchers have told me that vitamin E is more beneficial to rodents than to canines.

Vitamin C is increasingly being considered important to canine reproduction. One Eastern veterinarian feels that he has seen excellent results from administering vitamin C during periods of stress and for treating prostate problems in the stud dog.

As I read and speak to breeders, one recommendation is reiterated over and over—the B vitamins found in Brewer's Yeast. The recommended supplement for Collies is three 7-grain tablets daily for an adult. One of the B vitamins, B 12, is known to be a metabolic stimulant for impotent or infertile males. Vitamin B 12 can be added in the diet or given as an injection (Cyanocobalamine) under veterinary supervision.

Although it is difficult to find evidence to support the theory, I believe that zinc, a mineral, has some effect on fertility. Kelp and iodine have been used by breeders because of the suspected effect on the thyroid, pituitary, and other endocrine glands necessary for normal sexual activity.

Certain amino acids in protein are known to affect reproduction. If arginine is inadequate the formation and mobility of sperm is decreased. Lack of tryptophane causes testicles to degenerate, or atrophy, and females to lose their young. Of the two kinds of protein, animal and plant—animal protein in general is higher in essential amino acids, particularly lysine, methionine and tryptophane.

Probably every nutrient required to sustain life plays some role in stimulating normal hormone production and normal reproductive function. Supplementation of a good basic commercial dry ration with natural supplements seems to be the best policy. Perhaps old-time breeders were on the right track when they added liver, alfalfa, eggs, meat, Brewer's Yeast, and kelp to the feed of their breeding animals.

About seven years ago a dog breeding kennel that had just relocated in Kansas began to experience problems with infertile dogs, lack of normal growth in puppies, and heavy puppy losses. Investigating veterinarians came up with one clue: the water in this new location contained a high nitrate level. This episode and three other quite similar ones initiated a study on the effect of high levels of nitrates on reproduction in dogs. The results of the study are not available at this time, but efforts are directed at determining if the high level of nitrates in the water interfered with the utilization of vitamin A and at the link between high nitrate levels and the production of thyroxine, a hormone produced by the thyroid gland. [Low thyroid levels (hypothyroidism) are a common cause of low sex drive and infertility in the dog.]

SPERM CHECKS

Sperm checks are the best way of determining if your stud dog is fertile and they should be done once or twice a year on an active stud. You will especially want to do sperm checks if you have wormed your dog, if he has been ill, or if you live in a hot climate. Certain worming medicines can affect spermatogenesis. An illness accompanied by an elevated body temperature can affect sperm.

In 1976, tests conducted at the University of Missouri proved that heat reduces fertility in male animals. Nature has her own method of air conditioning. The dog's testicles are drawn closer to the body for warmth in cold weather. As warm weather approaches, the testicles descend for better air circulation. In coated breeds, it is wise to thin the hair around the scrotum during hot weather.

In the studies at the University of Missouri, bathing the testes of mice for fifteen minutes in water heated to 60 degrees centigrade prevented impregnation of females for up to fifty days after repeated bathing. Histologic studies revealed a complete absence of sperm production in these animals, but there were no hormonal imbalances or behavioral changes. When spermatogenesis resumed, there were no cellular mutations, and the animals sired normal offspring.

You can learn to do your own microscopic examination of semen to see if you have live sperm. Unless you are trained in further, more sophisticated evaluation, leave the rest to your veterinarian.

The dog ejaculates in a three-stage sequence. The first ejaculation lasts from six to twenty-six seconds, then is succeeded by a second ejacula-

tion lasting about the same amount of time. This second ejaculate contains most of the sperm. The third ejaculation lasts from four to sixteen minutes, and produces mostly clear prostactic fluid. For purposes of a sperm check, only the first and second stage are collected.

The head of the sperm contains the hereditary material while the tail is responsible for locomotion. The sole purpose of the sperm is to fertilize the egg, thereby reproducing its kind.

By examining the sperm under a microscope you, or your veterinarian, can determine approximately how many sperm are present and whether they are motile. A trained observer can also count the number of sperm that are deformed and those that are normal, healthy cells.

As long as there are a good number of normal, live sperm present, you do not need to be overly concerned with the difference in sperm count. We have observed a variation of sperm per cc of semen from individual studs, but with similar litter size resulting when they were bred. One stud might have two million sperm per cc of semen, while another would have a much lesser count but with good mobility and formation.

Many males also have a fluctuation of sperm production during the year. A yearling male may

145

Fig. 2. Ch. Hazeljane's Bright Future.

have a low sperm count as he blows his first coat, and may possibly follow a pattern of low count with each shed. It has been a known fact that many misses occur from summer breedings. This could be attributed to low hormone production accompanying the blowing of coat, coupled with the heat of the summer months. A stud dog should not be kept in temperatures over 82 degrees Fahrenheit. With air conditioning it is now possible to keep males in temperatures conducive to optimum sperm production.

In addition to sperm checks, periodic cultures should be taken from the sheath of the male to be sure that he is not harboring any harmful bacteria or infection. Periodic Brucellosis checks are also a must for the dog used at stud. For the protection of your male, require all incoming bitches to be cultured and have a current negative brucella titer.

TRAINING THE YOUNG STUD

Keep your young male a happy, outgoing extrovert. Never pen him with domineering, aggressive puppies or older stock where he will be intimidated by many battles to establish dominance. Naturally, he should have discipline from peers and elders—you don't want to raise a hermit—but be cautious how long he spends exercising and with whom.

Introduce the young stud to bitches in season at an early age and encourage his reaction. He may not quite know what to do about this stimulating excitement, but he knows something pleases him. Lavish praise on him. Don't allow him to run with bitches that are in season and then admonish him for attempting a breeding. Mismanagement at this time can result in psychological impotence. Once a psychological barrier has been established, it is almost impossible to reverse the situation. Be sure that the first bitch he breeds is not one that snaps, snarls and fights as this can do the same kind of harm to some males.

At what age to first use a dog? Depends upon the maturity of the individual. Some are ready at ten months of age (some have been used younger). We have observed that when males start lifting their leg to urinate, they are about ready to start being used at limited stud.

How often? At the May 1974 Symposium sponsored by Beecham Veterinary Products in England, the theme was "Infertility in the Dog and Bitch" and the advice for early use in a young male was repetitious of what we have heard many experts say. Use him for the first time at about ten months of age if he is well matured physically. Then the figures given were quite arbitrary, but every one of the speakers stressed that overuse in a young dog can cause him to go sterile at a much earlier age. It is far better to have one's dog functional for 8, 9 or 10 years than to make money to the time he is six and then come to a full stop.

There have been studs that have been used extensively with very little harm and a high ratio of conceptions. There is a good correlation in other species between the size of the testes and the number of sperm produced. It may be that a dog with bigger testes is capable of more services than a dog with smaller testes. He produces more sperm and these are available for fertilization.

HANDLING THE MATING

If you have an aggressive male without any psychological hangups, you can usually get any bitch bred, barring any physical impediments. Most of the bitch's problems stem from being a spoiled housepet, regardless of the fact that they may be shown. You must be aware that the bitch creates many of the breeding difficulties, compounded by novice owners inexperienced in breeding but who freely give directions to the stud owner. Too many owners present their bitch, demanding that she be bred on a certain day because "that is when she was bred before" or "that is when her sister (daughter, mother) was bred."

Eliminate set patterns and expectations. Bitches can vary from one season to the next, and there is most surely variation from one bitch to another.

A male may refuse to breed a bitch or dilly-dally around for a lengthy time, walking around the bitch, nibbling her ear, playfully grasping hair on her back or rump, but delaying any attempt to mount. The bitch is probably not ready. Give him some credit. HE is probably smarter than the bitch's owners about this matter.

Some bitches will reject a male throughout their season. It may be necessary to hold her to consummate the breeding. More bitches either reject a male or have no interest than are eager and willing to breed.

Procedure

Accustom your stud to work in a designated place such as the kennel, garage, or laundry room. Rubber matting or carpeting should be used to give firm footing for both dog and bitch.

Do not feed either animal prior to breeding. If the bitch is not clipped as an everyday sanitary precaution, it is wise to trim the hair around the vulva. She should have been checked for any strictures by the veterinarian who performed the culture. If not, you can use a rubber-gloved finger lubricated with *KY Jelly*® to dilate and lubricate the vulva. (Other kinds of lubricants may be spermicidal.)

It is helpful if the first several bitches the young male breeds are willing and cooperative. Just because a bitch is proven (has whelped a litter) does not necessarily indicate she will be a good tutor for your male. Many maiden bitches will also stand and court a male and not show resistance. Only observation of a bitch's reaction will let you know whether she is the one to use to introduce your stud to the world of reproduction.

As a safeguard, muzzle the bitch with one-inch masking tape wrapped around the muzzle. This prevents her from opening her jaws, but allows proper breathing. Even the best dispositioned Collie can strike out at handler or stud if frightened.

If two people are handling the dogs, one can hold the bitch by the head, near the collar and shoulder. If one person is handling the dogs alone, the bitch's leash can be tied so that her head and shoulder movement are restricted.

The following procedure applies for right handed handlers. Reverse if you are left handed.
1. Handler kneels on right side of bitch, right knee on the floor.
2. Place right arm under loin of bitch.
3. Place left hand around rear of bitch in the vulva area. If the bitch is not flagging, hold the tail to one side with the left thumb.
4. The male mounts, grasping the bitch around the flanks with his front feet. The handler's left hand manipulates, as necessary, to guide the penis to the vulva.
5. When penetration is accomplished, the male treads rapidly with his rear feet. The handler

Fig. 3. Ch. Lick Creek's Drummer Boy.

Fig. 4. Ch. Lick Creek's Pizzazz.

rises, moves behind the male and wraps arms around the male, holding the bitch by her flanks. Handler presses a knee firmly against the male's rear to assure the male is swelling inside the bitch.

After intromission, the gland at the posterior end of the penis (bulbus glandis) swells several times normal size and is held inside the bitch by the vaginal constrictor muscles. This is referred to as the "tie" and can last anywhere from two to three minutes to an hour or more. The usual time is about fifteen to thirty minutes.

Once the dog has stopped treading, he may rest before indicating he wishes to dismount. The pulsating spasms of the scrotum can be felt and you know the male is ejaculating. You can feel whether he has swollen completely inside the bitch. If not, hold the male in place for several minutes, or as long as you possibly can to allow ejaculation. Do not allow the dog to dismount!

If the bitch has been a most seductive and willing partner, you will notice a "rippling" along her back. These contractions literally pull the sperm forward to the uterus where they fertilize the ova.

If there is a good "tie" it is safe to allow the male to dismount by lifting his front legs to one side of the bitch. The male usually indicates whether he wants to dismount to the left or the right. Be sure the bitch's tail is out of the way and very slowly lift one of the dog's rear legs over the bitch's rear so that they are standing rear to rear. Holding both tails close to the base will prevent the dogs pulling at each other and possibly causing injury to either partner.

If the tie is so prolonged that everyone involved is getting bored, frustrated and fidgity, return the male to the mounted position on the bitch and press firmly against his rear. This may release the constricting vaginal band so that the male is freed.

Some owners elevate the bitch's rear to encourage the flow of semen up to the uterine horns. This procedure is of undetermined value, but we always do this if there was a very short tie or an outside tie.

Immediately after breeding, put the bitch in a confined place such as a crate to prevent her from urinating, and keep her quiet for about an hour. Then take her to a secure run with fresh water and a meal.

As soon as you have confined the bitch, turn your attention to the male. Take a sterile gauze pad soaked with hydrogen peroxide and swab the penis. Be sure it retracts properly into the sheath. (You may also use a syringe filled with diluted peroxide or any cleansing agent recommended by your vet to flush out the sheath.)

Problems With A Mating

Collies do not have the disparity in size between males and females that some breeds have, but if you should have a bitch that stands much higher than the male, you can elevate the male by furnishing a platform for his rear feet. This can be made of wood, rolled carpeting or towels, or you can have the bitch stand downhill on a grassy slope. The latter placement not only gets the bitch into a more desirable position, but also provides firm footing for the male.

A short vaginal tract in some bitches can prevent a tie. Some studs, particularly young, aggressive males, swell very rapidly, before complete penetration, thus preventing a tie. Some breeders and veterinarians have felt that unless there is a tie the breeding is not considered bona fide. This statement appears in the code of ethics adopted by some clubs and is a controversial topic when discussed with experienced Collie breeders. There have been many litters conceived when an actual tie never occurred. In fact, in some breeds, noteably Terriers, a tie is seldom experienced but high conception rates prevail.

If you are observant and have a reasonably good microscope, you can learn quite a bit about stud dogs. In examining many samples of semen, we have found excellent sperm counts in the initial ejaculate, contrary to reports by experts in canine reproduction who state that the second fraction contains the sperm. A higher ratio of conception does occur when there is a tie, probably due to the larger amount of semen in the second ejaculate. But, if you cannot get a tie with a particular dog and bitch, but penetration and ejaculation did occur, do not breed the bitch to a second dog as the semen deposited, even in min-

148

ute quantity, could very well impregnate the bitch. It is best not to take chances.

Sometimes the lack of a tie results when the person handling the breeding is not aware that some males have a slower swelling process of the bulbus glandis and the dog is turned or allowed to dismount too soon. Holding the dog against the bitch may accomplish the tie.

ARTIFICIAL INSEMINATION

Artificial insemination (A.I.) is not a replacement for natural breeding but may have to be employed for a variety of reasons. It avoids the spread of infection, especially if the stud is popular and breeding more than one bitch during the same week, or if the bitch's owner did not provide a negative culture. One collection of semen can be used to inseminate two bitches, thus saving a popular stud from overuse. For bitches that do not have good vulvar swelling or that are just plain mean, A.I. may be the only way to accomplish a breeding.

It has been predicted by several authorities that A.I. will comprise a high percentage of breedings within the next decade, especially since the use of frozen semen has proven successful and the American Kennel Club has approved the registration of litters from breedings done with frozen semen.

HOW MANY SERVICES?

I do not think there is any aspect of this subject that is not controversial. Some stud owners allow only one service. If the male is popular, there may be difficulty accommodating all the bitches accepted in one week. If the owner is thinking of monetary loss or trying to establish a siring record, he may accept far more bitches than he should. We cannot set a universal rule to follow, for as soon as we say that a male cannot be used more than two to four times a week, someone comes up with an example of a dog used excessively for a number of months or years with no apparent difficulty.

Some males solve this dilemma for their owners by refusing to breed a bitch a second time. I do not have the statistics, but it has been our experience that if the bitch is receptive (and particularly if vaginal smears have been done to determine ovulation) and the stud willing, the conception rate from one service has been very high.

Abstinence is advised by some authorities as the frequency of copulation with one bitch does not assure conception nor a large litter. Litter size is determined by the bitch, and since sperm can live for a number of days in the reproductive tract of the bitch, one breeding close to ovulation should be sufficient. When we study animals in the wild that often mate only once during a season, it is easy to see that we are trying to overwork nature.

I feel it is a stud owner's responsibility to assure a bitch owner that the particular female will be bred at the optimum time, but overuse can decrease the libido in the male, particularly if the stud is an excellent specimen and in demand. Also, if one bitch comes into season it appears to hit epidemic proportions and they all arrive at once.

By spacing wisely and not overworking the male, you should be able to accommodate the selected bitches. It has been our experience that many breeders (sometimes encouraged by their veterinarian) are so fearful that they will miss a bitch that they want to "try the bitch" every day or twice daily. If this happens to be a bitch that resents the male and most vociferously, the stud may decide to wait for a more docile creature. By the time this cantankerous one decides she is ready, the stud refuses to have anything to do with her. This is just too much human interference.

Reports from the University of Pennsylvania School of Veterinary Medicine and the work in England of J. E. Cox and presented as "The Research Worker's View" on the topic of infertility in dog and bitch, confirms that sperm survive in the uterine horns seven to eight days. To quote Cox, "It seems a golden rule that so long as a bitch stays in oestrus, the sperm will survive, but whether they are capable of fertilizing eggs, say up to eight days after having been mated, is doubtful."

We have found a high count of mobile sperm 24 to 36 hours after collection when the sample was kept in a room temperature in the sixties.

Eng. Ch. Magnet

Ch. Eden Emerald

150

Ch. El Troubadour of Arken

SIRE CHART 1

ENG. CH. MAGNET
(2 AKC CHS.)

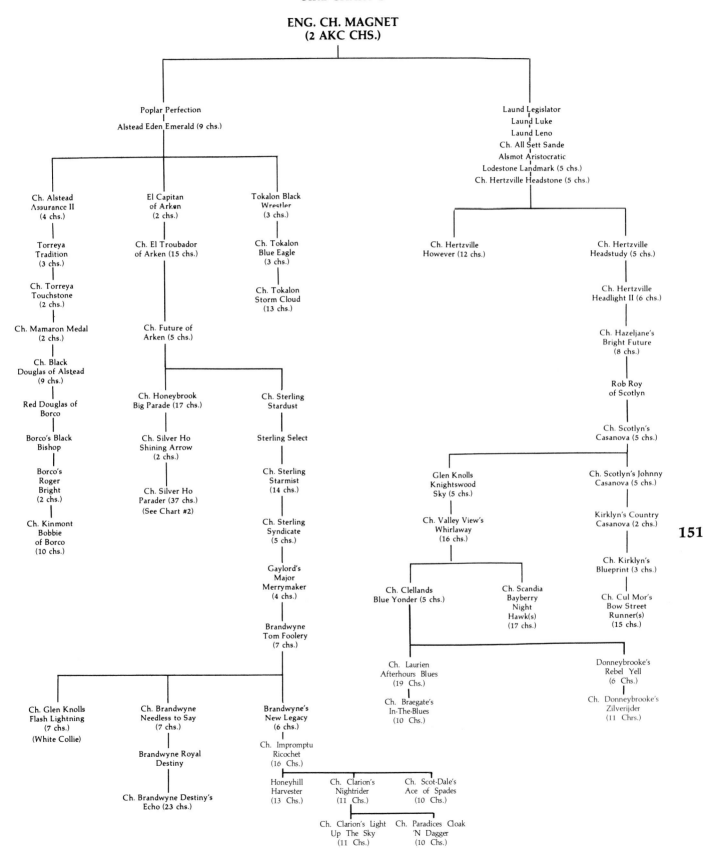

Poplar Perfection
Alstead Eden Emerald (9 chs.)

Laund Legislator
Laund Luke
Laund Leno
Ch. All Sett Sande
Alsmot Aristocratic
Lodestone Landmark (5 chs.)
Ch. Hertzville Headstone (5 chs.)

Ch. Alstead
Assurance II
(4 chs.)

El Capitan
of Arken
(2 chs.)

Tokalon Black
Wrestler
(3 chs.)

Ch. Hertzville
However (12 chs.)

Ch. Hertzville
Headstudy (5 chs.)

Torreya
Tradition
(3 chs.)

Ch. El Troubador
of Arken (15 chs.)

Ch. Tokalon
Blue Eagle
(3 chs.)

Ch. Hertzville
Headlight II (6 chs.)

Ch. Torreya
Touchstone
(2 chs.)

Ch. Tokalon
Storm Cloud
(13 chs.)

Ch. Hazeljane's
Bright Future
(8 chs.)

Ch. Mamaron Medal
(2 chs.)

Ch. Future of
Arken (5 chs.)

Rob Roy
of Scotlyn

Ch. Black
Douglas of Alstead
(9 chs.)

Red Douglas of
Borco

Ch. Honeybrook
Big Parade (17 chs.)

Ch. Sterling
Stardust

Ch. Scotlyn's
Casanova (5 chs.)

Borco's Black
Bishop

Ch. Silver Ho
Shining Arrow
(2 chs.)

Sterling Select

Glen Knolls
Knightswood
Sky (5 chs.)

Ch. Scotlyn's Johnny
Casanova (5 chs.)

Borco's
Roger
Bright
(2 chs.)

Ch. Silver Ho
Parader (37 chs.)
(See Chart #2)

Ch. Sterling
Starmist
(14 chs.)

Ch. Valley View's
Whirlaway
(16 chs.)

Kirklyn's Country
Casanova (2 chs.)

151

Ch. Kinmont
Bobbie
of Borco
(10 chs.)

Ch. Sterling
Syndicate
(5 chs.)

Ch. Kirklyn's
Blueprint (3 chs.)

Gaylord's
Major
Merrymaker
(4 chs.)

Ch. Clellands
Blue Yonder (5 chs.)

Ch. Scandia
Bayberry
Night
Hawk(s)
(17 chs.)

Ch. Cul Mor's
Bow Street
Runner(s)
(15 chs.)

Brandwyne
Tom Foolery
(7 chs.)

Ch. Laurien
Afterhours Blues
(19 Chs.)

Donneybrooke's
Rebel Yell
(6 Chs.)

Ch. Glen Knolls
Flash Lightning
(7 chs.)
(White Collie)

Ch. Brandwyne
Needless to Say
(7 chs.)

Brandwyne's
New Legacy
(6 chs.)

Ch. Braegate's
In-The-Blues
(10 Chs.)

Ch. Donneybrooke's
Zilverijder
(11 Chrs.)

Brandwyne Royal
Destiny

Ch. Impromptu
Ricochet
(16 Chs.)

Ch. Brandwyne Destiny's
Echo (23 chs.)

Honeyhill
Harvester
(13 Chs.)

Ch. Clarion's
Nightrider
(11 Chs.)

Ch. Scot-Dale's
Ace of Spades
(10 Chs.)

Ch. Clarion's Light
Up The Sky
(11 Chs.)

Ch. Paradices Cloak
'N Dagger
(10 Chs.)

Ch. Sujim's Mr. Onederful

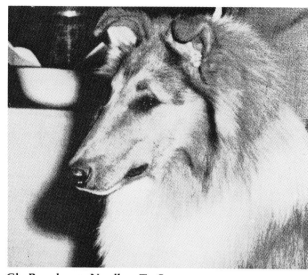

Ch. Brandwyne Needless To Say

Ch. Impromptu Ricochet

Ch. Hi Vu The Invader

152

Ch. Vi-Lee's Parading Chieftain

Ch. Cherrivale Darn Minute

Ch. Parader's Country Squire

SIRE CHART 2
CH. SILVER HO PARADER (37 CHS.)

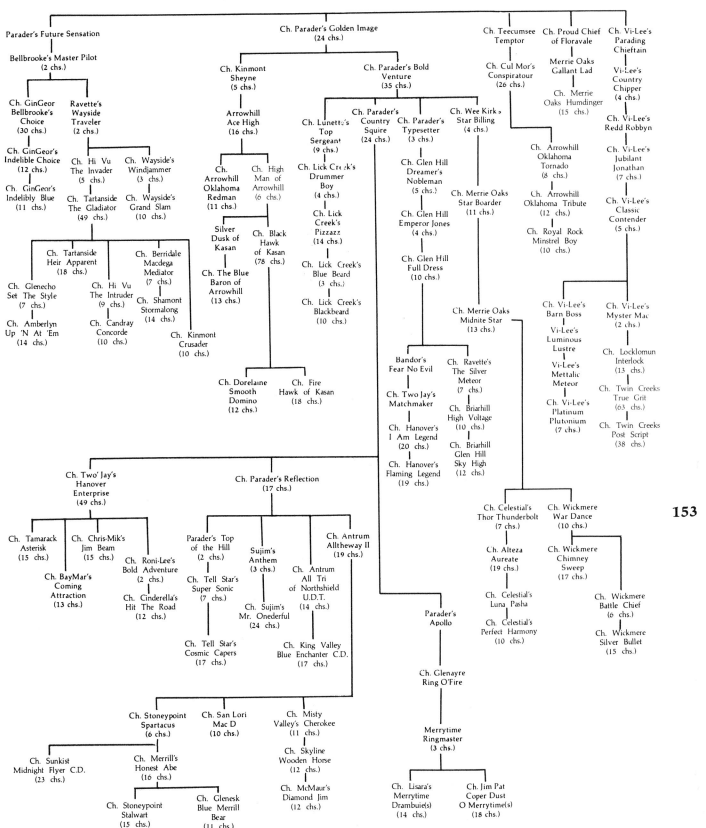

153

CANINE BRUCELLOSIS[1]

Brucellosis is the general name given infectious systemic bacterial diseases affecting a number of different species and caused by a member of a group of related organisms called *Brucella*. The bacterium isolated from aborted canine fetal tissues was named *Brucella canis*.

The disease signs are abortions, reproductive failures in both sexes and generalized enlargement of the lymph nodes. Animals also may show fatigue, poor condition, or behavioral abnormalities. Abortions in dogs occur most frequently between the forty-fifth and fifty-fifth day of gestation. Occasional litters may be born with some pups alive and some dead.

An important aspect of the disease in males is infertility, with abnormal sperm and a severe reduction in motility. This suggests that a semen examination is an essential portion of the diagnostic procedure for male animals.

The most common mode of transmission is by ingestion of placental tissue or vaginal excretions which generally last from 1 to 6 weeks following abortion. The vaginal discharge following an abortion may contain several billion organisms per milliliter. Infection of the dog can occur via all mucous membrane surfaces, such as the eye, nose, mouth and vagina. Transmission via urine or other body secretions seems unlikely since the number of organisms shed is very low.

Once the disease becomes established in the male, brucella may be transmitted at the time of breeding as a true venereal disease. Males and females are affected with equal ease.

To test for brucella, an agglutination test is required. Most veterinarians now have available to them the rapid slide agglutination test, which allows a presumptive diagnosis within minutes. As with all laboratory tests, results of a single test must be interpreted with caution since nonspecific reactions may occur. Thus far, the rapid slide agglutination test has been highly accurate in identifying uninfected animals, for "false negatives" are extremely rare. All positive slide-test reactions should be followed by additional laboratory and clinical studies.

It is strongly advised that you:
1. Test all females with a history of recent abortion or infertility.
2. Test males with scrotal irritation, enlarged and painful testes or a poor semen quality.
3. Test any new dog that is to be introduced into a clean kennel.
4. Test dogs that have been boarded for prolonged periods or used in field trials.
5. Test dogs as a portion of their pre-breeding examination.

In order for effective treatment for elimination of brucella infections from the body, one must be able to spend a great deal of time and money with no guarantee of the outcome. In kennel situations, the infected animal should be destroyed.

There is little opportunity for spread in non-breeding animals. This suggests that castration of infected males or the spaying of infected females, followed by a course of antibiotic treatment, would be of value to control spread of infection in household pets.

The bacterium does not survive long on kennel floors, or outside the host. Disinfection with strong household detergents or commercial disinfectants rapidly inactivates *Brucella Canis*.

[1]Cornell Research Laboratory for Diseases of Dogs, *Laboratory Report*, Series 2, Number 7, September, 1976.

154

17

The Brood Bitch

"Nature is a revelation of God; Art a revelation of man . . ."   Longfellow

A breeder is both geneticist and artist. Perhaps we can say thirty percent science, thirty percent artistic sense, and forty percent pure luck will make you a successful breeder of superb Collies.

To inaugurate your plan, find a bitch with a desirable pedigree of quality individuals so that she will be more likely to reproduce her background. A female that shows a family tree of "inbreeding" or "linebreeding," preferably from individuals that are known to have outstanding virtues, will no doubt be a shortcut to success.

"Inbreeding" has been falsely accused of *causing* temperament problems and low mentality. It surely can IF the stock being used has a poor disposition and low intelligence. Conscientious breeders are just as concerned about temperament and intelligence as they are with physical beauty.

If I were looking for a foundation bitch, I would be pleased to find that some inbreeding had been practiced, which would mean there had been a brother-sister mating, or father to daughter or mother to son. If not astute inbreeding, then linebreeding could help assure a genetic pre-potency. Linebreeding would be the mating of animals who are closely related to one ancestor. Advice given to us many years ago was to breed a granddaughter back to her grandsire (considering that this grandsire has the qualities you will wish to compound); and, if he was not available, breed to his best son or grandson. Then there is excellent latitude for "family breeding" by criss-crossing progeny back and forth—an elemental example of how a breeder can establish type and genetic gene pools.

Bitches resulting from several generations of well planned breedings are a valuable asset. Many owners are reluctant to part with them; and, if available, they can command high prices.

Dahlis

155

If your budget is limited and what you really covet is beyond your pocketbook, settle for a bit lesser female and allow more time. I have far more respect for a person who is willing to "grade-up" than for one who anticipates knocking the show world on its ear with a champion from a first litter. This has happened, but it is not the usual occurrence.

By the term "lesser female" it is not implied that a cheap Collie harbouring every distasteful fault is going to be the dam or granddam of your blue ribbon winners. If you have studied the Standard and know what a good Collie is, then you will be aware of the value of your first bitch and have to compensate for her faults and stress the virtues.

One of the best booklets available for the novice breeder is *Planned Breeding* by Lloyd C. Brackett. It is a compilation of his articles that appeared in an all-breed magazine in the 1960's. Mr. Brackett was a very successful German Shepherd breeder and all-round judge. The advice from his experience is easily understood and, if applied, could surely give excellent results.

SELECTING A STUD

After you acquire your bitch, the stud selection is made. A "universal" stud dog does not exist. When you study the production record of a male that has champion progeny, you will learn which bitches were compatible. Were they closely related (genotype) or were they of a certain physical type or appearance (phenotype)?

Quality should be virtues that are agreeable to the *practiced* eye. Merit and excellence are only discernible through cultivated appreciation. Seek virtues of significance and distinction, not an indifferent specimen of neutral, moderate appearance overshadowed by pageantry or advertising. Many dogs are overlooked because they lack the championship prefix. Keep in mind that the title does not alter or improve the potential of a dog's hereditary traits.

Aesthetic breeders of experience are connoisseurs of excellence and are not fooled by scintillating showmanship. We have attached such importance to a dog's self presentation and to astute handling that we have sacrificed many

156

Fig. 1. Ch. Impromptu Repartee at nine months. She was the first futurity finalist, BOW, CC of A, 1967; BOS 1969.

Fig. 2. Repartee at three months of age. *Petrulis photo.*

virtues for an extroverted dazzler with ring stamina. A dog that lacks flamboyant showmanship, perhaps not flashily marked or having an unattractive color, is described as being an "honest dog." Honest is an honorable state. Although they possess a minimum of nature's adornments, these dogs deserve to be scrutinized more closely for full appreciation. Personality, handling, or color should not overshadow breed characteristics. Do not settle for a happy medium—*juste milieu*—Collies without distinction. You want to produce individuals with exalted virtues.

Contact with the stud owner is by personal visit, letter or telephone. Abide by the stud owner's request concerning what tests the bitch must have prior to breeding. Generally, vaginal cultures are a must and can help prevent disappointments since these can reveal some infections which could cause abortion, early puppy deaths, or misses. This protects your investment in a stud fee, which can range from $125 to $300, and gives your bitch a clean bill of health and a better assurance of a healthy litter. The stud owner is particularly interested in the results of these tests as he does not want to expose his valued male to an infection that could quite possibly render the dog sterile or be passed on to other visiting bitches.

Your veterinarian can explain which bacteria are harmful, as a completely negative vaginal culture is nearly impossible.

Accompanying the vaginal culture, the bitch should have a Brucellosis test. *Brucella canis* can cause fetal (embryonal) deaths and is spread by oral contact or venereal transmission (see pg. 154). Conception failure can be noted, usually due to embryonal death or to aborting the litter at 45 to 52 days. If a stud is entertaining many visiting bitches, it is a wise owner who has the male tested for Brucellosis every three to six months.

Some bitches come into season as early as four months or as late as thirty-two months. The latter is the one that can cause concern. We do not recommend inducing a season by using hormones. If a bitch appears to be perfectly normal and healthy and misses the first seven- or eight-month-cycle, wait until she is eighteen to twenty months before you get too alarmed. You may easily miss a first season if you were expecting a full blown swelling of the vulva with a lot of dis-

charge. The signs of a first season may be very indistinct, so a "silent" season can slip by unobserved. The next season, six or seven months later, may be the "full blown heat." The cycles usually are repeated every six to seven months, on the average, or up to a year. The cycles depend upon the individual and vary with different breeds of dogs. A bitch that normally cycles only once a year may be converted to two cycles a year by exposing her to a two-cycle-a-year bitch.

What happens if the bitch goes through a pregnancy? Dr. Stephen Fels in California reports that it will add approximately two weeks to the cycle interim. We used to think in terms of "spring births," but now bitches are cycling every month of the year. We can expect to breed during any month.

As a bitch gets older, there is a tendency for the intervals between cycles to lengthen. It can be a subtle change at four or five years of age, but is quite noticeable when she reaches about eight years of age.

At the very first sign of the bitch coming into season, increase food intake by ten percent; and, as soon as she accepts the male, cut back to regular consumption. It is thought that the elevated amount of feed prior to breeding increases the number of eggs released and available for fertilization. This increase in food intake is called "flushing" and has been practiced successfully in

157

Fig. 3. Ch. Kimblewyck Tara of Tedjoi, one of the first Smooths to place in a Working Group.

sheep. If food intake is kept high after breeding, however, embryonic deaths can result.

TIMING

When is the right time to breed? Dr. Jacob E. Mosier reported that, when 350 breeders were questioned, the results were: 22 percent bred for the first time on the ninth day, 13 percent bred on the tenth day, 46 percent bred on the eleventh day, and 18 percent bred for the first time on the twelfth day. A range of nine to twelve days for the first breeding emerges. Then these breeders were asked when was the last breeding they counted on. Five percent bred the last time on the eleventh day, 5 percent on the twelfth day, 21 percent on the thirteenth day, 58 percent on the fourteenth day, and 10 percent on the fifteenth day.

There is a lot of variation as to when you can breed. When we talk about *averages,* we can say the tenth and the eleventh day; but it is reported that if you breed for the first time on the tenth or eleventh day, you would get about 80 percent conception.

Vaginal smears are very useful in determining just when a bitch is ovulating and are recommended especially for problem bitches. It has been our personal observation that the use of the test tape to determine ovulation is practically useless and this has been confirmed by several authorities in reproductive seminars. Test tape is probably accurate about 16 percent of the time.

To be useful, the tape has to be inserted fairly close to the cervix into the anterior vestibule of the vagina. The day it shows a positive sugar reaction, the bitch should be ovulating. The reason for this is that some of the follicular fluid contains a lot of sugar. Under the influence of certain estrogen levels, some of the sugar is combined with other products in the vagina and secretions are suddenly released, so there is a positive sugar reaction. If you are unsanitary or not very careful you could traumatize the vaginal wall and quite likely induce infection.

As you are observing the bitch externally for the optimum breeding time, you can tell quite a bit by examining the vulva. It becomes very swollen and has a normal proestrual discharge. It is not recessed. The amount of swelling reflects the amount of hormone level. If the bitch *never comes into a good swelling,* she may be a fertility problem and in all probability will not even ovulate. The proper hormone levels necessary to produce a good external manifestation of heat are lacking. We have discussed this phenomenon with other experienced breeders; and, if you can get these bitches bred (some experienced stud dogs ignore these bitches), they usually miss. We have also found that some of these bitches do not swell their first season but swell adequately at a subsequent season. Perhaps with "maturity" comes a natural change in hormone production. If the bitch has successive seasons of minimal swelling, consult your veterinarian to perhaps try a series of shots to intensify the hormone level. Our vet has used follicle stimulating hormone (FSH) at first show of season, five days later half the dose of FSH, then estrogen to induce a good swelling. Next he does a vaginal smear and gives a luteinizing hormone to induce ovulation.

This treatment may solve the difficulty and subsequent seasons and conception can be normal; but, if the bitch's dam, granddam or littermates also had to have medical assistance, I feel the young bitch is too much of a breeding risk. You could continue to perpetuate an expensive, time consuming and disappointing familial reproduction problem. This type bitch can be a harrassment; and, if she is presented for breeding to a *novice male,* which is owned by a novice "stud owner," the difficulty is compounded. The handler can become impatient and cannot under-

Fig. 4. Ch. Country Lane M'Liss, Best of Breed 1960 CCA Specialty.

stand why the male does not perform and consummate a breeding.

If a bitch is being shipped in by air, we like to know that she is having a "normal" season. No stud owner appreciates having someone else's problems dumped on them. If the bitch is not progressing in a normal pattern of swelling, cancel the shipment.

Let's look on the positive side—a good, healthy bitch coming into a season. You want to be sure of optimum breeding time, so a series of smears are taken. The veterinarian will look for a decreasing number of erythrocytes, for cornified epithelial cells (they resemble a fried egg with a curled outer edge), a few leukocytes near the end of the estral period, and no debris. Ovulation normally occurs two to four days AFTER first acceptance. Where the estral period is more prolonged, ovulation may occur later in that period. Generally, the bitch will accept the male no later than 72 hours following ovulation or 48 hours after appearance of the leukocytes.

Everything goes nicely and you get a good breeding. A second breeding in 48 to 72 hours, or every other day if the bitch is receptive, can give you a better chance of conception, *but* many experienced stud dogs take care of this matter themselves and refuse to breed a bitch a second or third time. Evidently the dog feels the bitch was bred at the right time, and he will just wait for another wench to come along. This reaction usually occurs as a male gets older and more experienced.

POST-BREEDING CARE

You have the bitch bred and now you are just too impatient and excited to wait until nature's obvious signal that the bitch is in whelp. One common method has been to palpate abdominally at twenty-one to twenty-eight days, but Dr. Mosier suggested an even earlier test for the "antsy" bitch owner. Check her vaginal discharge about ten to twelve days after breeding or last acceptance. If she is *not* pregnant, the discharge is thick and tenacious and white blood cells appear in large clumps. If she is pregnant, the discharge is thin and watery and any white blood cells are well distributed. I thought this was an interesting aspect timewise as implantation of the fertilized egg occurs at about fifteen to twenty days post breeding.

How many puppies will she have? Litter size is fifteen percent heredity, eighty-five percent environment and management. It is extremely prudent that during the time between breeding and subsequent implantation of fertilized ova that your bitch should be given cautious care to see that she does not undergo undue stress, exposure to disease or become ill, thereby preventing implantation.

Several breeders have felt that their bitches were "stressed" by shipping or just being in a different environment for breeding, and then subsequent traveling—another reason to look for a very stable disposition in a prospective brood bitch.

159

Fig. 5. Ch. Shamont Sabrina, dam of seven champions.

Fig. 6. Ch. Marnus Evening Breeze, BOS 1968 and 1970 CC of A.

At about the twenty-fourth to twenty-fifth day, segmental enlargements can be felt by palpation. If you still do not know or for some reason could not palpate at that time, at thirty-five days take a blood sample, and submit it to the laboratory for a hemoglobin check—it drops.

A series of visible reactions to pregnancy also occurs between the thirty-second and thirty-fifth day. The bitch may become restless, appear to be experiencing discomfort, and she may vomit. We have jokingly remarked that several of our bitches had "morning sickness."

Sometimes a bitch may appear to be in whelp between three and four weeks and then, like a deflated balloon, the signs disappear. If a bitch reabsorbs prior to the thirty-sixth day, resorption is usually complete. If this occurs later at about forty-eight to forty-nine days, the fetus mummifies and it may or may not be aborted. Any obstruction such as a mummified fetus or material remaining after whelping can act like an intra-uterine contraceptive device and keep a bitch in anestrus for many months. A mummified fetus may be passed as part of a litter in which other puppies are perfectly normal, vigorous whelps and there are no complications with the dam.

Generally your expectant mother is between two and six years of age—the prime reproduction age. When a female puppy is born, she has 700,000 potential ova in her ovaries. By the time she reaches puberty, the number has declined to 250,000, and by the time she is five years of age, it is 33,000, and at ten years she has only 500 potential ova. In litter-producing mammals, there is a high incidence of embryonic deaths. It would appear, then, with decreased ova as age advances and embryonic deaths increase, that it is risky to breed bitches nine years or over, or to purchase a bitch beyond the age of five or six if you are looking for a large litter size. Not all bitches follow the predicted breeding pattern, but it is wise to take this into consideration when contemplating a purchase or investing in an expensive shipping and stud fee even for a proven, older matron.

Your bitch was in optimum condition when bred. Now you are feeding a self-contained "family." If you want to improve the health and vigor of the puppies, increase the animal protein by two to four percent. Do not try to save money by purchasing a cheap dog food. If you want to raise strong, healthy puppies with good fertility in bitches (and studs), do not try to economize on dog food.

Twenty-four to twenty-six percent protein is required for reproduction in the average dog. Cheap feeds provide only about twenty-one percent. Dr. Mosier states he likes to take the twenty-four percent protein diet and add some cottage cheese, hamburger, or eggs to bring it up

160

Fig. 7. Ch. Mayoline Welcome Reflection, BOS 1962 CC of A.

to about twenty-six percent. Mosier is convinced that the best single supplement is plain, raw liver several times a week. The quality of the protein is *very* important. Mosier would rather see fish meal as a protein ingredient than *meat by-products*. A label of twenty-five percent protein and seven percent fat does not tell you much. Someone jokingly remarked that you could take one old leather boot, a gallon of coal oil and some coal, beat them up, emulsify, and send that off to be analyzed and it will come back twenty-five percent protein, ten percent fat, etc., yet it contains nothing that a dog can utilize.

If you keep a bitch on *restricted protein,* (not *average* but *restricted protein*) this will show up in her puppies' BRAIN size. You are trying to feed this prospective mother (or a finicky show prospect) so she will produce vigorous puppies, but she turns her nose up at the feed pan. Add a little more meat and moisten the dog food (we always use a warm broth, particularly in winter months) and she will consume twenty percent more calories. One part meat to ten parts meal is a good balance. An all-meat diet is disaster for any dog as meat is deficient in some essential nutrients such as phosphorous, calcium, and vitamins A and D.

About the fifth or sixth week of gestation, food intake should be increased by fifteen to twenty percent beyond the maintenance diet.

This is usually when over-zealous owners start adding a variety of vitamins and minerals. *Judicious* supplementation is recommended! Excess calcium can produce a zinc deficiency. Low zinc levels affect uterine contractions and can possibly be the reason some bitches must have caesarians.

Milk as a supplement has already been mentioned; and it is usually fortified with vitamin D so you should be cautious about adding more vitamin D if the bitch is already receiving an adequate supply via the milk and kibble or meal. Vitamin D is essential for the utilization of calcium and phosphorous, so these three ingredients are combined in one capsule as a supplement.

PREPARATION FOR WHELPING

The week prior to whelping, the bitch is using up a lot of energy to produce all the milk necessary for the impending litter. She needs a diet of high caloric density. For the last week of gestation and first week of lactation, substitute puppy chow for the regular kibble and add some extra fat and protein.

Excitement mounts as you prepare for the litter. A whelping box four feet by four feet (or four by six) will accommodate a Collie and her family. A "pig rail" around the inside of the box

161

Fig. 8. Ch. Regaline's Blue Intuition, dam of eight champions, six rough and two smooth.

will help prevent puppies being crushed by the dam when she lies down. An alternative to a wooden box is a child's plastic wading pool that can be easily washed and disinfected.

Do not try to compete with TV ratings. Whelping is no time to invite the neighbors. Allow the prospective mother solitude and privacy. She will usually try to locate her own secluded "den" by frequenting closets, under beds, or any nook or cranny that offers privacy. I have watched bitches that were going to have their own nest outside. They would find dense underbrush or low hanging limbs, select an opening, then set about preparing a den, turning in circles to tamp down the leaves that had accumulated and usually digging a small depression or hole. This is a very natural way that animals in the wild state keep the young together. So, curb your temper if you find your favorite rose bush almost uprooted by the energetic prospective mother who is responding to the call of the wild.

Collect some or all of the following in preparation for the nursery:

Stack of newspapers	Alcohol
Paper Towels	Scissors
Bath Towels	Hemostat
Hot Water Bottle	Iodine
Heating Pad	Dental Floss or Carpet
Pampers® disposable	Thread
diapers	Eye dropper or syringe
Measuring Cup—water and sugar	
Cardboard carton (preferrably with a top)	
Scale, notebook, pen	

162

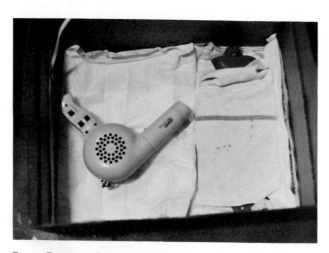

Fig. 9. Prepare a box to put the first puppies while others are arriving. Dryer is used to dry newborns.

Large trash bags for soiled papers
Lamp to hold infrared heat light (brooder type) for above-box heat *or* the commercial kennel heating pad which is placed on the floor of the whelping box

Layers of newspapers spread on the floor of the whelping box will help absorb the fluids. After the litter arrives and are comfortably settled with the dam, substitute the papers with soft blankets, disposable diapers, large towels or mattress padding that is cut to fit the floor of the box. We prefer blankets to indoor/outdoor carpeting. These materials provide good traction for the newborns to nurse. I feel that many skeletal problems can be avoided if the puppies do not slip and slide on a slick surface.

The moment you have waited for is drawing near. Bathe the bitch or if it is not possible to bathe her all over, wash off the breasts and nipples with soap and water, and rinse with clear water. Cut the long hair off the abdomen and rear pantaloons. This trimming makes whelping more sanitary, minimizes odor, and prevents the puppies from becoming tangled.

Five to seven days before the due date of sixty-three days, the bitch will become restless and her rectal temperature may fluctuate from the normal reading of 101 to 99. Her appetite decreases and a clear, mucous vaginal discharge becomes quite copius as actual whelping becomes imminent. The rounded, hard flank area becomes concave and the back bone and hip bones are prominent, indicating the puppies have dropped.

We have had bitches that continued to eat hearty meals right up to presentation of the first puppy and bitches with temperatures that never dropped from a normal reading. However, if the rectal temperature takes a sudden dive to 99 or 98 degrees and food is refused, keep close observation for accompanying signs of labor to begin within twelve hours.

THE PUPPIES ARRIVE

Dilation of the cervix takes place in the first stage of labor. During this time the bitch will shiver, pant, tremble and noisily chatter her teeth together. She becomes increasingly restless and may make several trips outdoors to urinate.

Chaperone her on these forays with a towel just in case she should have a puppy outdoors.

Some bitches will go through quite a prolonged production at this stage.

As the cervix dilates the panting can become more rapid and then you can observe the bitch straining, accompanied by grunting sounds, the flanks fill out as she literally holds her breath and "pushes."

The puppy is moved from the uterine horn into the central cavity and is now against the cervix. When the cervix is dilated the puppy enters the vaginal canal, preceeded by the water bag which may break before you see it protruding from the vulva. Arrival of the puppy occurs immediately.

Some bitches whelp lying down and others alter their position to standing or squatting. Don't interfere. Let her choose her position for delivery.

The water bag acts as a natural lubricant and the puppy literally slides out. If there should be difficulty with a first puppy or an unusually large whelp, and part of the head is out, don't panic. Quietly encourage the bitch to strain to expel the puppy.

If the pup disappears back up into the birth canal then you must step in to help. As the head appears again, roll the lips of the vulva back over the pup's head. This gives you an opportunity to grasp the puppy by the skin (don't pull on the neck or head!) with a very soft rag, (old T-shirts or large sterile gauze pads) and pull gently. KY® lubricant rubbed around the rolled back lips of the vulva will help assist expulsion.

If it is a breech (rear end presentation) use the same procedure and grasp the skin. Don't pull the tail or rear legs. Always pull slightly down toward the bitch's stomach, never straight out or upward.

Subsequent puppies usually arrive with ease.

Don't be surprised or alarmed if the bitch seems to be frightened by the first pup and attempts to escape from this "lump" and does not do anything to clean or care for it. You will have to assume her duties, at least initially.

Remove the sac from the head, cut the cord and get that first lusty cry. As you rub the puppy, encourage the dam to sniff and lick it. The odor from the fluids and this licking helps to establish the maternal bond.

Another puppy may arrive immediately or it may be as long as two hours.

Check the new arrival for any defects, mark down time of birth, weight, sex and any other pertinent information for later identification.

Be sure a placenta is passed with each puppy. The bitch may or may not eat the placentas. This is natural. Whether the placenta has any nutritional or hormonal value I'm not sure, perhaps this behavior is just left over from the wild state and general house-keeping on the dam's part to keep a tidy nest.

If arrival of another puppy is not imminent, leave the first one with the bitch. It may start nursing, which helps to stimulate contractions. When contractions and straining start coming close again, move the first puppy to the box prepared with a heating pad and towels so the bitch will not step or lie on it as she becomes preoccupied with the delivery of the next puppy.

Intervals of fifteen minutes, one-half hour, or one hour between puppies are usual. If the bitch strains hard and continues for two hours without delivering a puppy, call your veterinarian. Definitely do not allow a bitch to labor longer than three hours as one whelp may be sideways, blocking all traffic. Veterinary assistance is mandatory if this happens. Simple assistance may be all that is needed, but it is safer to sound an alarm than to get into serious trouble and lose puppies or endanger the dam's life.

163

Fig. 10. Ch. Alteza The Silver Lining, dam of eight champions.

If the bitch seems to be "lazy" and stops laboring, she may have uterine inertia, which can stem from various causes. Lack of exercise and overfeeding result in an obese prospective mother. Muscle tone can be maintained by allowing the bitch to play with other dogs up to the fourth and fifth week of gestation. Chasing sticks, balls or plastic bottles is excellent exercise. From the sixth week to whelping, violent running and bumping is discouraged, but as the bitch becomes heavier and more reluctant to move, take her on daily walks.

Fig. 11. During prelabor, bitch becomes restless and shreds newspapers.

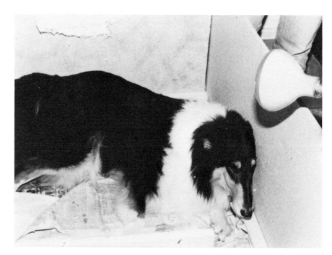

Fig. 12. As arrival of puppy is imminent, bitch arches her tail and strains with each contraction.

164

Fig. 13. A large pup is helped along by gently pulling with each contraction. Keep nose and mouth free.

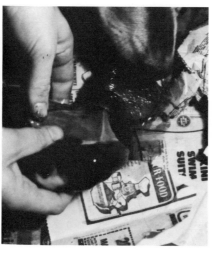

Fig. 14. Puppy born completely in the sac with placenta attached. Attendant removes the membrane from pup's head.

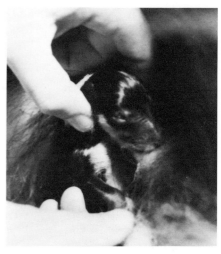

Fig. 15. A lusty cry expands the lungs. Puppies that start out vigorously give you fewer problems.

Non-productive labor to expel one large puppy can result in fatigue, or if the litter is large the bitch may become weary at some point and quit straining. Barring any mechanical blockage, your veterinarian may recommend a hormone shot, oxytocin, or calcium to stimulate contractions.

A brisk walk may be refreshing to the bitch and she might welcome a bowl of milk to which you can add an egg yolk or two and honey or sugar. This "egg nog" can be a real energy booster!

Cessation of labor also can result if the bitch is upset by strangers in attendance or by a parade of curious onlookers. It is prudent to limit the midwives to those the bitch knows and trusts.

Public display of the dam and her young can also result in the bitch becoming so upset that she resorts to cannibalism and devours her young. As revolting as this seems to our aesthetic sense, it should be taken into serious consideration as a natural reaction of the bitch to a stressful situation. Do not subject the bitch to undue stress from visitors, or unnecessary handling of the puppies either by yourself or strangers.

When the bitch appears to be through whelping she will settle down peacefully, with a most serene countenance, to care for her new brood. The puppies nurse, getting the vital colostrum, which contains antibodies for temporary immunity to disease. It is important that every puppy

Fig. 16. Puppy arrives easily.

Fig. 17. Second contraction pushes shoulders out.

Fig. 18. Puppy is fully out. Sac was broken.

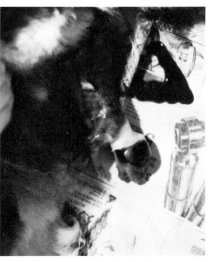
Fig. 19. The puppy starts to move and breathe.

Fig. 20. Hold the puppy with head down and rub briskly.

nurse within the first twenty-four hours after birth to receive these antibodies.

POST WHELPING PRECAUTIONS

Your bitch should be examined by a veterinarian within twelve hours after completion of whelping. Your notes will tell you if the bitch passed all the placentas. If not, the veterinarian will probably give an injection of oxytocin. This hormone will not only assist in expelling all retained material in the uterine horns, but will also encourage let-down of milk. Ergot, oral or injectable, can be an alternative to oxytocin for this purpose.

Fig. 21. The pups are now several days old. Note how much they have grown and gained weight. They find that Mom's leg is a comfortable pillow.

If you have experienced hemorrhaging with a proven brood matron following a previous litter, the veterinarian may prescribe vitamin K the last ten days of gestation or give a shot at the same time the oxytocin is given. Vitamin K is a coagulant that causes the blood to clot. Some breeders speculate that this is of benefit to newborn pups in preventing excess loss of blood when the umbilical cord is severed and they theorize that vitamin K may play a roll in the "fading puppy syndrome," as hemorrhaging of vital organs is often discovered during post mortem examinations.

Check the bitch's milk to avoid problems. Any discoloration or consistency varying from normal could indicate an infection. If the milk is discolored or very thick and stringy it can cause illness or death to the puppies.

If antibiotics are administered to the dam we always give lactobacillus acidophilus and yogurt to encourage the desirable intestinal bacteria necessary for good digestion. It is a known fact that oral antibiotics, particularly, can destroy beneficial intestinal bacteria.

As added protection when the dam is on antibiotic therapy the puppies are also given lactobacillus acidophilus. Capsules available at health food stores, are dissolved in sugar water and administered two or three times daily with an eye dropper.

Following the post partum veterinary visit, continue to keep a watchful eye on the dam. An elevated rectal temperature, 103 degrees Fahrenheit or higher, can indicate serious problems. There will be a copius vaginal discharge for the first two to three days, then it lessens and usually lasts three to four weeks. Veterinarians have now learned that it is not unusual for a light discharge to continue for four to eight weeks. If the discharge is not odorous and rectal temperature is normal and the bitch has a good appetite there is little to cause concern. It takes some bitches much longer to evacuate all the uterine residue.

Fresh water should be available at all times as the bitch needs adequate liquids for milk production. Water is equally as important as the increase in quality meals. Frequent recesses from the puppies should be allowed for elimination.

Watch carefully to be sure puppies are nursing from all breasts. If you find one breast that is hard, express the milk by hand. Hold one of the strongest pups to suckle to empty the breast. An inverted nipple may be difficult for a puppy to grasp. Again, the use of one of the most vigorous, aggressive pups can help to remedy the situation.

If one or more breasts are very hard and a color other than the normal pink and the bitch has an elevated temperature, have your veterinarian check her immediately. This could indicate mastitis. Antibiotic treatment should be started immediately. The puppies can usually continue to nurse from the unaffected breasts if the bitch is not toxic. The affected breasts can be taped over, or some breeders have been ingenious in designing "jackets" to cover the breasts.

Puppies' nails should be trimmed regularly to avoid scratching and bruising of the dam's breasts.

A large litter causes such a strain during lactation that a bitch can develop eclampsia, a lack of calcium balance. The dam becomes quite uncoordinated and can even have convulsions. Veteri-nary assistance is required immediately. Intravenous calcium solution is usually required; and, if the dam is physically able to return to nursing her litter, di-calcium-phosphate is given as a dietary supplement.

Several conscientious breeders have experienced this phenomenon with bitches that received what they felt was adequate calcium supplement during pregnancy. It could possibly be due to faulty individual utilization of calcium/phosphorous and a breeder should not harbour guilt feelings over such an episode.

References
1. Dr. Jacob Mosier, Reproduction, Neo-Natal Care, University of Pennsylvania Symposium, 1973. Virginia Dog Owners Seminar, 1978.
2. Dr. Donald F. Patterson, University of Pennsylvania Symposium, 1977.
3. Dr. Joseph S. Hansen, University of Pennsylvania Symposium, 1977.

167

Fig. 22. Ch. Wickmere Wedding Bell, winner of six working group first and a specialty winner.

Ch. Wickmere Noblesse Oblige, a sable merle.

Ch. Wickmere Chimney Sweep as a puppy.

Ch. Lisara's Morning After, Best of Opposite Sex to Best of Breed at the 1984 and 1985 Collie Club of America National Specialties, "Dutch" compiled a show records which includes nine Best In Show, All Breeds, sixteen Specialty wins and is the dam of six champions, three smooths and three roughs.

18

The Nursery

"The mother's heart is the child's schoolroom."   Beecher

Breeders have varied methods and equipment for whelping and raising litters. Your own routine will evolve by trial and error and finding what works best for you by opting a system or equipment that you see is successful for others.

Up to about five days of age, the puppies should be kept at a constant temperature of eighty-five to ninety degrees. The temperature can then be dropped gradually until it is about seventy-five degrees at the end of the fourth week. Overheating is as detrimental as lack of heat because newborn puppies do not pant. They are dependent on the temperature of their environment, so heat must be carefully controlled.

We have tried both overhead heating with an infrared lamp and the commercial kennel heating pad. The dam can lie to one side of the pad and she seems to be more comfortable with this type of heating unit rather than the suspended light. If the bitch has well developed mammary glands, the puppies will not utilize the heating pad as much as they will huddle together next to the dam's breasts. This bodily contact furnishes natural warmth.

When the bitch has finished whelping, newspapers should be replaced with turkish towels or lightweight blankets on the floor of the whelping box. When we use the commercial kennel electric pad, a towel is wrapped securely around it and white paper towels or disposable diapers are placed on top. They can be removed promptly when soiled and the towels or blankets are laundered with a disinfectant. Towels or blankets give the pups strong footing as they struggle to nurse. The hind legs brace and push back, while the front paws move in a kneading action which stimulates the milk flow. Their heads move back and forth in a pumping action. If the floor has a slick covering, such as paper, the rear legs slip and slide and the pups

Dahlis

just cannot get traction to nurse efficiently. Many experts feel that lack of proper muscular action has something to do with the etiology of hip dysplasia.

Body contact is important. A litter may seem to be intertwined (the "maggot" reaction), as they lie in a heap. If the room temperature is comfortable and they have a full tummy, you may find them draped over their mother's leg or foot.

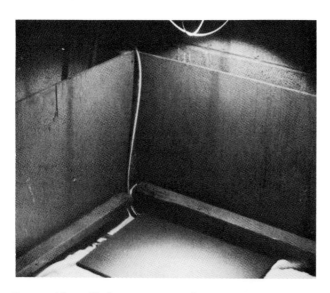

Fig. 1. After all the puppies are born, remove the soiled papers and put clean bedding in the box. A thick layer of newspapers acts as insulation. Cover them with towels, mattress padding, or blankets. Overhead heat lamps are good, but the commercial kennel pads are even better.

Fig. 2. We prefer to cover the heating pad with a towel or disposable diapers. Pups will lie contentedly on the pad unless they get too warm. The dam can lie to one side where it is cooler.

HEALTHY PUPPIES

A healthy puppy seldom cries. It spends about ninety percent of the time in activated sleep.

Twitching and involuntary leg and body movement is necessary for muscle development. For the first two days a puppy will extend his head when sleeping. If it does not do this and continues to curl its head into the chest area, there is trouble.

The mucous membranes of a newborn puppy are bright red for the first few days. The coat looks sleek and dry, and the body feels warm to the touch. A puppy's rectal temperature is approximately ninety-six degrees Fahrenheit. Its breathing rate is about 20 per minute, and the heart rate is 200 to 300 beats per minute. When stimulated, the healthy puppy shows good muscle activity. Rubbing the back will stimulate vigorous activity and some high-pitched squeals. The pup is able to suck vigorously, and if placed near the dam it has no difficulty in moving toward her, and becomes quiet.

For careful monitoring of health, puppies should be weighed at birth, at twelve and twenty-four hours, and then daily for at least the first week. Normal pups may lose up to ten percent of their birth weight in the first two days, after which they rapidly and steadily gain. Puppies should double their birth weight by nine to twelve days of age.

Table 1. Landmarks of Maturation in Normal Pups

Occurrence	Time Postpartum
Umbilical cord dries and drops off	2-3 days
Birth weight doubled	9-12 days
Eyes open	12-14 days
Ears open	15-17 days
Standing and walking	21 days
Weaning	5-8 weeks

FADING PUPPIES

The "Fading Puppy Syndrome" is a set of clinical problems, not a single cause. The syndrome represents the limited responses an ill puppy can have to a number of different disease processes. These general signs of illness include crying and restlessness even in a warm (not hot) environment, rough coat, weight loss, hypothermia (body feels cool to touch), tendency to lie on sternum, slowed breathing or heart rate, poor reflexes when stimulated, failure to move in contact with the bitch and to nurse vigorously. Common causes of death in newborn puppies include overheating, hypothermia, failure to nurse, trauma, hookworms or roundworms transmitted in utero, colibacillosis, B-hemolytic streptococcus, septicemia, brucella, herpes, infectious hepatitis, toxoplasmosis, congenital malformations, and inborn errors of metabolism.

Most newborns are on the verge of hypoglycemia (low blood sugar) since they have no body fat or glycogen store to call upon.

If you are concerned about a puppy that does not appear to be thriving, check the stools. A green stool indicates over feeding, and the green is bile. The food passes through the intestinal tract so rapidly that the normal bacteria did not get a chance to change its color. A grey stool indicates the liver is depleted, and a white stool tells you that the entire digestive tract is depleted. The worst thing you can do is feed this puppy. Give it glucose and amino acids.

If the puppy is dehydrated, 50 percent concentration of glucose is given under the skin (subcutaneously); or you can mix one teaspoonful of sugar into one ounce of water, warm to 100°F and give a dropperful every half hour. Honey and water or *Karo*® Syrup can be used. Breeders have used *Gatorade* in an emergency to combat dehydration. A commercial product, *Pedialyte*® is a ready-to-use oral electrolyte solution for replacement of body water and minerals lost in diarrhea. Since a puppy is eighty-two percent water, it is imperative that dehydration (skin loses elasticity and if you pinch the skin together, it remains pinched, see Ch. 18) be avoided.

HAND FEEDING

If the puppy has been chilled and is not nursing, separate it, warm it until its temperature is back to at least 96°F, continue the glucose, then use a supplemental feeding. DO NOT USE A FORMULA until the puppy's temperature is definitely up. The digestive system is usually "paralyzed" and the formula will just remain in the stomach.

Hand rearing or supplemental feedings may be required for various reasons. A bitch may reject her puppies, she may become ill, or supplementing may just provide a temporary boost for an ineffectual nurser. The latter will expend a lot of energy moving around with littermates and when it finally grasps a nipple, it never gets the suction with the tongue. After fussing and smacking around, it usually tires and falls off. Soon it is suffering from lack of nutrition.

A small or weak puppy will benefit from tube (gavage) feeding to introduce food immediately. (An older, vigorous puppy should be bottle fed as the sucking reflex is very important.) The gag reflex is developed at about nine days, so you do not have too much difficulty inserting the tube. Tube size #5 French is recommended for small pups, #8 French for larger pups. If you continue to tube feed, increase the tube size as the puppy grows (for instance, a #15 French for a one-pound puppy).

We have been very pleased with the disposable human infant feeding tubes. Federal law restricts these to a physician's order.

Cold sterilization (*Zephiran*®—follow instructions for dilution) is recommended for the equipment, which would consist of the tubes or catheter and the plastic syringe (20 to 50 cc).

A home formula[1] that can be mixed in an emergency has proven adequate:

    1 cup milk
    3 egg yolks (no albumin)
    1 tablespoon corn oil
    1 dropper liquid baby vitamins
    Salt (a pinch)

Mix and blend uniformly. Warm to 90-100°F (human body temperature) for puppies less than two weeks of age. The formula can be fed with a dropper, baby bottle, spoon, or by stomach tube. A Monoject 412 syringe is a helpful piece of equipment to administer formula or medication at any age.

If you are forced to hand raise a litter and feed around the clock, the formula can be heated very rapidly in a microwave oven. When the puppies graduate to a bottle, the formula can be heated right in the plastic or glass bottle.

Each puppy must receive the attention normally provided by the dam. Take the time to rub each puppy individually prior to feeding. This

---

[1]*Purina Kennel News,* Volume 74, Issue I.

massage with your hands or a soft cloth is a form of exercise and assures that the puppy is fully awake for a feeding.

Measure the tube so that it will extend into the puppy's stomach. The tube should reach from the last rib to the tip of the nose. Mark the correct distance with a piece of tape. Continue to measure and move the marker tape as the puppy grows. Attach the tube to a 20 cc syringe filled with warmed formula. After attaching the tube, expel air. Formula will drip from the tube. Insert gently into the mouth while holding the head firmly. The tube should enter easily and go right down the throat and esophagus into the stomach. If the puppy fights, withdraw the tube.

When the tube has been inserted to the marker, gently push the plunger to inject the formula into the stomach, then just as gently remove the tube. After feeding, if the dam is not available, clean the puppy by dampening a cotton ball with oil or warm water and massage the anal and urinary orifices to stimulate defecation and urination. This procedure should be continued for the first two weeks.

Bottle feeding should be used as soon as you can switch the puppies. Tubing is definitely a time saver, taking about one minute per puppy, but the puppies need the sucking action. Lacking it may result in non-nutritive body sucking.

When artificially rearing pups, it is essential that they have the same leg activity as if they were nursing (Figs. 4, 5 and 6). A towel placed on your lap or a firm surface will allow them to brace the rear legs, when being tube fed or nursing from a bottle. "Preemie" nipples are softer and more pliable than regular baby nipples. To provide adequate flow, heat a needle and puncture two additional holes. Using a formula that closely approximates the bitch's milk should allow you to feed at eight-hour intervals. Hand-reared puppies should be slightly underfed for the first couple of weeks but should have a steady weight gain.

Digestive disturbances complicate matters. We keep *Biosol-M®* on hand to administer according to package instructions at the very first sign of diarrhea. Re-evaluate the feeding schedule and amount of formula given. Close observation of the litter will indicate whether it is just one puppy or more that is having difficulty.

172

Contamination can be a cause of diarrhea. All utensils and equipment should be kept as clean as possible through boiling or the cold germicide, *Zephiran®*.

Fig. 3. Tube and syringe filled with formula for tube feeding weak puppies.

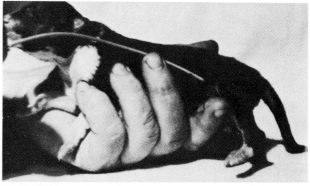

Fig. 4. Measure from the tip of the nose to the last rib and mark that position on the tube.

Fig. 5. With the pup lying in nursing position, head up, slowly insert the tube to the position previously marked.

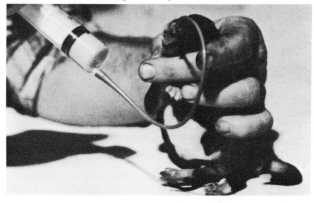

Fig. 6. Slowly inject the premeasured amount of formula.

Some breeders have made an initial supplement to bolster the pups by thawing liver or allowing it to stand and the blood which accumulates is given as a nutritional boost. We have gone a step further and at two to three days of age start a litter on raw liver.

Chop, or cut up 12 ounces of liver. Drop into a blender or processor in which you have one cup of whole milk. Blend on high for about four minutes. Strain through a fine colander or tea strainer. Pour into a covered container and refrigerate. We gave this mixture two to three times daily with an eye dropper. One teaspoon per puppy (5ML).

The amount needed for one litter feeding is warmed to room temperature. Then we added one to two acidophilus capsules and several drops of liquid Vitamin C to the warmed broth.

The stools were watched very carefully in the event the liver mixture caused diarrhea. The puppies have never had loose stools and liked the liver "soup" so much that the amount given was increased. The treat was so anticipated that the pups would automatically open their mouth when we touched their heads in preparation to feed them.

For some years we had given a liquid vitamin-iron supplement obtained from our veterinarian but learned that it upset their stomachs and they would vomit the supplement and milk. We wanted to have an iron supplement without nausea.

This liver broth was used to pour over the soaked kibble or meal as the pups were being weaned.

The litters raised with this supplement had exceptional firm body development at eight weeks of age.

Cut small chunks of raw liver. Kitchen shears are easier than using a knife. Twelve ounces of raw liver to one cup of whole milk. Blend liver and milk on high for about four minutes.

Strain through a colander when the puppies are very young so that you can administer with a syringe or medicine dropper, one teaspoon daily for newborns and increased to two to three times daily as the puppies grow older. Squeezing the bulb gently the liquid is on the back of the tongue. The puppies soon accept this as a "treat" and look forward to it.

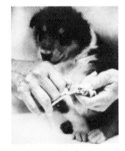

173

Daily checks should be made on the eyes. If there is any pus squeeze gently to remove it and swab with boric acid solution on a cotton ball. Check the nails and trim often to keep them short to avoid damage to the dam's breats or to the other puppies' eyes.

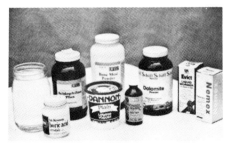

Assemble a collection of medical and nutritional aids ahead of time to have on hand when needed. Boric acid solution for cleaning eyes, calcium, yogurt, acidophilus, Nemex. Cod Liver Oil if calcium supplement does not have Vitamin D for assimilation. Cottage cheese as a protein source. Canned meat products.

A large cake pan is an excellent feeding container for a litter. Kibble, softened by soaking in warm water, with canned or powdered milk, and the addition of canned or fresh meat is a good meal.

Reusable ice substitutes and plastic water containers, which can be frozen, are placed in the puppy pens to cool the puppies when the heat is bothering them.

Just as they seek the warmth when newborn, the older puppies welcome the plastic container with the frozen water when the temperature escalates.

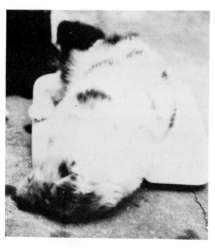

174

Sleep comes peacefully when a hot day is soothed by getting the underside draped across a cool container. Puppies will eat AND sleep better when comfortable, either with heat or cold.

CARING FOR THE NEWBORNS

When handling the puppies for feeding or just observation, check the naval for staphylococcus or streptococcus. If there is any distention of the abdomen or pus at the naval, accompanied by a bluish tinge to the skin, get veterinary attention immediately. Prompt antibiotic treatment can bring this under control.

Keep the puppies' nails cut back to the quick. If nursing on the dam, this can prevent scratches and sores from developing on the breasts and avoid injuries which puppies can inflict on littermates.

The eyes should open from the 10th to 14th day. If they should become swollen, soak a cotton ball or soft cloth in boric acid solution and squeeze the pus out. You may have to pull the lid apart but usually there is a small opening which allows removal of the pus. Ears, also sealed shut at birth, usually open a few days after the eyes, about the 15th to 17th day. Puppies crawl at birth, but usually get up on their feet to walk about eighteen to twenty-one days.

About the time the eyes are opening, pablum can be added to formula or diluted canned milk. We hand feed using a narrow demitasse spoon. Feed slowly so they do not aspirate the mixture. Ground meat, at room temperature, is rolled into a small ball and given along with the milk and pablum mixture. Cooked liver or hard-boiled eggs put through a food processor gives you the same consistency as strained baby foods and are an excellent additive easily handled by such a young puppy.

If the puppies are fussing even though they are receiving adequate milk from the dam, it could be a lack of the B-Complex vitamins in the bitch's diet. The puppies will fuss or cry for a short time only. (If the crying persists, over 15 minutes, the

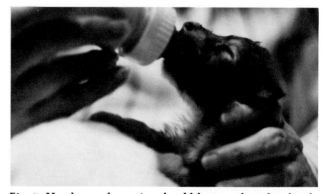

Fig. 7. Hand-reared puppies should be transferred to bottle feeding as soon as practical. Use a premature human baby nipple. Note that the puppy is held solidly with forequarters elevated, and sucking strongly.

pup undoubtedly is ill.) The addition of B-Complex to the dam's diet may quiet the puppies. If the bitch should become antagonistic towards the puppies about the second week of lactation, increase her vitamin C intake.

After three weeks, pan feeding can be started. We switch from pablum to kibble or meal soaked in warm water with meat and milk added.

During this three-week period, the puppies have been given a daily vitamin supplement, *Vi-Sorbin*™, particularly to avoid parasitic anemia in case they should have hookworms in spite of negative checks of the dam prior to breeding. If you suspect hookworm anemia, *Geritol*® can be purchased at a drugstore and administered until you can obtain a fecal check, a proper vermifuge and a vitamin-iron supplement from your veterinarian.

At about three weeks of age we have experienced a strange phenomenon and have heard from breeders across the country with similar experience. Puppies seem to be thriving. Then a strong and vigorous puppy will start to whimper and cry and refuse to eat from a pan or nurse. The whimpering progresses to a constant scream, and the puppy's abdomen becomes distended and very hard. Handling the puppy in an effort to console it or to alleviate the distress seems to make matters worse. Enemas or suppositories do not relieve the distress. When some breeders have presented puppies of this age to a veterinary clinic, the initial assumption has been that a three-week-old puppy in trouble must have hookworm anemia.

These symptoms were very similar to low blood calcium, a condition known as Tetany. I had heard of a breeder of another breed experiencing these symptoms and treating with injections of Calcium Gluconate. Usually, this medication is given intravenously or intramuscularly but can be given under the skin (subcutaneously) in emergencies. Liquid calcium is now available and has proven to be very effective in eliminating the distress which seems to be similar to the pain of muscle cramps in humans.

A veterinarian cooperated with us when these symptoms appeared in a three-week-old litter. Although there was skepticism, I asked if calcium gluconate could be administered. Following the calcium shot, the puppy quieted down and nursed. When two other puppies repeated the identical symptoms within twenty-four hours, the same procedure was followed with the same results.

These can be isolated cases due to inadequate calcium in the formula or the diet of the in-whelp bitch, or perhaps the bitch utilized much of the calcium and did not pass it on to the puppies. Whatever the cause, this situation has been experienced by many breeders. In several instances, this treatment has apparently solved the problem.

Heat has been of primary importance the first two weeks of life. At three to four weeks, puppies can become very uncomfortable from excessive heat. In hot weather, if you do not have an air conditioned area, place an electric fan over the pups and a container of ice on the floor. Coffee cans or plastic jars with screw top lips can be filled with water and frozen.

A fecal check should be done when the puppies are two or three weeks of age. The dam could have had a negative check, but the roundworm larvae could have been encysted in the bitch's muscles. Hormones activate the larvae about the fortieth day of gestation and the puppies are infected in utero. The earlier that fecal checks are made and medication is used, the healthier your puppies will be. They will seem to literally blossom!

WEANING

Between three and five weeks you will be preparing the puppies for weaning. Complete weaning age varies with breeders and circumstances. A majority of breeders complete the weaning process at four to five weeks of age.

We have experimented with early weanings, three to four weeks, weaning at five weeks, and a completely natural weaning by allowing the dam to follow nature and her own disciplinary manipulation of the matter and found that the situation was as variable with the dogs as it was with human interference.

If a litter consists of four to six puppies and the dam has a plentiful supply of milk, we like to have the puppies nurse twice daily through the fifth week of age. Not only does it satisfy the need for sucking, but I have felt it has an excellent psychological effect as the puppies are still interacting with siblings and their dam, plus it is the very best "weaning supplement" available.

Optimum nutrition and socializing develops a healthy extrovert. A radio near the whelping box and/or puppy pen accustoms the puppies to various noises. Also power lawn mowers and vacuum cleaners are excellent for conditioning puppies to noise. Do not isolate the puppies or become overly protective in regard to exposure to noise, strangers or a different environment.

Eyes are checked at five to eight weeks by a qualified canine ophthalmologist and the vaccination schedule is implemented (refer to accompanying schedule) so that the pets will be ready for a new home. You may wish to retain several pups until an older age for final consideration.

COCCIDIOSIS

As a young puppy leaves for a new home, another problem may be faced—coccidiosis. Coccidiosis is a problem of stress. As long as a pup is settled in a certain environment, adjusted to a particular regimen and diet, it gets along fine; but as soon as it enters a new home, particularly if a stress factor such as shipping is introduced, then coccidiosis appears as a bloody stool and a foul, odorous diarrhea. Coccidiosis is a protozoan infection of the intestinal tract.

Fig. 9. Healthy puppies will nurse strongly and often. Their bodies fill out and the coats look smooth and shiny.

Fig. 10. Note how these puppies are pushing with their rear legs as they nurse. Tails are extended for balance. These puppies appear vigorous and healthy.

176

CANINE VACCINATION SCHEDULE
(Reprinted from *Cornell Research Laboratory Report*, Series 2, No. 5)

Disease	Vaccine	Type of Vaccine	Age to Vaccinate
Canine Distemper	Measles Virus (MV)	Modified live virus	1st vaccination at 6-8 weeks of age. Do not use MV in breeding bitches.
Canine Distemper Canine Cough Canine Leptospirosis	Canine Adenovirus 1 (CAV-1, Infectious Canine Hepatitis Virus, ICH) or Canine Adenovirus 2(CAV-2) Canine Parainfluenza Virus	Modified live virus Modified live virus	1st vaccination at 6-8 weeks of age. Do not us MV in breeding bitches. Usually combined with CDV and CAV-1 or CAV-2.
Rabies	Rabies Virus	Modified live virus	1st vaccination at 12-16 weeks of age, revaccinate at 1 year and at least every 3 years, depending on product used.
Parvovirus	Canine Parvovirus (CPV)	Killed or modified live	Current information suggests vaccinating at 3 to 4, 8, 12, and 16 weeks with killed vaccine, then boosters every 6 months, or annually with modified live vaccine.
Canine Cough	Bordetella bronchiseptica	a) Modified live bacteria b) Inactivated bacteria	Intranasal inoculation of dogs 2 weeks of age or older, repeat every 6 months. Subcutaneous inoculation as recommended by manufacturer.
Canine Herpesvirus		None available	
Canine Brucellosis		None available	

Individual puppies can be treated very effectively. Strict sanitation is to be observed in a kennel situation. Some bitches can be carriers of coccidia and have negative stool specimens until the nursing litter is about four weeks old, at which time the dam's stools can be loaded with coccidiosis oocysts and the puppies are consequently infected. If you have had any resident coccidiosis infection, establish a strict sanitation program and pretreat a puppy for five days prior to sale or shipping. Coccidiosis, like fleas, can happen in the very cleanest environments as isolated instances, but continued occurrence indicates a review of kennel management is needed.

GIARDIASIS

This illness is caused by a protozoan and usually occurs in young dogs. Principal sign is diarrhea in which mucous and blood is visible. As in coccidiosis a puppy can become dehydrated, weak and debilitated. Diagnosis is made by finding the protozoan in the stool. If impossible to get a stool sample rectal swabs are a satisfactory method of obtaining a smear. Sanitation is a must as this is often endemic in kennels. There has been evidence that Giardia cysts from one species can infect other species. The infection responds well to Flagyl.

CANINE PARVOVIRUS

In 1978, two previously unknown diseases struck the dog population. The first was a highly contagious enteritis characterized by severe vomiting and diarrhea, the second was the sudden and unexpected death of seemingly healthy puppies. These two very different syndromes (enteritis and puppy death) are now recognized as two forms of a single disease, canine parvovirus, a new pathogen for dogs.

Dogs with parvoviral enteritis usually stop eating and act depressed twelve to twenty-four hours before they show other signs of disease. Prominent clinical signs are vomiting, often severe and protracted, anorexia, diarrhea, and rapid dehydration, especially in puppies. The feces are generally a light grayish or yellow-gray color at the onset of disease; however, fluid stools either streaked with blood, or frankly hemorrhagic may be present as the initial sign and persist until recovery or death. Most dogs have a fever; temperatures may exceed 105 degrees in puppies. Blood counts often reveal a leukopenia (low number of white blood cells). Animals with severe parvoviral enteritis require intensive fluid and electrolyte replacement therapy, antibiotics, antiemetcis, antidiarrheals, and skilled nursing.

The other manifestation of parvoviral infection is inflammation of the heart (myocarditis). Myocarditis occurs without concurrent diarrhea. The virus multiplies rapidly in muscle cells of the growing heart. The heart weakens and fails. There is no effective treatment. Puppies that survive may have permanently damaged hearts. Such animals may die from heart failure weeks or months after they have recovered from infection.

Feces are the most important source of virus. There may be over a billion infectious virions in a diarrhetic stool. A susceptible dog can become infected by ingesting less than one-thousandth of a gram of infected fecal material. The virus survives for several days after being passed in the stool. Hence, canine parvovirus is readily transported on the hair and feet of infected dogs and by contaminated cages, shoes, and other objects. Even animals that have mild disease can shed millions of infectious virion. The duration of viral shed is brief; virus has not been recovered from dogs for longer than two weeks after clinical illness. Dogs that recover are immune to reinfection. The best known disinfectant available is *Clorox®* in thirty parts of water.

Vaccination of bitches before breeding is suggested as the antibody to canine parvovirus is transferred from an immune bitch to her pups. However, the same antibody that protects pups also interferes with successful immunization. The higher the dam's antibody level, the older the pups must be before vaccination will be successful.

Pups that receive little or no maternal antibody can be successfully immunized at six weeks of age. Pups born to mothers that have recovered from infection do not respond to vaccination until they are fourteen to sixteen weeks old.

177

Cornell Research Laboratory for Diseases of Dogs, Laboratory Report, Series 3, Number 1, March, 1979.

178

Fig. 11. Ch. Bandor's Twila's Twilight. Head study at nine years. Best Opposite Sex to Best of Breed Collie Club of America 1974 and 1977.

19

The New Generation

"Nature gives to every time and season some beauties of its own . . ."   Charles Dickens

In order to select a quality puppy, one must have studied the Collie standard and developed an impression of an ideal Collie. Know your line. Pick the parents in relation to what you have learned from the Standard. Find out as much as possible about how they developed and watch for this in your puppies. Parents from a pedigree of quality ancestry will increase the probability of better quality offspring. Many excellent specimens are not champions or even exhibited. This can be due to lack of interest by either the dog or owner or perhaps an injury that prevents exhibition.

At birth, the puppies may appear to be very similar. Look for a blocky head with the muzzle and skull almost equal in fullness (Fig. 1). Some puppies have a very blunt finish which may round off very slightly in a few days.

Run your fingers in an up-and-down movement and from ear to ear (arrows, Fig. 2). It should be very smooth. If there is a definite protuberance of bone (I call it the "bent coat-hanger curve") it is likely this head will broaden or coarsen.

Look for a fairly flat profile. As you run your finger from the nose button to skull, you may feel two very slight "stair steps." The smoother the plane from nose to skull, the better the chances that the mature parallel planes will exist. Many plump newborns will have a "drop off" on the nose. This corrects itself within a few days and should not cause alarm, as it is cartilage and not associated in any way with the faulty Roman head, which is curvature of bone and which does not appear until months later.

Big puppies may have had a difficult trip into the world, and they look like they are frowning on the entire episode. The foreface is wrinkled into several folds like a stewed prune. If the cheek area is smooth, we wait four or five days to check them again.

Dahlis

Although many breeders attest to picking at birth, we like to scrutinize the litter closely at four to five days and make **cursory** assessment, only, at birth.

The underjaw should be strong and run roughly parallel to the foreface. Ears are pressed back against the head, and like the eyes, are sealed shut. Eyes and ears will be later considerations. We have not found that ear size is safely predictable until the puppies are approaching five to six weeks of age.

Chunky, husky puppies are your best bet for good substance. A blocky body with spring of rib and firm chest are desirable. The legs are firm with a good "roundness" right up to the elbows. Rear pasterns are also firm, and as the puppies nurse, you can see how they dig in for leverage and foothold.

You can see these virtues as the puppies lie in the whelping box, but use the "braille system" and feel the contours of the body with your fingers. From the back of the skull, you can feel the length of neck (also watch puppies as they nurse for neck length), the angulation of shoulder, and along the back to the tail, which is like a strong whip attached solidly to a slightly rounded croup. There is very slight tuck-up in loin at this time.

Barbara Schwartz, of Impromptu Collies, has done an enormous amount of personal observation, testing, study and working with Rachael Page Elliott and has concluded that there are some interesting evaluations of the muscles in infant puppies which can be an indication of mature development affecting movement.

Barbara's well-founded attention to this aspect of Collie structure reveals that the balance of muscle, length of bone and degree of angle is visible at birth. These are genetically determined traits. Environment and nutrition enhance or deter the development of these traits—but correct exercise and nutrition cannot build balanced muscling, bone and angulation if the genetic propensity for such is not present at birth.

In the rear, the muscles on both the interior and exterior sides of Femur should be of equal density, size and mass. These muscles can be felt at birth in a Collie. It is important to note that these muscles, obvious within the first few days of life, will feel and look similar to the muscling found on new-born Whippets, Borzoi, and Greyhounds. Since these breeds have very little diagnosed hip dysplasia, it is relevant that Collies, too, have had little problem with dysplasia in the past. When this rear muscling pattern is compared to that of puppies from such breeds as German Shepherds, Golden Retrievers and Bloodhounds, where there is little muscling at birth, and where dysplasia is a major breed problem, the quality, quantity and placement of rear muscling in the Collie is significant.

Barbara adds that the lack of breeder concentration on this development lately has produced many Collies that are either unevenly muscled behind or lack the proper muscle density. The muscles on little Collie puppies should stand out visibly when they are nursing and should be of equal size on both the inside and outside of the Femur bone.

If the animal has larger muscles on the inside of the Femur, it will move cow-hocked or close behind. It will appear to be narrow in the rear. If the animal has more muscling on the outside of the bone, it will stand spread behind, toes perfectly straight or slightly "toed-in." Its legs will be placed as wide or wider than its hips. It will have a stance like an "A," similar to that of a Boxer or Doberman Pinscher—both leaping and attacking dogs, not herding animals. Many new Collie breeders and judges think that this is a correct stance and praise it. Such a dog cannot single-track adequately. It will be "spread-hocked" in some degree and will move parallel, limiting its ability to "change its direction of travel almost instantaneously," as called for in our Standard.

Muscling is important in the front assembly. The muscles over the withers as well as the spring and length of rib will determine the width and angle of the shoulder. The dog has no collar bone, so the angle of the shoulder is determined by the muscling and spring of rib.

Undoubtedly many of us, previously, had not been aware of the impact the muscles had on total structure and movement. It is a relevant fact that Dot Gerth, authority on color inheritance and known for her astute work with Collie skulls, was speculating about the genetic factor of muscles and the effect on the Collie head, particulary the back skull.

At two weeks, the puppies have grown a great deal. The head has lengthened, eyes and ears are opening, and the ears are beginning to come away from the head, falling forward (Fig. 3). Do not evaluate the eyes as they are opening. The membrane has not yet receded and may give the appearance of a large white haw. Wait for another week, at least, after the eyes are fully open to pronounce judgment. Eyes are a deep blue initially and not the adult dark brown eye.

The more prominent "puppy stop" is lessening now as the backskull and foreface start to come into their proper relationship.

At five weeks, the ears fall down to the side like a hound's ear (dotted line, Fig. 3). Within a short time, you can see the muscles working and pulling the ear base up on the skull; and about three quarters of the ear starts to swing around towards the skull. From this age and stage on, the ears are like semaphore flags and can change placement and carriage rapidly.

Some breeders start to work with the ears at this time. This is personal preference. The larger, floppy ear is most desirable because it is easier to work with.

The end of the muzzle seems to narrow and give the "coffin" appearance to the head (Fig. 4). This is true even on pups with good muzzle. The backskull is slightly rounded. At this time, you can feel the occipital bone. The foreface should be smooth and run back into flat cheeks. A nice rounded curve downward from eyes to lips will indicate good curvature of muzzle and good eye set. You do not want a fall-off under the eyes.

Since the puppies are now well up on their feet, you can evaluate the rear quarters, the hocks and rear pasterns, plus turn of stifle for the same adult qualities.

A home "test" breeders can give to see if their dogs have excellent rear angulation can be accom-

plished by moving the hock joint "A" up to the ischium (B). If "A" touches "B" with ease you can be assured the dog has proper angulation and the length of tibia/fibula is equal and in balance to the femur. This is particularly an appropriate test for an adult dog.

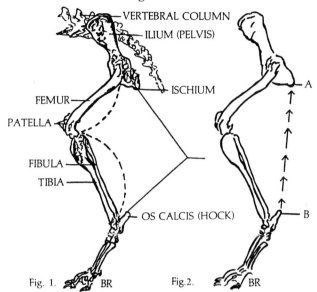

Fig. 1.   BR   Fig. 2.   BR

Through all of these physical observations, each puppy shows its own personality traits. Watch for that clown that shows an excellent disposition. A happy, bold, inquisitive youngster is a delight. Through supplemental pan feeding and weaning, there will be those who establish dominance and aggressiveness. This is a good sign and should be encouraged.

Guard hairs begin to show at five to six weeks and indicate a more profuse coat. The longer hairs are visible along the back, across the shoulder, and are especially plain to see if the puppy is endowed with a white collar. Ruffle the coat up from pastern to elbow and it is usually thicker with a slight swirl.

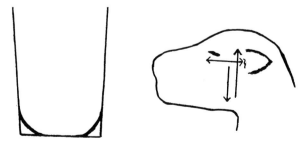

Fig. 1. At birth, muzzle and skull should be almost equal in width.
Fig. 2. Cheeks should feel smooth when you run your fingers over them (see arrows).

Fig. 3. At five weeks, the ears drop down (dotted line).

Fig. 4. Five-week-old pup's head has lengthened and narrowed.

Between eight and twelve weeks, the adult Collie head in miniature is seen. The head has flattened considerably, the backskull has lost the puppy roundness, and the ears are now on top of the head. Ears tip forward more than is desirable in an adult. Expression becomes more visible as the puppy fuzz retreats. The hair can still be misleading, so wet the coat down on the head, stand back and look, THEN go over the puppy with your hand.

An eye that looks too round and protruding, like a small button, can seem to flow and blend into the more desired shape as the head lengthens in a series of spurts.

Three months is a significant age. Choose your pup, or narrow your choice to two or three, and let them alone for awhile. Do not scrutinize them daily as they can go through "teething" lumps and bumps. Some muzzles can become pinched only to fill in later.

At about four months, the head can rise at the eyebrows and the backskull recedes. It depends on the *degree* of rise and fall whether you want to weather this storm of doubt. Many puppies straighten out by a year of age. If the stop remains clean and the eye shape is pleasing, these skulls usually flatten at least to the point where it is highly acceptable. If the puppy holds its skull through the fourth to sixth and eighth month stage but goes off at nine or ten months, it is best to discard this one as soon as an appropriate home is found.

A few years ago, when the bloodlines were closely bred and supervised, predictability was more definitely assured. Some of the dogs were slower in maturing and did not make a ring appearance until they were two-and-a-half or three years of age. Not many exhibitors expected their Collies to be a finished product, according to the Standard, at ten to twelve months and had the patience to wait for the propitious time of development to show their dog.

THE TOOTH FAIRY

One of the most perplexing and formidable problems is that of bite. It is difficult to become a prophet in this department!

The dog has twenty-eight deciduous (puppy) teeth and forty-two permanent teeth, twenty teeth in the upper jaw and twenty-two in the lower jaw.

The natural occlusal pattern for Collies is referred to as a "scissors" bite. The maxillary or upper incisors overlap the mandibular or lower incisors.

The deciduous teeth gradually loosen and are replaced by the permanent teeth during approximately the puppy's third through eighth month. If an adult tooth comes in before the deciduous tooth has loosened, the permanent tooth may grow at the wrong angle. In such cases your veterinarian may need to remove the deciduous tooth.

Following is an approximate schedule for the permanent teeth to replace the deciduous teeth:

Teeth	Eruption
Incisor	2-5 months
Canine	5-6 months
Premolar	5-6 months
Premolar	6 months
Premolar	6 months
Premolar	4-5 months
Molar	5-6 months
Molar	6-7 months
Molar	6-7 months

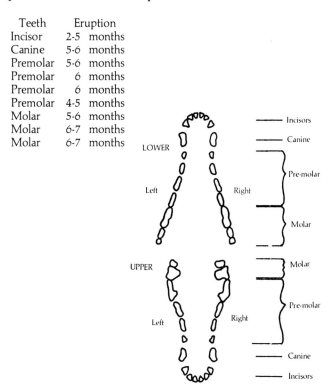

Fig. 6. **Permanent teeth of the dog.**

Bites can shift around as the puppy matures and many breeders have apprehensively watched an excellent specimen go through various stages of faulty bites. Some malocclusion can occur during puppyhood to become a correct bite at one year to eighteen months of age, while some bites can become worse, either under or overshot, and the dog can be severely penalized in the show ring.

182

The accompanying illustration (Fig. 6) will help you in watching your puppies progress through the teething period and to check for full dentition.

There have been reports of missing teeth, but I do not feel that the incidence has been enough to cause alarm to breeders. It is wise, however, to be alert. The Doberman Pinscher standard is very explicit, requiring forty-two teeth correctly placed. Four or more missing teeth is a disqualification.

The similarity of the Collie and Doberman Pinscher is that both breeds evolved from shorter-headed dogs and, in elongating the head, we can have weak (slack) jaws and incomplete or faulty dentition.

A slightly overshot mouth (upper teeth protrude beyond lower) can eventually become a scissors bite and may not close adequately until eighteen months of age. An even bite at five or six months can develop into an undershot (lower teeth protrude beyond upper) mouth. If the stop fills in at that age, then you know the bite will only become worse. I have witnessed bites that were even at less than twelve months to settle in and not go undershot but remain level.

The bites of littermates can vary. I have not been able to discover a hereditary pattern that would offer worldly wisdom on how to select or breed a high percentage of scissor bites.

Fig. 7. Twelve-week old male. Dark rims make eye appear to be larger than actual size. "Teething bumps" are clearly visible under the eyes. This puppy has just entered the first of a few stages that require patience as the smooth muzzle is temporarily lost during teething. Eye shape can change as the head lengthens.

Gait can be assessed as early as eight or nine weeks, and by ten weeks you can be very critical

Fig. 8. The same puppy a month or two later. As the head lengthens, the backskull and stop go through unattractive stages. Now the teething bumps are smoothing, but the skull recedes ("falls off") in front of the ears and the area behind the eye rises.

183

Fig. 9. This view more clearly shows the section of skull that rises and the lateral indentations behind the eyes. Eye shape has become more eliptical. Depending upon the family line, the skull usually flattens to become the desired two parallel planes. In some pups the condition will correct in a few months, and in others it does not flatten until the dog is two to three years of age. If the skull starts to recede close to one year it is unlikely that it will correct. Edwin L. Pickhardt (Sterling Collies) felt that dogs which went through the least changes were the better producers.

of body faults which can affect gait or be offensive to the eye, such as a poor top line, slabside, cowhocks and narrow fronts. The movement may be a little loose and soft, but the rear in particular can be evaluated.

Choose your puppy by all-over balance, not piece by piece. It is always simple to see the faults. Look for the outstanding virtues. Stephen Field wrote, "To know the faults is comparatively easy. Almost any novice can soon pick the faults and glibly discuss them. The parallel task of knowing and evaluating points of merit is usually more difficult."

What I have given you is merely a guideline and is a generalization. Different bloodlines develop in different ways and have various char-

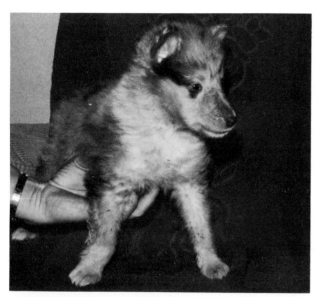

Fig. 10. Blue female. Smallest pup in a large litter, development was delayed. Adequate bone for size. Prick ears common in a tiny pup. Eye shape good, nice round muzzle. Age five weeks.

184

Fig. 12. Eleven weeks. Excellent age for her. She has caught up with her littermates. Square, solid body, bone, ears over, very small eye.

Fig. 11. Seven weeks. Round, full muzzle, pretty eye, bone coming along nicely and ears starting to break. Many novice breeders overlook a puppy like this because of the early appearance.

Fig. 13. Five months. Well-balanced, lovely puppy with nice arch of neck. Caught up to littermates in size and substance.

acteristics and patterns of development. No one can guarantee the evolution of a fuzzy puppy into a top calibre champion.

Call it spunk, grit, nerve or a stout heart—it takes all of that and something extra to look at a litter and admit that it does not contain anything of merit. Some of the best planned breedings of quality parents do not produce the hoped for progeny with superior virtues.

Fig. 14. Blue merle male littermate, five weeks. Decidedly male.

Fig. 15. Eleven weeks. Well-balanced body, style, ears coming up, eye shape still good.

Fig. 16. Six months. Very puppyish but still masculine with a long head, round muzzle, and good bone. Top line is off at this stage, common in the growth pattern of his line.

185

Fig. 17. Seven months. Nice length of head, pretty eye, ears wide set.

Fig. 18. Seven weeks. A winsome look, ears not as tight as they could be. Head is coffin shaped and still masculine.

Fig. 19. Nineteen months. Matured with a long, lean head, full muzzle, plenty of bone and coat. Ears still wide. This dog won minor points.

Fig. 20. Ch. Rosslane Amelia at eight weeks. A sturdy puppy showing a firm rear with excellent turn of stifle, good slope of croup, and proper tail set.

Fig. 21. Amelia at four months. Nice depth of chest, well-fitting coat. Some puppies do not carry a full puppy coat while others can compete with adults because they have a lovely "puppy bloom."

Fig. 22. At two years, Amelia is a nicely balanced bitch.

Fig. 23. Rosslane Vignette at eight weeks. Note the full, rounded muzzle.

Fig. 24. Note how the head has lengthened in just one week. Vignette at nine weeks.

Fig. 25. Rosslane Spring Song at five weeks.

Fig. 26. Spring Song at four months. Muzzle less full than littermate.

Fig. 27. Spring Song at eleven months. Note the head changes as the skull lengthens.

20

Don't Hide Your Light Under A Bushel

"Every one stamps his own value on himself."   Schiller

Now that you have bred and raised a marvelous litter of Collie puppies, you will have to think about selling them. This does not always come easily, and may take some creative thought and energy.

After you have been breeding or showing Collies for a few years, you will want to think about your image as a breeder. Strive for something unique and easily identified and build on repetition in keeping your kennel before the public.

RCA's famous dog and phonograph symbol came out of semi-retirement in 1978 to star in an $8 million a year advertising campaign. The logo had been inspired by a painting called "His Master's Voice" showing a white terrier-type dog with black, floppy ears, and head cocked to one side as he listened to the phonograph. This commercial symbol had been in use since 1901, but a revamping in 1968 placed Nipper and "His Master's Voice" in a state of limbo for almost ten years. Now Nipper and the horn are making a comeback and will be seen on RCA products, trucks, stationery, shipping cartons, newspaper ads and TV commercials. This logo has eye appeal.

Another product used an eyecatcher with a clever phrase. *Bon Ami,*™ a household cleanser, pictures a newly hatched chick accompanied by the declaration "it hasn't scratched yet."

Turn the pages of a magazine and notice the impact that various advertisements have on you. Which ones do you remember? Of the many dollars spent on advertising campaigns, it appears that cosmetics, liquors and cigarettes particularly use color, simplicity and a well-turned phrase to sell a product.

In advertising our dogs, the use of color is limited. There just are not many dog publications that use it, and the cost is prohibitive to many fanciers. You can, however, use the example of simplicity and an excellent photograph accompanied by a motto or slogan.

Dahlis

189

Avoid trite, hackneyed bromides. Such platitudes as "Quality Begets Quality" and "We are a small kennel, Quality Not Quantity" have become a familiar tune. You want to penetrate the minds of those you wish to impress without antagonizing.

It pays to call attention to personal attributes and thereby enhance one's public image. If you have a consistent winner, the fancy is well aware of it; so, conserve space on statistics. If you do use statistics, be sure they are correct. Some boastful claims have been exploded by doubting readers who have checked facts and circumstances.

An exhibitor may be thrilled to have a win over a particular Best In Show special or a dog that has set an enviable record, but to use that one win as an announcement is in poor taste. With the vagaries of judging and showing consid-ered, the gloating advertiser/exhibitor may find himself at the bottom of the heap at the next show.

Advertising can be witty and entertaining, but humor can fall flat. In national coverage the humor may be completely missed or misinterpreted because it is an "inside" or "local" joke.

Selling the pet stock is vitally important as it will help defray the expenses of a hobby. Usually, the best source is the newspaper classified section. Separate yourself from the mundane advertisements such as: "Collie pups. AKC. Shots and Wormed."

Since this seems to be the message of most ads, pick out something unique and different using as few words as possible. Get your point across that yours are well bred and expensive considering some of the competition.

190

Fig. 1. Puppy, seven weeks. Huge bone, large pup. Head is lengthening, ears dropped, eye becoming more almond shaped. Stop full. Littermate to blue male in previous chapter.

Fig. 2. The same male at sixteen months. Head finished with good eye. Smooth, round muzzle, stop full, ears acceptable. Still needs maturity of body and more coat.

Collective efforts are beneficial. Club secretaries can send a list of members to area veterinarians; or, if your club has a newsletter or bulletin, include veterinarians on a complimentary basis.

Pet shops which specialize in fish, birds, and supplies usually appreciate referrals for purebred puppies.

A yellow page listing is an excellent source for a good clientele, but there are disadvantages. When the telephone is installed, it is considered a "business" listing, which many hobby breeders would prefer to avoid; and it is expensive. The cost can be prohibitive for just a single subscriber. This type listing is more conducive to a metropolitan area where there is a larger population from which to draw. If you have the time and patience, these yellow page listings seem to fulfill a service and are a way to provide information if you are a knowledgeable person with skill and diplomacy.

When you decide upon a logo or prefix that your dogs will carry, have stationery, notepaper and business cards printed.

If a sale is made as a result of a referral, a written thank you on your stationery or notepaper will foster good will and is one of the best types of advertising for you and your Collies.

Fig. 3. Playing and socialization are as important for the mental health of a puppy as for its muscle development. **191**

Ch. Tell Star's Cosmic Capers, Best of Breed, 1983, Collie Club of America.

192

Ch. Lee Aire's Flambeau Monobo, Best of Breed, 1975, Collie Club of America.

21

Hereditary Defects in the Collie

"Nature has perfections, in order to show that she is the image of God; and defects, to show that she is only his image."
Pascal

Our breedings are gambles. We can't be assured that everything we desire is going to appear in one litter or one dog. Many fanciers are lost when less than desirable aspects must be faced—defects.

If Collies were placed on a scale of one to ten, we might find we would be willing to cope with the genetic defects existing in the Collies when compared to the blemishes that appear in other breeds. Some of these impairments can be treated with medication, enabling a Collie to be sustained and lead a "normal" life. Other genetic faults, however, are so debilitating that euthanasia is the wisest course to follow. Yet another disorder, such as the semi-lethal gray puppy, carries an unwarranted stigma.

It is not a disgrace when any breeder experiences a problem or a genetic fault. How the problem is faced when it appears is important. Is it placed in a proper perspective? How are priorities arranged? To place perspectives and priorities, it is imperative that we more thoroughly understand the dark side of the moon.

Some problems are simply inherited tendencies that are more prevalent in one breed line than in another. A susceptibility to bloat is definitely found in families. However, families of dogs are often fed in the same manner which may increase the susceptibility. All large dogs are prone to bloat, and in recent years we have heard enough cases in Collies to indicate that it is more common than previously expected. Older dogs are particularly prone.

Feeding twice a day, not immediately before or after violent exercise, and withholding water for an hour after feeding will help prevent bloat. Expanded foods swell more than biscuit or meal and are less desirable for this reason. Spoiled or moldy food should never be used.

Dahlis

Some Collies have a "nervous stomach" and tend to burp up their food after eating. They should be fed several small meals.

Fortunately, the Collie is not prone to diarrhea as are some breeds, and when observed it is usually due to worms or bacterial or viral infection.

The breed does seem to be more prone than some other breeds to reproductive problems. When choosing a brood bitch make sure she is from a line of proven producers with no history of reproductive failure. If you do not intend to breed your Collie bitch, it may be wise to spay her to avoid uterine infections.

The following section on actual genetic defects was prepared by Linda Sparks, a Collie breeder and exhibitor who has done considerable research in this area.

There are a vast array of known or suspected genetic abnormalities in the canine world. Some of these hereditary problems affect all or nearly all breeds and crossbreeds alike, while others are confined to specific breeds. The concerned Collie breeder needs to be aware of the genetic anomalies most likely to appear in our breed as well as the mode of inheritance, when known. The following disorders have been ordered from the most generalized (appearing most often in numerous breeds) to the more specific (appearing only or primarily in Collies).

PATENT DUCTUS ARTERIOSUS (PDA)

194

PDA is the most frequently recognized congenital (present at birth) heart defect in the dog. In order to understand PDA one must first realize the fundamental difference between the circulatory system of the unborn fetus and that of the newborn animal. Because it is impossible for the fetus to breathe "in utero" it receives fully oxygenated blood from the dam through the umbilical cord. There is, therefore, no need for fetal blood to pass through the unborn's lungs. Instead, blood flows straight from the right atrium and ventricle into the left atrium and ventricle through temporary valves (holes) and through a small temporary vessel, the ductus arteriosus, located between the pulmonary artery and the aorta. At birth or shortly thereafter these three temporary passages must close in order that the blood can be oxygenated by being pumped through the newborn's lungs.

When the openings in the ductus arteriosus remain open (patent) the full volume of blood never reaches the lungs. Without fully oxygenated blood the pup may experience poor brain development and will surely experience varying heart problems, although he may live for a long time without showing symptoms. The condition can be corrected surgically, preferrably before six months of age.[1*]

The mode of inheritance of patent ductus arteriosus is polygenic[2,3] and an affected pup indicates that the trait is inherent in the family of that animal. Of interest is the fact that approximately eighty percent of the affected animals are female.

CANINE HIP DYSPLASIA (CHD)

Listed in one reference[3] as the most common genetic defect in dogs, hip dysplasia has received a vast amount of study. While CHD has been termed a polygenic trait with environmental modifiers, researchers have been unable to determine exactly which genes or what environmental factors are the causative agents,[5] nor have they been able to recommend a breeding program which will eliminate the anomaly.

Hip dysplasia is manifested in varying quantitative degrees as befits a polygenic trait. It is graded from I to IV with grade IV being the worst expression. These expressions include increased synovial fluid and enlarged ligaments, a

*Refer to references at end of chapter.

shallow or flattened acetabulum ("ball socket"), remodeling of the femoral head ("ball") and neck, and accompanying joint laxity.[4] While these changes may be determined as early as 3-6 months in some animals by means of x-ray, there are large numbers of dogs who are dysplastic but show no outward signs, even to the trained eye of a veterinarian. Conversely, many dogs who "move funny" are not dysplastic. The best method of diagnosis is hip x-ray under general anesthetic, which cannot be certified until the dog is at least two years of age.

Studies have shown that, although breeders will have a hard time eliminating Canine Hip Dysplasia from some breeds where it is wide spread, the incidence and severity of the disease can be controlled. While limiting one's breeding animals to only those who x-ray normal does not prevent the occurrence of CHD affected animals, it does lower the number affected and the severity of expression. Breeding one normal animal to an affected one does not greatly increase the risk—indeed as a whole these offspring resemble their normal parent more than their dysplastic one. Finally, the breeding of two borderline or Grade I animals has been shown to produce very little more severe hip dysplasia in the progeny than was produced by parents with normal hips.[6] These results should lead breeders to the same

conclusions reached by the researchers: that hip x-rays alone are inadequate as a breeding selection mechanism. The concerned breeder must include progeny testing to determine which specific sires and dams transmit the least affection, both in numbers of offspring affected and in severity of affection.[6]** This is true for all polygenic traits.

_____

**These studies were done on German Shepherds and Golden Retrievers where CHD is extremely common. With the lower incidence in Collies (probably due to the Collie's slower growth rate), we should attempt to use those animals with normal hips and a low or non-existent occurrence rate in the progeny.

(Ed. Note.—Patellar luxation, or wobbling of the knee joint, is probably as common a cause of faulty gait in the Collie as is hip dysplasia.)

EPILEPSY AND EPILEPTIFORM SEIZURES

The term epilepsy refers to all intracranial (inside the skull) disorders which are characterized by recurrent seizures. The term is applied to both the acquired and inherited forms. Sources differ as to the exact mode of inheritance in specific breeds[7,9,10] and it appears that in one group of breeds epilepsy is recessive while in several

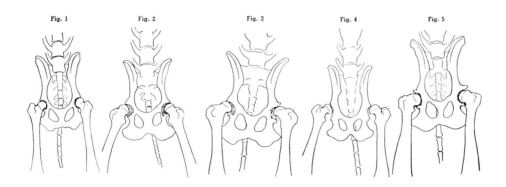

Fig. 1. Drawing of a radiograph of a dog's pelvis. Left: normal, well-formed acetabulum and femoral head.
Second from left: Grade 1 dysplasia in one hip and grade 2 in the other. Both sockets are shallow but one is worse than the other.
Center: Sockets shallow and ill-formed. The destructive elements of wear are beginning to show.
Second from right: Grade 4 dysplasia. Sockets have no cupping and the epiphyses of the femoral heads are poorly formed.
Right: Grade 1 or 2 dysplasia. The roughness of the joint surfaces and the "spurs" illustrate the reason for the crippling lameness of osteoarthritis.

(from Popular Dogs, 1962)

others it is polygenic.[7,10] (No English language documentation of a specific study pin-pointing inheritance in Collies could be found by this writer.)

An owner who witnesses a generalized seizure usually recognizes it for what it is. The animal suffers loss of consciousness for a few seconds to two to three minutes. There may be excessive salivation, urination or defecation; this is usually followed by several minutes of running or walking movements. When consciousness returns, the dog may appear normal or he may be frightened, fatigued or dazed.[7]

Inherited epilepsy does present some guideposts for identification by its age of onset. It is very rare to find a pup younger than six months who exhibits seizures due to hereditary causes. Most hereditary seizures first appear between 10 to 20 months of age and while they may occur later than this the first episode is almost always prior to three years of age.[7]

Acquired epilepsy, however, can have an extensive variety of causes and may occur at any time in the dog's life. Since the brain must have a prescribed amount of sugar and oxygen in its blood supply to function normally, any disease or event which appreciably decreases these supplies may bring about seizures. Among these are included: a difficult birth with accompanying oxygen starvation to the brain, severe liver disease, cardiac or pulmonary diseases and hypoglycemia. Hypoglycemia is a common cause, particularly in pups, and is often evidenced by seizures shortly before mealtime when blood sugar is at its lowest ebb. In older dogs sudden onset may be evidence of a brain tumor. Toxic agents ingested or inhaled by

196

Fig. 2. Ch. Rosslane Bronwyn at nine months. Note feminine appearance, nice coat, good topline, firm, straight front legs. *Rulin photo.*

the dog are also frequent causes of a seizure—unless the dog remains in constant proximity to the agent, exposure would probably result in a single episode or grouping of seizures. Toxic agents include: lead, carbon monoxide (auto exhaust), organophosphates (found in flea powders, dips and collars), chlorinated hydrocarbons and other pesticides, as well as rat and mouse poisons containing strychnine or cyanide. Additional causes may be any type of brain injury or skull trauma such as being dropped as a puppy, or being in an auto accident. Furthermore, seizures may appear anytime from a few weeks to two years following the initiating injury.[7]

Because of the wide range of causes it is most important for the owner or breeder whose dog suffers a seizure to have kept a medical history of their animal from babyhood. The veterinary exam, lab tests and possible neurologic workup might be spared, at least in part, for the owner who has his dog's medical history written down. This is especially true for breeding animals since hereditary epilepsy is usually suspected when no discernable cause can be found in testing of history.[7]

UMBILICAL HERNIAS

Umbilical hernias are common and of hereditary origins in many breeds, of which Collies are one. The exact mode of transmission is not agreed upon but may be either recessive or polygenic.[10] Umbilical hernias are due to failure of the umbilical ring to close properly after birth. If the hernia is large and allows the protrusion of the peritonium and intestines it should be repaired, otherwise a small hernia will fill with fat and cause the animal no trouble.

CANINE CUTANEOUS (SKIN) IMMUNOLOGIC DISEASES

This rather impressive heading covers numerous cutaneous diseases which affect most breeds as well as one, nasal solar dermatitis - "Collie nose", which affects primarily Collies and Shetland Sheepdogs. While canine immunogenetics is in its infancy, several researchers and numerous breeders acknowledge at least a familial predisposition for many of these problems. Because this writer believes that continued research will prove the genetic mode or modes of transmission these diseases are briefly presented in this chapter.

CANINE DEMODICOSIS

Canine demodicosis is commonly known as demodectic mange and is the reaction of the dog to the demodex mite which normally inhabits, in small numbers, the hair follicles. Localized demodicosis generally occurs in dogs three to ten months old and consists of small, well-defined scaly areas of hair loss around the eyes, lips or forelegs. Generalized or pustular demodicosis is usually a severe disease which is difficult to control or cure. In this form the scale areas of hair loss may spread over large areas of the body accompanied by itching, edema, bleeding and frequently invasion of secondary bacterial infection. Dr. Danny Scott of Cornell University has hypothesized that "Generalized demodicosis is the manifestation of an hereditary, specific 'T'-cell defect for Demodex canis..." which allows the mite to multiply in large numbers.[11]

AUTOIMMUNE SKIN DISEASES

Dr. Richard Halliwell, University of Florida, has also implicated a defective suppressor "T"-cell function in the development of autoantibodies in deleterious quantities. Dr. Halliwell implicates these autoantibodies as causitive agents in these autoimmune skin diseases:[12]

Pemphigus Vulgaris symptoms range from newly ulcerated areas to crusty, non-healing erosions

Dahlis

197

located on or immediately adjacent to mucous membranes: mouth, eyes, nose, anus and vulva. This disease may become systemic, attacking the connective tissue of internal organs and can prove fatal without immuno-suppressant treatment.[13]

Pemphigus Foliaceus is not as systemically debilitating as pemphigus vulgaris. It is characterized by crusty scaling eruptions extending up most of the bridge of the nose and around the eyes. Similar lesions often appear on the ear tips, toes, scrotal skin and near the anus and vulva, as well as elsewhere on the body. These eruptions are not centered on mucous membranes. The disease sometimes resembles generalized demodicosis, however, lack of demodex mites in scrapings will clarify the diagnosis.[12,13]

Dr. Victor Austin, veterinary dermotologist, adds two more diseases of this type seen in Collies: *Epidermolysis Bullosa Simplex* (EBS) which is also evidenced by hair loss, erosions, ulcers, crusts, edema and pigment changes, and a similar appearing disease also seen in Collies and Shelties, *discoid lupus erythematosus* (DLE).[13]*

It should be noted that few cases of these auto-immune diseases have been positively diagnosed. This may be due to genuine infrequency or the the general veterinarians' unfamiliarity with the diseases and the diagnostic tools.

Other sources[2] list as possible hereditary immune system disorders *Atopic Dermatitis* and *Nasal Solar Dermatitis*. *Atopic dermatitis* is a genetically determined immunologic disorder which is allergic in nature and most usually attacks the skin. Flea bite allergy (or eczema) is an atopic disease. *Nasal Solar Dermatitis* (or Collie nose) has been diagnosed as *Discoid Lupus Erythematosus*. Originally thought to be an allergic reaction to sunlight, the condition is aggravated by sun exposure. The dog should be kept out of bright sunlight as much as possible and the nasal area covered with a sun screening lotion. This is not indigenous to the Collie as it appears in the Shetland Sheepdog and mixed breed farm shepherd type dogs.

198

Fig. 3. Ch. Rosslane Bronwyn at four-and-one-half months. Note good rear angulation.

CYCLIC NEUTROPENIA**

The single genetic anomaly which occurs naturally in only the Collie is cyclic neutropenia, also know as the Gray Collie Syndrome. Because the disease also affects children, this anomaly has now been bred into a Collie-Beagle cross for experimental purposes. Cyclic neutropenia is inherited as a single autosomal recessive so that the appearance of a "gray puppy" in a litter implicates both parents as carriers.

Puppies suffering from cyclic neutropenia are usually identifiable at birth by their characteristic coat color. This ranges from dark pewter gray (in tricolors) to silver (in sables). The white areas are unaffected but the tan areas in tris are nearly white. About half of the pups die at birth or are stunted, and even with intensive medication few survive past three months of age. The disease, which is brought on by basic defects in the animal's bone marrow, is characterized by the cyclic destruction of the neutrophils in the blood at eleven-day intervals. Without these blood elements the animal has no immune response and is stricken with fever, diarrhea, gingivitis and respiratory infections. These cyclic episodes generally begin between eight and twelve weeks.[14,15,16]

Dr. Yang discovered that by transplanting the bone-marrow of normal animals into those suffering from the disease, he could halt the cycles of neutropenia in the affected animals. To his surprise, two years after curing two of these "grays" the animals began to grow hair of normal coat color. Although the color recovery was incomplete and appeared only on tails and portions of the body, this was strong evidence to support the theory that the gene which causes the bone marrow defect also causes the coat color modification.[17]

**also termed *cyclic hematopoiesis*

REFERENCES

1. DiFruscia, R.: "Cardiovascular Diseases of the Dog." *Pure Bred Dogs, American Kennel Gazette.* April 1980.
2. Foley, C. W.: "Genetic Defects in the Dog." *Pure Bred Dogs, American Kennel Gazette.* May 1980.
3. Erickson, F. et al: *Congenital Defects in Dogs.* Veterinary Practice Publishing Company. 1978.
4. Hedhammer, A.; Olsson, S-E; Andersson, S-A et al: "Canine Hip Dysplasia: A Study of Heritability in 401 Litters of German Shepherd Dogs." *JAVMA* 174:1012-1016, 1979.
5. Lust, G. and Farrel, P. W.: "Hip Dysplasia in Dogs: The Interplay of Genotype and Environment." *Cornell Veterinarian.* 67:447-466, 1977.
6. Hutt, F. B.: *Genetics for Dog Breeders.* W. H. Freeman and Co. 1979.
7. Holliday, T. A.: "Seizure Disorders." *Veterinary Clinics of North America; Small Animal Practice.* February 1980.
8. Cunningham, J.: "Canine Seizure Disorders. *JAVMA* 158:589-597, 1971.
9. Falco, M., Barker, J. and Wallace, M.: "Genetics of Epilepsy in British Alsatians." *J. Small Animal Practice,* 15:685-592, 1974.
10. Foley, C. W., Lasley, J. and Osweiler, G. D.: *Abnormalities of Companion Animals.* Iowa State University Press, 1979.
11. Scott, D. W.: "Canine Demodicosis." *Veterinary Clinics of North America, Small Animal Practice.* February 1979.
12. Halliwell, R.: "Skin Diseases Associated with Autoimmunity." *Veterinary Clinics of North America; Small Animal Practice.* February 1979.
13. Austin, V. H.: "Bullous Dermatoses—A Review." *California Veterinarian.* September 1979.
14. Cheville, N.: "The Gray Collie Syndrome." *JAVMA* 152:620-630, 1968.
15. Lund, G., Padgett, G. and Gorhan, J.: "Additional Evidence on the Inheritance of Cyclic Neutropenia in the Dog." *J. of Heredity.* 61:47-49, 1970.
16. Jones, J. B., Lange, R. D. and Jones, E. S.: "Cyclic Hematopoiesis in a Colony of Dogs." *JAVMA* 166:365-367, 1975.
17. Yang, T-J: "Recovery of Hair Coat Color in Gray Collie (Cyclic Neutropenia)—Normal Bone Marrow Transplant Chimeras." *American Journal of Pathology.* 91:149-153, 1978.

200

Fig. 23. Ch. Bay Mar's Coming Attraction, a lovely dark shaded sable.

22

The Collie Eye Problem

by Linda Sparks

"How disappointment tracks the steps of hope."   Landon

The most misunderstood defects in the Collie are the eye problems. They have caused potential pet owners to become unduly apprehensive because of misinformation from well-meaning laymen and medical advisors.

Two primary eye problems appear in the Collie, the Collie Eye Anomaly (CEA) and generalized Progressive Retinal Atrophy (PRA). While the intent is to present factual data, as currently known, where opinions of the author are included, they are clearly identified as opinion.

ANATOMY OF THE EYE

The gross structure of the eye is fairly simple (Fig. 1). For the purposes of this discussion, we will be primarily concerned with the retina, choroid, and optic nerve as these are the areas most often affected by the hereditary eye diseases in the Collie.

The eye is encased in a tough fibrous coat called the sclera. This is very similar to the dura which covers the spinal cord and brain. This is not surprising since during early embryonic development the eyes arise directly from the brain. Inside the sclera is a lining called the choroid which is a densely pigmented membrane carrying the blood supply to the outer layers of the retina. The choroid also contains a section of iridescent pigment (called tapetum lucidum) which serves to reflect additional light back to the visual cells (rods and cones). (This tapetum lucidum is what causes dogs' eyes to shine in the dark.) Inside the choroid is a third layer called the retina, which contains the highly sensitive receptor cells, the rods and cones. The rods are most sensitive to dim light and also serve to detect motion. The cones are most sensitive to bright light and allow the dog to see sharp bright images.[20]

Dahlis

Light reflected from an image enters the eye by passing through the cornea and lens and falls upon the retina in the rear of the eye (this field is called the fundus) (Fig. 8). This iris regulates the size of the pupil, thereby determining the amount of light that enters the eye. The retina then transforms this light into a nervous response which is transmitted to the brain by way of the optic nerve.

COLLIE EYE ANOMALY

Collie Eye Anomaly (CEA) or Collie Eye Problem (CEP) is the common term used to group several defects found in the rear (fundus) of the eyes of many Collies. While grading systems may differ, most veterinary ophthalmologists recognize three major categories of defects as most important.

The most minor of these categories is *chorioretinal change* (often called choroidal hypoplasia, choroidal dysplasia and occasionally choroidal hypopigmentation). At one time this defect was believed to be linked with the merling gene because many merles have hypopigmentation (decreased pigmentation) of the choroid.[4] This linkage, however, has been disproven.[2]

When the ophthalmologist examines a Collie with chorioretinal change he/she sees a pale area or areas on the fundus where the cells of the tapetum are abnormally developed or missing, pigment is diminished and fewer blood vessels exist in the choroid. The defect, regardless of size, does not interfere with vision.

The second category is a more serious defect and is termed coloboma, staphyloma or ectasia. During embryonic development an opening in the eye tissue (choroidal fissure), through which the retinal blood vessels grow, closes. If this fissure fails to fully close, the area in or around the optic nerve remains undeveloped and the condition is called a coloboma.[20] In the Collie eye these areas usually appear as an indentation or hole in the region of the optic nerve. When viewed microscopically it is found that the sclera is thin and the choroid, tapetum and retina may be absent or abnormally formed.[3] A staphyloma is an area of similar appearance elsewhere on the fundus. A staphyloma can be most easily visualized by pushing one's finger through a balloon, stretching and thinning one small spot.

Although some researchers have stated that staphyloma is found only in the presence of chorioretinal change,[5] this author has owned a sable male Collie who was found to have colobomas in both eyes but no chorioretinal change.

Neither chorioretinal change nor staphyloma are progressive with age. However, retinal holes which lead to retinal detachment frequently develop in eyes that have very large colobomas or staphylomas.[5]

Retinal detachment constitutes the most serious form of CEA. A dog with a detached retina is blind in that eye, since the retina is not properly attached and cannot perform its sensory function.

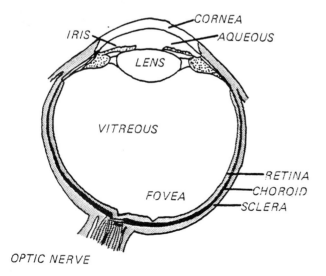

Fig. 1. Structure of the eye.

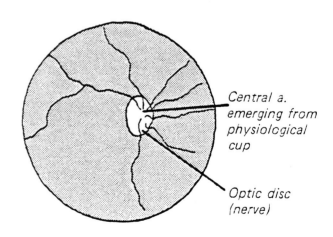

Fig. 2. Fundus of the eye showing optic disc.

Mode of Inheritance

Most researchers have reported that CEA is inherited via a simple autosomal recessive gene.[1,5,7,8] If we assume a simple recessive inheritance, it is possible to determine the genetic makeup of a normal-eyed dog. A normal-eyed dog is either a carrier (one normal gene, one affected gene) or a non-carrier (two normal genes). Since an animal only requires one normal gene to be normal-eyed, the carrier will produce approximately 50 percent normal-eyed dogs while the non-carrier will produce 100 percent normal-eyed dogs when bred to affected animals. With apologies to the geneticists for my unorthodox symbols, these breedings are illustrated in Figure 9. For purposes of illustration, the normal-eyed parent was the sire. In actuality, either sire or dam may be normal or affected with the same results.

It is my opinion that if the CEA is a simple autosomal recessive in its presence or absence, then there are several other genetic possibilities which govern the *degrees* of expression. For instance, if the degree of expression of CEA is inherited polygenically, the following would apply: Within the affected animal are a group of genes which are coded for chorioretinal change or staphyloma or detachment. When these are divided up in the process of reproduction, the offspring receive some number from each parent. The greater the number of genes with severe coding the animal receives, the greater degree of

the CEA it will display. I think this may also hold true with the normal-eyed carrier. If he carries severe coding with the affected gene, affected offspring have the possibility of being severely affected. The coding of the affected parent also plays a part (see squares in Fig. 3). Not only will he contribute coding to the affected offspring, he may determine entirely the coding of the normal-eyed carrier offspring. Epistasis (as described in Genetics) might be an equally valid explanation to the degree of expression of the CEA.

COLLIE PRA

What is commonly known as Progressive Retinal Atrophy (generalized PRA) in the Collie is

Fig. 3.

a — affected gene

N — Normal-eyed gene

Na — Normal-eyed *dog*

aa — affected *dog*

		dam				dam	
		a	a			a	a
sire	N	Na	Na	N		Na	Na
	a	aa	aa	N		Na	Na

sire-carrier   sire—non-carrier

½ normal-eyed   All normal-eyed
carriers   carriers

½ affected

203

Fig. 4. Ch. Wickmere Chimney Sweep at four months. A colt-like appearance with knobby knees when all parts seem to be connected with rubber bands and springs is common at this age. This dog finished at eleven months and became a Best in Show winner.

almost identical clinically to that found in the Irish Setter. As such, it is more correctly termed "rod-cone dysplasia." This means that both the rods and cones were abnormally formed during development and only become progressively more abnormal with time after birth. This is different from the Miniature Poodle, whose rods and cones develop normally and achieve functional maturity before experiencing premature degeneration.

Examination of the retinal tissue via the microscope showed that the rods generally appeared more abnormal than the cones in the Setter. As was pointed out earlier, the rods are the receptors most sensitive to dim light. When these are abnormally developed and marginally functional, it is understandable that the first signs of this disease in Collies, as in Setters, would be night blindness. Since cones are also involved but to a lesser extent, affected animals eventually become blind in daylight, resulting in complete blindness.

Mode of Inheritance

The mode of inheritance for PRA in all breeds to date is simple autosomal recessive.[9,10,11,12,13,14] The Collie breeding studies support the simple autosomal process of inheritance in Collies.[15] This means that a PRA blind Collie can pass on only the genes for PRA and that a carrier will produce offspring, fifty percent of whom will also be carriers. It also means that a Collie who has a PRA blind offspring is a carrier.

OTHER EYE ANOMALIES

Pupillary membranes may be found in the eyes of a number of breeds including the Collie. These may first be seen by the breeder as fine blue streamers in the pupil when he holds his pups up in the sunlight. These are simply remains of a membrane which covers the pupil during embryonic development and is normally completely resorbed. In some animals, these membranes remain past the first three to four weeks of age and are then termed *persistent pupillary membranes.* Although it is rare in Collies, these membranes can cause problems. If a persistent pupillary membrane becomes attached to the cornea, it can

cause clouding and opacity of the cornea. Should it become attached to the lens, a cataract may develop.

During the ophthalmoscopic examination the veterinarian may find a *physiologic cup.* This is a very small pit in the optic disc which is also a remainder of embryonic development. There is no known connection between the physiologic cup and CEA and this cup is not a coloboma. Whether or not this anomaly is inherited is unknown to this author. However, several Collies in one family have exhibited this anomaly in succeeding generations.

Cataracts can have numerous causes. The incidence of cataracts in Collie puppies known to this author have been believed to be from two primary causes. One type of cataract is believed to be caused by hand-rearing of puppies on a commercial milk substitute. Breeders who have experienced this type of cataract report that the cataract eventually disappears as the pup grows up.

A second type of cataract seen in Collie pups has been attributed to some type of "insult" to the pup during a critical growth period.[21] This insult may occur while the pup is in the womb or may occur shortly after birth, especially in the case of slightly premature births. The insult could be in the form of a viral infection or fever in the bitch while she is carrying the pups. Following whelping it is believed that some of these cataracts may be caused by feeding anything other than the

Fig. 5.

a — PRA affected

N — Normal

NN — Normal, non-carrier

Na — Normal, carrier

aa — affected (BLIND)

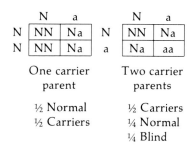

	N	a
N	NN	Na
N	NN	Na

One carrier parent

½ Normal
½ Carriers

	N	a
N	NN	Na
a	Na	aa

Two carrier parents

½ Carriers
¼ Normal
¼ Blind

204

dam's own milk to the whelps during a critical "window" in their early development.

This type of cataract, unlike those attributed to hand-rearing on the commercial product, either remain unchanged or progress as the pup grows up. The presence and prognosis of these cataracts can only be determined by a veterinary ophthalmologist on an individual basis.

The cause of the majority of cataracts, however, is unknown. It is possible that some cataracts in Collies are inherited by a yet unknown mode of inheritance.

Special thanks go to Dr. Gustavo Aguirre for insuring the accuracy of this paper and for his comments. Thanks also to Dr. Aguirre and Dr. Lionel Rubin for providing quantities of research material. Both of these men and Dr. Elias Souri have spent many patient hours answering the questions of this author and they have my deep gratitude.

Illustrations for this chapter were done by Charlotte Kestler.

REFERENCES

CEA

"Reports and Comments From a Symposium on Collie Eye Anomalies," July 21, 1968, *J.A.V.M.A.*, Vol. 115, No. 6, Sept. 15, 1969. 859-878:

1. Roberts, S. R., "The Collie Eye Anomaly."
2. Rubin, L. F., "Comments."
3. Wyman, M. and Donovan, E. F., "Eye Anomaly of the Collie."
4. Cello, R. M., "Comments."
5. Donovan, R. H., Freeman, H. M., and Schepens, C. L., "Anomaly of the Collie Eye."
6. Vainisi S. J., "Comments."
7. Catcott, E. J., "Summary and Conclusions."
8. Yankely, W. L., Wyman, M., Donovan, E. F. and Fechheimer, N. S., "Genetic Transmission of an Ocular Fundus Anomaly in Collies." *J.A.V.M.A.*, Vol. 152, March 1, 1968; 457-461.

PRA

9. Aguirre, G. D. and Rubin, L. F., "Rod-Cone Dysplasia (Progressive Retinal Atrophy) in Irish Setters," *J.A.V.M.A.* Vol. 116. No. 3, 157-164.

10. Aguirre, G. D. and Rubin, L. F., "The Early Diagnosis of Rod Dysplasia in the Norwegian Elkhound," *J.A.V.M.A.*, Vol. 159, No. 4, 429-433.
11. Aguirre, G. D., "Inherited Retinal Degeneration in the Dog," 8th Annual Meeting– American Academy of Opthalmology and Otolarnygology, Sept. 21-25, 1975.
12. Aguirre, G. D. and Bistner, S., Cornell Research Laboratory for Diseases of Dogs, "Lab Report," Cornell University, Series 2, No. 2, 1972.
13. Fisher, T. M., "PRA - A Genetic Study," *Sheltie Pacesetter*, May 1979, 92-138. As reprinted from Poodle Variety.
14. Black, L. "Progressive Retinal Atrophy; A Review of the Genetics and an Appraisal of the Eradication Scheme," *J. Small Animal Practice*, Vol. 13, 1972, 295-314.
15. Wolf, E. D., Vainisi, S. J. and Santos-Anderson, R., "Inherited Retinal Dysplasia in the Collie," *J.A.V.M.A.* (from the Summary as reprinted in *Paw Prints*, April 1979.)

GENETICS

16. Merrell, D. J. *Introduction to Genetics*, Norton, 1975.
17. Burns, G. W. *Science of Genetics, Introduction to Heredity*, Macmillian, 1972.
18. Crow, J. F. and Kimura M. *An Introduction to Population Genetics Theory*, Harper and Row, 1970.

ANATOMY

19. Gray, H. *Anatomy of the Human Body*, Lea and Febiger, 1973.
20. Zuidema, G. D. (ed.). *Johns Hopkins Atlas of Human Functional Anatomy*, John Hopkins University Press, 1977.

206

Fig. 4. Ch. Blossom Heights Tammy, A specialty winner.

About the Author

The Roos's and Wickmere Collies have been a part of Collie history for almost four decades. They have also helped to *create* Collie history.

An astute eye for a dog, intuition, hard work, dedication and some luck parlayed Wickmere into an acknowledged, identifiable branch of the Parader line with a chain of events that set some of the breed records.

The key acquisition was the tri male, Ch. Merrie Oaks Midnite Star (litter mate to three champions, one of which finished for the title by going best in show, all breeds) from Dick Warren, who was retiring from Collie activities.

Midnite Star was named sire of the year in 1965. It is interesting to note that three of the top producing bitches owe so much to Midnite Star. Ch. Alteza The Silver Lining produced six of her eight champions by Midnite Star. Ch. Regaline's Blue Intuition, dam of eight champions, produced three champions when bred to the Midnite Star son, Ch. Wickmere Chimney Sweep. When Ch. Wickmere Battle Chief (by War Dance) was bred to Ch. Wickmere Cotillion (line bred to Midnite Star) they produced Ch. Shamont Sabrina, dam of seven champions.

Spanning the generations, through the tail male line, the Battle Chief son, Ch. Wickmere Silver Bullet, was the sire of four champions in one litter out of Ch. Highefields Debutante and the contemporary Bullet daughter, Ch. Courtesy of Aryggeth (out of Hallie of Aryggeth) is the dam of five champions with additional progeny anticipated to complete the title to place Courtesy in the elite sorority of top producing dams.

Ch. Wickmere Reveille (Midnite Star son) was bred to his half-sister (she by Midnite Star) to produce Ch. Wickmere Rapunzel, a pure for sable possessing the most incredible head and eye virtues.

207

Line breeding produced the qualities of the ideal Collie as envisioned by George, Bobbee and Shelley Roos.

Experience and knowledge gleaned through the years has been shared by means of seminars, club programs, magazine series and now, COLLIE CONCEPT. Grooming, training, nutrition, reproduction, history and trivia—all of the facets which are an integral part of breeding and exhibiting or just enjoying a family companion.

There has been recognition by peers and contemporaries and a collection of awards, but Wickmere was not established with particular goals as they did not set out to win the national specialty, best in shows, or to breed X number of champions. Perhaps this is why they have endured.

> "Nor Fame I slight
> nor for her
> favors call,
> She comes unlooked for
> if she comes
> at all."
>
> ....Alexander Pope

Sign at entrance way.

Ch. Lemels Sno Job O'Wildwood.

Index

211

...Photo of Ch. Ransom's Regency...

"WHAT IS BEAUTIFUL
            IS A JOY FOR ALL SEASONS
                        AND A POSSESSION
                                    FOR ALL ETERNITY."

Oscar Wilde

Back Cover Photo
A Picture is Worth a Thousand Words!

As advertising chairman for the 75th Anniversary show for the St. Louis Collie Club, Robert D. Collin, a professional photographer, visualized a photo representing rough and smooth, coat color, obedience and conformation. A white Collie was unavailable.

The models selected were Robert D. Collins' rough sable male, Collins' Shepherd O'Brian C.D. (Shep); Joyce Norris' smooth sable male, Ch. Charmant's Electric Horseman (Ely); Mrs. Dan Eilers' and Dana D. Eilers', Ch. Kalstrom's Darth Vador (Darth); and My-T Asgard Aires C.D. (Danny) owned by Lisa Schmidt.

Locating a suitable site led Collin to about five places before this park setting impressed both he and his wife, Barb. The main concern was lighting as harsh shadows would ruin the photo. Collin took his dog, Shep, and photographed him in every position—sitting, right, left, on top of the steps, below the steps, standing etc. He then cut out all the pictures of Shep and tried various combinations on a plain shot of the back ground. The decision was made as to just how each of the four dogs should be placed.

Another decision was to be made. When would the lighting be best? Collin spent many hours in the park watching shadows and it wasn't until he saw the sun rising, just above the horizon but still behind the lower half of the trees, that the lighting was perfect.

Using fast film there was just enough light for the exposure.

The time span they had to work within was from 5:50 A.M. to 6:15 A.M., twenty five minutes. Everyone involved had to be at the site no later than 5:45 A.M. with their dogs groomed, ready to assume their assigned positions and pose.

The photographer lived within a few blocks of the park, two others lived ten miles away but Joyce Norric and Ely had a three hour drive!

The weather cooperated. A beautiful sun rise and the four dogs took their assigned positions. Getting eight ears up and four dogs looking in the right direction at the same time was an arduous task.

Seventy two black and white pictures in fifteen minutes! Short break to load film. Then a change to color and thirty additional shots. From one-hundred two shots *one* was unanimously selected as the pick.

Collin remarked, "I hope you can visualize all the hard work that five people went through who truly love Collies."